Advertising Media Workbook and Sourcebook

THIRD EDITION

Advertising Media Workbook and Sourcebook

THIRD EDITION

Larry D. Kelley

Donald W. Jugenheimer

and Kim Bartel Sheehan

M.E.Sharpe
Armonk, New York
London, England

Library of Congress Cataloging-in-Publication Data

Kelley, Larry D., 1955–
  Advertising media workbook and sourcebook / by Larry D. Kelley, Donald W. Jugenheimer, and Kim Bartel Sheehan.—3rd ed.
  p. cm.
  ISBN 978–0–7656–2638–7 (pbk. : alk. paper)
  1. Advertising media planning. 2. Advertising media planning—Problems, exercises, etc. I. Jugenheimer, Donald W.
II. Sheehan, Kim. III. Title.

HF5826.5.K456 2012
659.13—dc22   2011012297

Printed in the United States of America

The paper used in this publication meets the minimum requirements of
American National Standard for Information Sciences
Permanence of Paper for Printed Library Materials,
ANSI Z 39.48-1984.

SP (p)   10   9   8   7   6   5   4   3   2   1

Contents

Introduction   vii

Part I. Marketing and Communication Planning   1

1. Working with a Communication Work Plan   3
2. Outlining the Components of a Communication Plan   7
3. Working with a Communication Planning Worksheet   13
4. Working with a Situation Analysis   21
5. Working with Communication Objectives   27
6. Working to Define the Target Market   33
7. Working with Geographic Marketing Information   43
8. Working with Seasonality Marketing Information   53
9. Working with a Communication Budget   57

Part II. Media Objectives and Strategies   63

10. Working to Define Media Objectives   65
11. Working with Reach   71
12. Working with Combinations of Media   75
13. Working with Frequency   81
14. Working with Frequency Levels   85
15. Working with Emotional versus Rational Appeals   91
16. Working with Test Cities and Standards   95
17. Working with Quintiles   101
18. Working to Define Media Strategies   115
19. Effectiveness, Engagement, and Commoditization   119

Part III. Media Tactics   127

20. Working to Define Media Tactics   129
21. Working with Media Cost Comparisons   133
22. Working with Estimating   143
23. Working with a Media Calendar and Flowcharts   151

Part IV. Broadcast Media   **159**

24. Working with Broadcast Media Estimates   161
25. Working with Broadcast Media Costs   171
26. Working with Broadcast Negotiations   199

Part V. Print Media   **205**

27. Working with Print Media Estimates   207
28. Working with Print Media Costs   217
29. Working with Print Negotiations   227

Part VI. Out-of-Home Media   **233**

30. Working with Out-of-Home Media   235
31. Working with Out-of-Home Media Costs   239
32. Working with Out-of-Home Negotiation   245

Part VII. Digital Media   **251**

33. Working with Online Display Media Estimates   253
34. Working with Online Display Media Costs   257
35. Working with Search Engine Marketing   263
36. Working with Social Media   267
37. Working with Mobile Media   271

Part VIII. Media Tools, Analysis, and Resources   **275**

38. Combining Sources and Data   277
39. Manipulating Data   281
40. Working with Basic Media Math   287
41. Working with Media Websites   301
42. Working with Competitive Media Information   307

Appendix A. A Primer to Media Math   313
Appendix B. Some Commonly Used Advertising Media Formulas   321
Appendix C. Advertising Media Glossary   323
Appendix D. Steps in the Media Decision Process   345
About the Authors   349

Introduction

Advertising Media Workbook and Sourcebook, Third Edition

To be successful in the advertising industry, you need at least three things: knowledge, skills, and experience. This workbook and sourcebook are designed to help you gain all three.

Knowledge hinges on information. You need to know how to find information, how to read it, how to interpret it, and how to apply the information in advertising contexts. Many different sources of advertising media information are available from a variety of firms that collect and distribute syndicated research. In this book you'll learn about many of these sources and the data they provide, as well as how to read, interpret, and apply the information to real-world (and real work) situations.

Organization and communication skills are essential to success in advertising. Specifically, these include skills in writing, reading, planning, and executing plans and programs. Two of the most useful skills are quick thinking and problem solving. Again, this workbook will help you develop these skills through exposure to real advertising media situations and problems.

Experience is critical. It is the trait that every employer wants from employees. Experience on the job is important, but it is also important to gain experience working with the actual tools, sources, and situations that you will eventually encounter on the job. Additionally, the constantly changing digital world means that media planners and buyers today encounter new types of media offerings. Understanding similar or comparative media to compare new offerings too is invaluable. So, if you have real-world job experience, that's great; but even without it, exposure to real-world tools and sources, like those shown in this workbook, will still be helpful to you.

Organization of Each Unit

This book is composed of 42 individual units, each one dealing with a specific item of knowledge, type of skill, and realistic experience that will be useful to you working in advertising media. Each unit begins with information about the area of knowledge being discussed. Following that, there are actual examples of research from current advertising cases and problems. Explanations follow, with detailed notes on how to read the data in the examples and how to apply that knowledge. Finally, each unit contains exercises that take you through actual advertising media problems, in which you seek a solution and apply it to the situation at hand.

Workbook

Workbooks are designed to let you work at your own pace on real problems. They also allow you to keep a record of your own progress, so you will know where you have difficulties, how you overcame them, and what you accomplished along the way.

This workbook does exactly those things: explains how to do the work, shows you the available resources, and allows you to maintain your record of achievement while learning about advertising media.

Sourcebook

This sourcebook includes actual advertising media information sources, explains how to understand and interpret the information they give, and presents real problems from real advertising situations—just like the ones you will eventually face while working on the advertising business.

Organization

Advertising Media Workbook and Sourcebook starts out with an overview of the development of a media plan, and discusses in detail each strategic element of the plan. The section on media objectives and strategies helps you understand the importance of a strong base for a media plan. Following that, the units delve into various types of media tactics, including broadcast, print, out-of-home and digital. You'll be introduced to complex kinds of information and work situations, where you'll often be tasked to integrate multiple sources of information.

In this third edition, we have included new units in media negotiation. The topic of media negotiation is often overlooked or given short shrift in media planning class work, yet is an essential skill for anyone entering the media profession. Such information will also be extremely valuable to anyone considering a career in media sales.

The final part, Media Tools, Analysis, and Resources, provides important information into the basic concepts and numerical tools used in media planning and buying. You may wish to visit this section first, just to familiarize yourself with the concepts used throughout the book.

For many problems there is only one solution; but as you progress to problems and questions that are more complicated you will discover that there may be several ways to approach the problem. You may recommend one approach, whereas someone else may recommend a completely separate approach, one perhaps that is quite different from yours. There is no single best way to advertise, so there can be different paths to achieve success. The important thing is that you can explain and justify your decisions and recommendations in order to support your solutions.

Although the units are arranged to correspond generally with the accompanying textbook, this workbook can be used with or without the text, just as the textbook can be used with or without the workbook.

So as you go through this book, be thinking about how you can apply information you are learning, how you might use it in your class work and in your advertising career, and how you would use it to help you make decisions, explain those decisions, and justify those recommendations.

Acknowledgments

The authors express their deep appreciation to our colleagues who supported us with the writing and preparation of this edition. In particular, we acknowledge Harry Briggs and the staff at M.E. Sharpe for their valued assistance. We especially thank our spouses and families for all their support, without which this project would not have been possible.

Part I
Marketing and Communication Planning

Unit 1
Working with a Communication Work Plan

Before a media plan is developed, many media teams request a work plan that solicits input from the client and/or the account management or account planning groups. Just like a creative brief, the media work plan serves as the road map for media planning development.

The communication (or media) work plan contains simple facts as well as brand strategies. The simple facts included on the document are:

1. What the media budget is.
2. When the campaign is to start and to end.
3. When the media plan is due internally and to the client.

There is also a background briefing on the situation facing the brand. This usually consists of a synopsis of marketing and advertising research that gives a picture of where the brand is today and what issues face the brand for reaching its goals tomorrow.

Some key factors that influence media plan development include the advertising objectives and overall ad strategies of the target market and creative messaging and execution. All of these strategic decisions greatly influence the outcome of a media plan.

Many media planners have moved to a contact plan or a media touchpoint plan that takes into account a wide array of traditional and nontraditional media. One key question in the media work plan is how the brand is bought—is it in a store, through a catalog, online, or a combination of all of these channels? The answer to this question greatly impacts the media team's thought process. There are many factors regarding target market influence and timing that can also play into media strategies.

Media planning is a natural outgrowth of a marketing plan, so factors such as seasonality of sales, geographic strengths and weaknesses, along with competition, influence the outcome of all media plans.

A media work plan also contains a section for any mandatory or prior commitments that the client or brand may have. For example, there may be existing media commitments that the media planner must consider or account for in the plan. Or the client may request that the media team use a certain medium or media vehicle. Media planners must know all these facts before embarking on developing a media plan.

Exhibit 1.1 **Media Workplan**

Media Work Plan		
Client:	Brand:	Date:
Media budget only (net/gross):	Campaign start:	Campaign end:
	Plan due internally:	Plan due to client:

1. Background (What is the situation facing the brand?)
2. Advertising objectives
3. Target audience: List marketing target, including any relevant attitudinal, demographic, or psychographic data.
4. How is the brand bought? List factors on how it is purchased, such as target influencers or timing that could aid media planning.
5. Key marketing factors:
   a. Seasonality
   b. Geography (BDI/CDI)
   c. Distribution
   d. Competition
6. Creative considerations (new or existing campaigns)
7. Mandatories
8. Measurement

The final section of the media work plan contains how the campaign will be measured. This is vitally important to the media planner because there may be methods of modeling past sales or brand metrics that could lead the planner to develop a future outcome. Tying the media plan to some form of measurement is a fundamental aspect of media planning. With increasingly sophisticated databases and online metrics, media planning is becoming much more focused on return on investment (ROI).

In Exhibit 1.1 you will find an example of a media work plan. It contains the fundamentals a media planner must know to develop the media plan. The work plan can also serve as a nice guide to what information you need before you can proceed to media strategies.

Unit 1 Exercises
Working with a Communication Work Plan

1. What is the significance of net or gross in the media budget section of the media work plan?

2. Discuss what target audience information you would like to see if you were developing a media plan for Cheerios cereal.

3. How do different sales channels impact a media plan? Discuss how you might approach a media plan for Dell computers where the brand is bought online, through a catalog, and in kiosks in malls.

4. Discuss what might be different on the media work plan for a business-to-business product such as a copier compared with a consumer product such as an automobile.

Unit 2
Outlining the Components of a Communication Plan

Every communication plan should begin with an outline. Outlining what is contained in the plan is an efficient way to begin the communications planning project. Whereas all plans are unique depending upon the advertiser, there are fundamentals that should be contained in any communication plan.

Exhibit 2.1 contains an outline for a communications plan. There are 10 broad areas that are covered. They range from an executive summary to how you would measure the results of your plan. Other than the executive summary, each component of the plan builds on the previous one. Marketing objectives/strategies lead into the role that communication plays in solving the marketing challenge. This leads to communication objectives which then lead to communication strategies and tactics. Each communication plan is not unlike a book. It tells a story. In this case, the story is how you plan to solve the brand's marketing challenge.

Communication Plan versus Media Plan

A communication plan and a media plan have similar components. The difference between a communication plan and a media plan is the approach to solving the marketing problem. In an advertising media plan, it is assumed that advertising is the solution to the marketing problem. Therefore, a paid media plan is necessary to convey the advertising message to the appropriate target market.

In a communication plan, on the other hand, advertising is only one of a myriad of alternatives to solve the marketing challenge. It may be the solution or it may not. Or advertising may be a part of the solution in combination with other communication alternatives. A communication plan then assesses advertising, promotions, publicity, direct response, and any other form of communication. The communication plan should be strategy neutral. It doesn't assume that one method of communication is better than another going into the planning process.

Exhibit 2.1

Components of a Communication Plan

1. Executive Summary
   a. Summary of Marketing Objectives/Strategies
   b. Summary of Communication Objectives/Strategies
   c. Budget Summary

2. Situation Analysis
   a. Marketing
   b. Communication
   c. SWOT

3. Marketing Objectives/Strategies
   a. Business
   b. Brand

4. Role of Communication
   a. Message

5. Communication Objectives
   a. Target Segment
   b. Geography
   c. Seasonal/Timing
   d. Reach/Frequency/Continuity

6. Communication Strategies
   a. Mix
   b. Scheduling

7. Communication Tactics
   a. Vehicle
   b. Rationale
   c. Costs
   d. Impressions

8. Communication Budget
   a. Dollars by Communication Channel
   b. Dollars by Month

9. Communication Flowchart
   a. Weekly Schedule
   b. Recap of Dollars
   c. Recap of Impressions
   d. Reach/Frequency

10. Testing and Evaluation
    a. Test Programs
    b. Evaluation Methods

Components of a Communication Plan

There are ten components to the communication plan, as highlighted in Exhibit 2.1. The following are brief descriptions of what is contained in each of these components.

1. Executive Summary

An executive summary of your plan focuses management on the link between the marketing objectives and strategies and the communication objectives and strategies. From a management viewpoint, it is crucial to understand how communication is tied to the business goals of the brand. Management will also want to understand the strategic nature of the plan and the budget necessary to implement it. All of that is contained in the executive summary.

2. Situation Analysis

The situation analysis forms the context for the plan. It should contain a marketing analysis as well as a communication analysis. Marketing analysis will contain a review of pricing, distribution, resources, and product differentiation compared with competing brands in the same category. Communication analysis will contain message, copy, and communication channel comparison with competing brands in the category. Both should roll up into a strengths, weaknesses, opportunities, and threats summary. This is called a SWOT analysis.

3. Marketing Objectives/Strategies

All communication plans derive from a marketing strategy. It is paramount to recap the marketing objectives and strategies. These objectives and strategies should have two aspects. One is business objectives, typically defined by the number of customers and sales. The second is brand aspects which may be defined by differentiation.

4. Role of Communication

The role of communication defines how communication is going to solve the marketing challenge or meet the objectives. The role of communication is how the brand is going to communicate with its consumers. Some typical roles of communication are to increase awareness, change perceptions, announce new "news," or associate the brand with quality perception. Within this section should be the role that communication plays as well as the creative message strategy. This is the foundation for the communication plan.

5. Communication Objectives

Communication objectives include whom you are going to target with the message, where you are targeting, when you are targeting, and how much pressure you plan to provide the message. The Big Four communication objectives are target market, geography, seasonal/timing, and reach/frequency/continuity.

6. Communication Strategies

Communication strategies are the ways you plan to achieve the objectives. Each objective should have a corresponding strategy. The two major strategies for a communication plan are the communication mix and scheduling. The communication mix is the mix of communication channels you plan to use to achieve the objectives. The scheduling strategies are the ways you plan to deploy each channel.

7. Communication Tactics

Communication tactics reflect the details of the strategies. For example, if a strategy to support a specific local market contains print and radio, then the tactics are the print vehicles and radio formats or stations that are recommended. Tactics are the specifics of the plan. They should address each vehicle recommended and the creative unit (rationale), costs, and impressions that the vehicle will deliver.

8. Communication Budget

Communication budget is a recap of the dollars allocated to each communication channel, not to the specific vehicle; for example, magazines as a category rather than *Vanity Fair, Wired,* and *GQ* individually. Communication budgets include not only dollars by channel but also a recap of dollars by month.

9. Communication Flowchart

A communication flowchart is a schematic of the plan on a single page. It contains a weekly schedule of activity, a recap of dollars by vehicle and category, a recap of impressions by vehicle and category, and a reach/frequency analysis. The communication flowchart is a summary of all activity, scheduling, and costs.

10. Testing and Evaluation

Testing and evaluation are optional aspects of a communication plan. Many communication plans have test programs. A test program may mean testing how increased media pressure might impact a specific market, or it might mean testing an emerging medium. Any test would be covered in this section. The other aspect of this section is how to evaluate the success of the plan. This may be a recap of a research method or a recap of the measure and methods to ensure that the communication plan reaches its impression objectives.

Summary

Before diving into any communication plan it is important to outline the components of that plan. Doing so will provide the best and most efficient method for developing the plan. It is vital that each section of the plan build on the prior section. A communication plan is a strategic road map on how you plan to solve a marketing challenge.

Unit 2 Exercises
Outlining the Components of a Communication Plan

1. What is the difference between a media plan and a communications plan?

2. Why is it important to tie the communications plan to the marketing plan?

3. Give an example of a test program?

4. Find an example of a communications plan on Slideshare.com and discuss its differences and similarities to the outline in Exercise 2.1.

Unit 3
Working with a Communication Planning Worksheet

Facing the prospect of preparing an advertising media plan for the first time, many novice media planners are lost, simply not knowing where to start.

It may be helpful to use a worksheet like the one presented here. It will help you begin to establish your objectives for marketing, advertising, and media goals, which are among the first steps required in a media plan.

To use this worksheet, you may first need to conduct some research on the competition and competitors' usage of advertising and media. It may be helpful to examine the overall marketing situation for your advertised item or service, too.

Then, using this media plan worksheet, you can begin to compile your objectives.

You may be given marketing objectives or you may need to develop them yourself. Similarly, you may be given advertising objectives or you may need to establish them. Certainly you will be responsible for the media objectives that will be used in establishing the advertising media plan.

After you use the worksheet, you will still need to write out the actual objectives. In addition, each objective needs full explanation and justification. It is not enough simply to state an objective; rationale is also required.

Communication Planning Worksheet

Fill in all the requested information.

Marketing Objectives

For the time period of the prospective campaign, provide the marketing objectives required on the next page.

1. Market share of _____ percent of [all U.S. dollars sales, units, etc.]

2. Dollar volume: $_____

3. Number of units to be marketed: _____ [number of sales, units/items sold, etc.]

   Now, check your figures by computing units to be sold per 1,000 (or per 100) households, and advertising per unit sold.

4. a. _____ units per 1,000 (or 100) persons or households (specify which)

   b. $_____ advertising investment per unit of one [sale/item/unit] each

5. Prices: FOB: $_____

             Wholesale: $_____

             Retail: $_____

6. Timing during year/by season:

7. a. General profile of potential customers:

   b. How many of them are there (rough estimate)?

8. Geographic patterns, if any:

Advertising Objectives

1. a. General target audience:

   b. _____ % that can reasonably be reached

   c. About how many people is that? _____

2. Advertising goals: _____ % awareness

   _____ % knowledge

   _____ % preference

   _____ % desire

   _____ % purchase

Media Objectives

1. Rank in order, 1–4: Reach   _____

   Frequency _____

   Impact   _____

   Continuity _____

2. Total advertising budget for this product/service: $ _____

3. Media efficiency goals: $ _____ cost per thousand (CPM)

4. $\dfrac{\text{Budget: \$}}{\text{CPM: \$}}$ = _____ number of times $CPM can be spent

5. _____ × 1,000 audience impressions for each $CPM

6. _____ total audience impressions (TAI)

7. $R\# \times F = TAI$, so $\dfrac{TAI}{R\#} = F$, or $\dfrac{TAI}{F} = R\#$.

   a. Reach: _____ persons (match to target audience size)

   b. Frequency: _____ times

   c. (Check figures: _____ $R\# \times$ _____ $F =$ _____ TAI)

8. Assess need for media mix vs. media concentration:

Note: The media to be used are not considered objectives; rather, media are strategies to help achieve objectives.

Unit 3 Exercises
Working with a Communication Planning Worksheet

1. You have an advertising budget of $2,350,000. If your CPM goal is $17.50, how many times could you spend that $17.50 CPM within your advertising budget? Show your calculations. You may need to round your answer to a workable figure.

2. Each time you spend the CPM amount, you will be purchasing 1,000 audience impressions (because the M in CPM stands for "thousand").

   Using your answer from question 1 above, multiply that answer by 1,000 to calculate the total audience impressions that you can afford with your advertising budget. Show your work. You may wish to round off your answer.

3. Reach (as number, not as a percent) multiplied by frequency will produce the TAI (total audience impressions) figure ($R\# \times F = TAI$).

   Then the corollary of that is:

   $$\frac{TAI}{F} = R\#$$

   and

$$\frac{TAI}{R\#} = F$$

So, using the answer from question 2, figure the numerical reach that is possible if you wish to achieve a frequency of 7 during the campaign. Show your calculations. You may wish to round off your answer.

4. Again, using the answer to question 2 and the information in question 3, calculate the frequency that is possible if the size of your target audience is 15 million (that is, a numerical reach of 15 million). Show your work. You may wish to round off your answer.

5. Like the TAI equations above, we can use our GRP to calculate other figures. Reach as a percentage multiplied by frequency gives GRP, or $R\% \times F = GRP$.

So, just as we did with TAI in question 3, we can also use these relationships to solve for percentage reach or for frequency.

$$\frac{GRP}{R\%} = F$$

and

$$\frac{GRP}{F} = R\%$$

Using these relationships, figure the percentage reach possible if we have a frequency goal of 10 times and our campaign will achieve 325 gross rating points. Show your calculations. You may need to round your answer to a workable figure.

6. Using the same relationships as in question 5, what frequency could we hope to achieve if we can afford to purchase a total of 280 GRP and we have a goal of reaching 27 percent of our target group? Show your work. You may wish to round off your answer.

Unit 4
Working with a Situation Analysis

Before providing a strategic recommendation, you should assess the situation. That is the first step in the planning process. A properly constructed situation analysis should provide you with the necessary information and insights to construct a communication plan that will meet the brand marketing objectives.

SWOT Analysis

The situation analysis is typically called a SWOT analysis. SWOT stands for strengths, weaknesses, opportunities, and threats. Exhibit 4.1 diagrams the SWOT analysis and the components of it. Here is a view of what each of the four areas contains.

1. Strengths

Strengths are something that the brand has that will be helpful in achieving the marketing objectives. For example, Frito-Lay has a sophisticated and highly developed distribution network for providing its products to all types of retail outlets including grocery stores, convenience stores, and institutions. If Frito-Lay is introducing a new product, this would be a great asset.

2. Weaknesses

Weaknesses are items the brand has that are detrimental to achieving the marketing objectives. For example, Cadillac has an old and stodgy reputation that would impact the company's ability to attract younger buyers to their automotive products.

Exhibit 4.1 **SWOT Analysis**

	Helpful	Harmful
Internal	**Strength**	**Weakness**
External	**Opportunity**	**Threat**

3. Opportunities

Opportunities are external forces that are helpful or that will aid the brand in reaching its objectives. For example, if birthrates for young women are rising by 5 percent, that is a good trend for Pampers. Or if the U.S. government taxes soft drinks, that could be an opportunity for bottled water brands.

4. Threats

Threats are external forces that are harmful or that will get in the way of the brand's achieving its objectives. For example, if Pepsi increases its marketing budget by 50 percent that could negatively impact Coke and other brands in the soft drink category. Or if the Pope decrees that all soft drinks are evil, that would be a threat to all soft drink brands.

Putting SWOT in Context

It is important to construct a SWOT analysis with a goal in mind. Otherwise, the SWOT analysis becomes a listing of unrelated items that do not impact the future strategy of the brand. So, if the brand's objective is to grow by 5 percent and the strategy for doing this is by expanding the user base of the brand, then the SWOT analysis should be done within that context.

In this case, it means looking at consumers who do not use the brand. Brand strength may be that the brand is accessible to new users. But a weakness may be that it is perceived as being too expensive. An opportunity could be that there is a movement toward quality within the category. A threat could be that another brand totally dominates this sector of the market.

Instead of just listing items to fill in each box in the SWOT analysis, always think about how each item will either help or hurt the brand's cause. That will make your SWOT analysis more powerful and actionable.

Integrated Marketing Communication SWOT

As you develop a SWOT analysis for an integrated marketing communication plan, you should identify both marketing and communication elements that can impact the brand. In addition, consumer trends may impact both marketing and communication. Here are examples of marketing and communication items that should be considered for the SWOT analysis.

1. Marketing

Marketing elements include distribution, pricing, and product comparisons between the brand and its competitors. Marketing can also include items such as how financially strong the company is, how experienced management is, and any patents or other proprietary items that the company has of value. It can also include brand perceptions by the consumer and other perceptual items related to the brand.

2. Communication

Communication elements include message, copy platforms, and communication outlet comparisons between the brand and its competitors. It can also include perceptual elements such as how strong the creative message is and if there are any media or sponsorships associated with the brand. There can also be cost or consumer trends in media consumption.

This is not an exhaustive list of items for either marketing or communication. The key is to identify all the elements that are relevant to the brand and its competitive set. It is also important to view the brand from the consumer's viewpoint. How the consumer sees the brand is crucial in determining how to tackle the marketing challenge. This should be captured in the SWOT analysis.

Summary

The SWOT analysis is a tremendous tool for determining future communication strategy. Keep in mind that the best SWOT analysis starts with an objective in mind. This puts the SWOT analysis in proper context. Ensure that the SWOT analysis contains both marketing and communication elements. These plus a thorough review of consumer trends will aid in developing a meaningful analysis.

Unit 4 Exercises
Working with a Situation Analysis

1. How would you describe the differences between each element of a SWOT analysis?

2. Why is it important to develop a SWOT analysis within the context of the brand's objective?

3. What is the difference between a marketing and a communication element?

4. If you were marketing the NIKE brand of athletic shoes, what are some external influences you might look at to develop your SWOT analysis?

5. Develop a SWOT analysis for NIKE to enter the geriatric shoe category. What makes this challenging, compared with merely introducing a new athletic shoe?

Note: A geriatric shoe is different from just another athletic shoe because it belongs to a new demographic, as well as to a new market where the NIKE brand may not have a track record or a perception of strength.

Unit 5
Working with
Communication Objectives

Every communication plan starts with overall communication objectives. Communication objectives derive from the overall marketing strategies. The key to a solid communication objective is to understand the role that communication plays in solving the marketing problem. The communication objective should be linked directly to the marketing challenge.

Communication objectives provide the road map for the entire integrated marketing communication planning process. These objectives will be reflected in the communication brief that will direct the creative team, the media team, and other stakeholders such as public relations, digital, and promotions.

Communication objectives contain two key elements:

1. The overall mission or goal of the communications. This is essentially the "what" that communications is designed to accomplish.
2. The target market. This is the "who" the communications are directed toward.

Specific objectives such as where and when are usually a part of the media brief and not necessarily a part of the overall communication objectives. The exception would be if knowing where and when becomes an overall communication issue that has creative as well as media implications.

There are five fundamental communication objectives that the majority of plans are built on. Following are brief descriptions of each objective and the target market implications of it.

1. Gain Awareness

Generating brand awareness is a classic objective for communications. Making people aware of your brand who aren't currently aware of it is the first step on the road to your brand's being purchased. An awareness objective drives the "who" you are going to target. It would be those who are unaware of the brand.

2. Convey New "News"

Imparting new information about a brand is another classic role for communications. It can be a new flavor, color, or way to use the current brand. In this case, conveying new "news" is a strategy that is typically directed at brand users or consumers who have some familiarity with the brand.

3. Encourage Brand Trial

Another classic role of communications is to persuade consumers to try the brand through some sort of short-term incentive. This objective suggests a target of consumers who are category users but may not be brand users. The goal of this communication is to meet the marketing strategy of increasing the consumer base.

4. Change Consumer Attitudes

Communication is heavily used to help change consumers' attitudes toward a brand. In this case, your target market is consumers who are aware of the brand but have a false perception of it. The role of communication is to get them to reconsider the brand.

5. Associate the Brand with a Specific Image

Communication is also heavily used to help develop an emotional connection with the brand's audience. To accomplish this, a brand aligns itself with a specific image. For example, Harley Davidson motorcycles are defined as an outlaw brand. Communication is used to reinforce that image.

These five communication objectives form the foundation for the communication plan. All strategies and tactics are aimed at fulfilling the objective.

Writing a Communication Objective

If your objective, then, is written in a fuzzy manner, your plan will suffer. A clearly written objective is paramount to developing a great communication plan. A clearly written objective begins with the word "To." A clearly written objective is measurable. And a clearly written objective is single minded.

The following are examples of clearly written communication objectives. Note the brevity and clarity of each. You can see from these objectives how a communication plan would unfold.

- "To increase awareness by 50 percent among urban teen men."
- "To convince working mothers that Pampers is worth the extra 50 cents."
- "To persuade conservative Democrats to vote for the Republican candidate."

All of these communication objectives are specific. They spell out the objective and the target audience. Some are straightforward while others evoke a sense of purpose. Regardless, they provide clear direction for the various team members to craft strategies and tactics that will meet the objective.

Unit 5 Exercises
Working with Communication Objectives

1. Why is it important that the communication objective be linked with the marketing strategy?

2. What are the two components of effective communication strategy?

3. What are the five fundamental communication objectives?

4. What are the components of a clearly written communication objective?

5. Write a communication objective based on the following marketing strategy for McDonalds: "to increase its usage among young men by offering $1.00 meal deals."

Unit 6
Working to Define the Target Market

Working to define your target market is the most important aspect of developing a media plan. If you are directing your advertising to the wrong target group or target audience, then you are not likely to meet your brand's marketing growth objectives. The task of properly defining the appropriate target audience is not confined to the media department. The target audience must align between the marketing objectives: the creative message and the media plan and buy. That is why defining the target audience is the most important facet of media planning.

The Target Triangle

There are three angles in discussing how to define the target audience. The first is the person who buys the product. This is called the *brand purchaser*. The brand purchaser may or may not be the one who is actually using the product. For example, a mother may be buying canned pasta for her children. The person who is actually using the product is called the *brand user*. Many times the brand purchaser and the brand user are one and the same. Other times, the user and the purchaser may be different persons, like the mother buying canned pasta for her children. She is the brand purchaser but the kids are the brand users. The third angle of the triangle is the *purchase influencer*. This is a situation that often arises, particularly when the brand is expensive. A purchase influencer is someone who neither buys the brand nor uses it but influences the one who is the brand purchaser. For example, a father may influence his wife's purchase of a car for their daughter. He may help direct the purchase, but he is not the one buying the car and he is not the one who will be driving it.

Each brand has a unique set of brand purchasers, users, and influencers. Some purchases are made and consumed by one person, such as buying yourself a cup of coffee. Others are more complex and involve other users or influencers. How your brand weighs each of these target areas is determined largely through primary research techniques. Nevertheless, there are a number of syndicated resources that can be used to help identify the purchaser of a brand and the user of the brand.

Syndicated Resources

We will cover three syndicated resources used by today's media planners to help define target audiences. The three resources are: Mediamark Research Incorporated, or MRI; Simmons Market Research Bureau, or SMRB; and Scarborough Market Research.

MRI is the primary resource for aiding media planners in defining target audiences and media habits. MRI is a national study with a huge sample of 26,000 adults ages 18 and over per wave. It conducts two waves per year, so the "doublebase," or combination of the two studies, yields a sample of over 50,000 adults, making the data highly projectable. MRI provides information on more than 500 product categories and over 6,000 individual brands, and its data can be used to help determine the brand purchaser and the brand user.

SMRB, also a large, nationally syndicated tool with a large sample, surveys many of the same product categories and brands that MRI does, but each study focuses on distinctive categories. SMRB has some unique questions that help media people and brand managers better understand the psychographics, that is, the psychological makeup of the consumer. Like MRI, SMRB allows the media planner to evaluate the brand purchaser and the brand user for a variety of products.

Scarborough is the largest of the three studies in terms of sample size because it is a local market study. Scarborough surveys the top 75 markets in the United States with a total sample size of 200,000 respondents. Whereas MRI and SMRB focus largely on national categories and national or large regional brands, Scarborough provides individual market-by-market information primarily in the retail, media, and entertainment sectors. As well, they offer market-level information on select consumer product categories.

Each tool has its merits and can be used in a wide variety of ways. With computer-aided software, each syndicated study can be manipulated to find target audience segments on demographic, geographic, and even psychographic levels.

Defining the Target by Usage

We have said that there are three types of people who may impact the purchase of a product. They are the purchaser, the user, and sometimes the influencer. One way to evaluate the importance of a target audience segment is by usage. This can be defined either by a household or by an individual. MRI and SMRB define many products and brands by heavy, medium, and light users.

The *Pareto principle* states that 20 percent of consumers purchase 80 percent of the products for sale in the United States. This 80/20 rule may or may not apply to the brand or category that you are studying, but, typically, there is some sort of heavy user segment for every brand. MRI and SMRB measure heavy users by purchase frequency. So, if a consumer buys five tubes of toothpaste in a month, they may be considered a heavy user of toothpaste. Likewise, if another consumer buys a tube of toothpaste once every two months, they might be considered a light user. The principle of heavy, medium, and light usage helps aid media planners in determining the relative importance of each segment and how much volume each one contributes to the purchase of the brand or category.

Before assessing the importance of heavy users, it is crucial to understand the volume they represent. If 20 percent of your brand users represent 80 percent of the purchases of your product, then the heavy user is crucial for the survival of your brand. There is another way to view these data: you may want to get the other 80 percent of your users to use more of your product so that you aren't as dependent upon those core heavy users.

Practical Application of Defining the Target Audience

As we have described, there are many ways to define a target audience. Because the common denominator for much of media buying research is demographics, at some time you will likely need to define your target audience demographically.

A typical demographic target comprises gender, age, income, and the presence of children in the home. For example, many grocery products have a demographic target audience of women, ages 25–54, with a household income of $40,000+, and with one or more children in the household.

As you review demographic targets, it is important to balance your definition between those who are most likely to use the product and a large enough population base to market to. For example, if women ages 25–34 had an index of 150, it might be tempting to market to just this group. They obviously are 50 percent more likely to buy your brand than any other age group. But women ages 25–34 represent less than 20 percent of all women, so even though they are highly engaged in your product, they represent only 30 percent of your brand's usage.

Most marketers want to market to the majority of their brand users, or, if they are introducing a new product, then to the majority of the category users. This means that marketers want their target audience definition to include at least 50 percent of the users of their product. As we described earlier, this may not necessarily mean 50 percent of the population. As you define your target, it is important to ensure that you have a target that represents the majority of users.

On the other hand, marketers want to target those most likely to purchase their product. In reviewing secondary research, most marketers set a benchmark of a 120 index or above as defining a group that is very likely to buy their product. Conversely, marketers view a group with an index of 80 or below as a group that is unlikely to buy their product. As you review the information defining a target audience, it is important to balance the size of the audience with the likeliness of their purchasing the product.

Tips for Reading the Information

Reading and properly interpreting MRI, SMRB, or Scarborough information can initially be a rather daunting task. There is a wealth of information available, but with it comes a tremendous amount of data to digest. With all of these resources, what once came in a library of printed publications now comes only online. Even with the sophisticated software that manipulates these data, there are some basic items you need to understand that will help you interpret the information.

For example, as shown in Table 6.1, MRI has five columns of information on the target group. The first is the total projected universe of the United States, that is, "Total U.S. (000)."

This serves as the base for all the other numbers. The base may be all adults or it may be just female homemakers. Consider the set of five rows to the right of "Ages 21–34" in Table 6.1. There are an estimated 52,558,000 adults ages 21–34 in the United States (52,558 × 1,000 = 52,558,000). The number above this projection is the unweighted sample size, abbreviated "Unwgtd." In this example MRI's sample size was 11,960. All the numbers in this row are the bases for understanding how the brand information relates to the general population.

Let's walk through one set of five rows of numbers. If you look at the (000) row for ages 21–34. Under the heading "Budweiser: all users" (meaning everyone who has had a Budweiser beer in the past six months) you will find the number 8,421. That means that 8,421,000 adults ages 21–34 have had a Bud in the past six months. The next row is called the horizontal percentage, or Horz %. This relates to the horizontal base, or, in this case, adults ages 21–34. The 16.0 percent here means that 16.0 percent of adults ages 21–34 have drunk Budweiser beer in the past six months.

The next row is the vertical percentage, or Vert %. This relates to the vertical base, or, in this case, the total Budweiser drinkers in the past six months. The 33.9 percent in this row means that 33.9 percent of adult Budweiser drinkers in the past six months are between the ages of 21 and 34.

The final number is an index. The index in this case is 132. This means that adults ages 21–34 are 32 percent more likely to be Budweiser drinkers than the general adult population. Another way to look at the index is that 12.1 percent of all adults drank a Budweiser in the past six months, but 16.0 percent of adults ages 21–34 drank a Budweiser over that same six-month span (16.0/12.1 = 1.32 × 100 = 132).

It takes some time to grasp this information, so don't be discouraged if you don't understand it all immediately. Many media professionals have a hard time communicating what each of these rows means. With some practice, you will be able to reliably interpret and apply the calculations that go into defining a target audience.

Table 6.1

The Target Group

		Total U.S. (000)	Total beer/ale: Budweiser all users	Budweiser heavy users	Total beer/ale: Miller Lite all users	Miller Lite heavy users
All	Unwgtd	51,774	6,271	1,413	3,040	592
	(000)	205,368	24,847	5,898	10,492	2,002
	Horz %	100	12.1	2.87	5.11	0.97
	Vert %	100	100	100	100	100
	Index	100	100	100	100	100
Ages 21–34	Unwgtd	11,960	1,911	431	1,001	212
	(000)	52,558	8,421	2,099	3,791	739
	Horz %	100	16.0	4.0	7.2	1.4
	Vert %	25.59	33.9	35.6	36.1	36.9
	Index	100	132	139	141	144
Ages 35–44	Unwgtd	11,901	1,694	407	802	149
	(000)	44,776	6,099	1,513	2,565	495
	Horz %	100	13.6	3.4	5.7	1.1
	Vert %	21.8	24.6	25.7	24.5	24.7
	Index	100	113	118	112	113
Ages 45–54	Unwgtd	10,109	1,139	252	565	117
	(000)	38,134	4170	967	1,904	356
	Horz %	100	10.9	2.5	5.0	0.9
	Vert %	18.57	16.8	16.4	18.2	17.8
	Index	100	90	88	98	96
Age 55+	Unwgtd	16,132	1,266	257	587	99
	(000)	57,504	4,306	925	1,666	293
	Horz %	100	7.5	1.6	2.9	0.5
	Vert %	28	17.3	15.7	15.9	14.7
	Index	100	62	56	57	52
Median age	Unwgtd					
	(000)	43.5	38.9	38.3	38.5	37.7
	Horz %					
	Vert %					
	Index	89	88	89	87	
HHI $0–$29,000	Unwgtd	12,809	1,414	394	393	83
	(000)	58,615	6,935	2,016	1,537	353
	Horz %	100	11.8	3.4	2.6	0.6
	Vert %	28.54	27.9	34.2	14.6	17.6
	Index	100	98	120	51	62
HHI $30,000–$49,000	Unwgtd	11,847	1,338	347	558	115
	(000)	43,895	5,261	1,397	1,845	366
	Horz %	100	12.0	3.2	4.2	0.8
	Vert %	21.37	21.2	23.7	17.6	18.3
	Index	100	99	111	82	86
HHI $50,000–$74,000	Unwgtd	10,737	1,330	288	655	137
	(000)	42,424	4,929	1,118	2,399	443
	Horz %	100	11.6	2.6	5.7	1.1
	Vert %	20.66	19.8	19.0	22.9	22.2
	Index	100	96	92	111	107
HHI $75,000+	Unwgtd	16,381	2,189	384	1,434	257
	(000)	60,434	7,722	1,366	4,712	839
	Horz %	100	12.8	2.3	7.8	1.4
	Vert %	29.43	31.1	23.2	44.9	41.9
	Index	100	106	79	153	142

(continued)

Table 6.1 *(continued)*

		Total U.S. (000)	Total beer/ale: Budweiser all users	Budweiser heavy users	Total beer/ale: Miller Lite all users	Miller Lite heavy users
HHI $100,000+	Unwgtd	9,715	1,269	197	874	157
	(000)	34,544	4310	694	2794	498
	Horz %	100	12.5	2.0	8.1	1.4
	Vert %	16.82	17.4	11.8	26.6	24.9
	Index	100	103	70	158	148
Median HHI	Unwgtd					
	(000)	$50,093	$51,053	$41,712	$69,193	$65,905
	Horz %					
	Vert %					
	Index		102	83	138	132
Married	Unwgtd	28,252	3,449	721	1,815	320
	(000)	117,121	13,211	2,960	6,142	1,069
	Horz %	100	11.3	2.5	5.2	0.9
	Vert %	57.03	53.2	50.2	58.5	53.4
	Index	100	93	88	103	94
Single	Unwgtd	10,983	1,740	428	756	172
	(000)	49,609	8,065	2,021	3,115	641
	Horz %	100	16.3	4.1	6.3	1.3
	Vert %	24.16	32.5	34.3	29.7	32.0
	Index	100	134	142	123	133
Race: White	Unwgtd	44,370	5,299	1,188	2,791	546
	(000)	171,788	20,205	4,690	9,490	1,853
	Horz %	100	11.8	2.7	5.5	1.1
	Vert %	83.65	81.3	79.5	90.5	92.6
	Index	100	97	95	108	111 *
Race: Black	Unwgtd	5,325	716	182	158	31
	(000)	24,335	3,549	973	648	108
	Horz %	100	14.6	4.0	2.7	0.4
	Vert %	11.85	14.3	16.5	6.2	5.4
	Index	100	121	139 *	52	46 *
Race: Asian	Unwgtd	1,334	168	25	56	12
	(000)	5,754	656	130	193	30
	Horz %	100	11.4	2.3	3.4	0.5
	Vert %	2.8	2.6	2.2	1.8	1.5
	Index	100	94	79	66	53 *
Spanish or Hispanic original or descent	Unwgtd	4,437	654	167	194	47
	(000)	22,534	3,441	845	850	232
	Horz %	100	15.3	3.8	3.8	1.0
	Vert %	10.97	13.9	14.3	8.1	11.6
	Index	100	126	131	74	105
Education: graduate college plus undergraduate		16,869	2,028	321	1,362	226
	(000)	48,773	5,655	906	3,797	600
	Horz %	100	11.6	1.9	7.8	12
	Vert %	23.75	22.8	15.4	36.2	30.0
	Index	100	96	65	152	126
Education: graduate high school	Unwgtd	13,714	1,641	434	614	138
	(000)	66,311	7,887	2,063	2,535	534
	Horz %	100	11.9	3.1	3.8	0.8
	Vert %	32.29	31.7	35.0	24.2	26.7
	Index	100	98	108	75	83

		Total U.S. (000)	Total beer/ale: Budweiser all users	Budweiser heavy users	Total beer/ale: Miller Lite all users	Miller Lite heavy users
Education: no college	Unwgtd	19,101	2,285	625	790	178
	(000)	100,824	12,264	3,349	3,661	809
	Horz %	100	12.2	3.3	3.6	0.8
	Vert %	49.09	49.4	56.8	34.9	40.4
	Index	100	101	116	71	82*
Marketing region: New England	Unwgtd	3,509	541	147	153	25
	(000)	10,370	1,585	422	395	73
	Horz %	100	15.3	4.1	3.8	01
	Vert %	5.05	6.4	7.2	3.8	3.7
	Index	100	126	142	75	72
Marketing region: Mid-Atlantic	Unwgtd	10,671	1,504	280	545	89
	(000)	33,289	4,677	878	1,430	223
	Horz %	100	14.1	2.6	4.3	0.7
	Vert %	16.21	18.8	14.9	13.6	11.1
	Index	100	116	92	84	69
Marketing region: East Central	Unwgtd	7,593	913	205	475	119
	(000)	26,817	3,190	872	1,504	338
	Horz %	100	11.9	3.3	5.6	1.3
	Vert %	13.06	12.8	14.8	14.3	16.9
	Index	100	98	113	110	129
Marketing region: West Central	Unwgtd	8,085	850	171	848	171
	(000)	31,062	3,591	814	2,839	565
	Horz %	100	11.6	2.6	9.1	1.8
	Vert %	15.12	14.5	13.8	27.1	28.2
	Index	100	96	91	179	187
Marketing region: Southeast	Unwgtd	7,070	792	185	382	74
	(000)	40,667	4,644	1,121	1,890	328
	Horz %	100	11.4	2.8	4.7	0.8
	Vert %	19.8	18.7	19.0	18.0	16.4
	Index	100	94	96	91	83
Marketing region: Southwest	Unwgtd	5,414	613	181	383	73
	(000)	23,633	2,743	749	1,514	306
	Horz %	100	11.6	3.2	6.4	1.3
	Vert %	11.51	11.0	12.7	14.4	15.3
	Index	100	96	110	125	133*
Marketing region: Pacific	Unwgtd	9,432	1,058	244	254	41
	(000)	39,531	4,417	1,043	919	169
	Horz %	100	11.2	2.6	2.3	0.4
	Vert %	19.25	17.8	17.7	8.8	8.4
	Index	100	92	92	46	44

Source: Doublebase Mediamark Research Inc.

Notes: weighted population (000).

*Projections relatively unstable, use with caution. Base: All.

All users = drank in last 6 months; heavy users = 6+ glasses past 7 days.

HHI = household income.

Unit 6 Exercises
Working to Define the Target Market

Use Table 6.1 on the previous pages to answer the following questions:

1. How many more adults ages 21+ have drunk Budweiser in the past six months compared with Miller Lite?

2. What percentage of Budweiser drinkers (all users) fall into the ages 21–34 category?

3. What household income (HHI) levels would you need to target to best reach 50 percent of Miller Lite's heavy users?

4. What is the index of usage for Budweiser versus Miller Lite among the ethnic audiences of blacks and Hispanics?

5. If you were going to try to gain market share for Miller Lite, which marketing region would you pick to "heavy up" (give extra weight or emphasis to) and why?

6. Would you target more users of Budweiser or Miller Lite by directing your message toward college-educated or not-college-educated adults?

7. If you changed the target emphasis for Budweiser from all users to heavy users, how would that impact your household income aspect of the target?

8. What is the minimum number of glasses consumed by Budweiser heavy users ages 21–34?

9. What would be your target audience definition for Budweiser?

10. How does the above target compare with Miller Lite?

Unit 7
Working with Geographic Marketing Information

A fundamental part of media planning is knowing where you should apply media pressure to get the best result. This involves understanding the geographic sales of the brand as well as the category sales. Like the seasonality indices, the sales information that you use as a basis for geographic analyses is proprietary information that is held by the brand.

You will want to do an analysis that measures the per capita consumption of your brand on a market-by-market basis. This is called a *brand development index* (BDI). A BDI is computed by dividing the percentage of sales in a given market by the percentage of that market's population to the total brand's universe. If we were dealing with a national brand, then it would be the percentage of the United States (see Table 7.1).

For example, let's take a look at New York in Table 7.1: 6.4 percent of Barton Springs sales are in New York, yet New York represents a little over 6.8 percent of the total population of the United States. So, the BDI for New York is 94, that is, 6.4%/6.8% × 100 as the BDI formula. With a 100 index being the average, consumers in New York are slightly less than average purchasers of Barton Springs.

Just looking at your brand without looking at the category it competes in may not reflect the true picture of how best to apply your advertising resources on a market-by-market basis. The category sales per capita is called a *category development index* (CDI). It is computed identically to the BDI. For example, New York's bottled water sales are 12.9 percent which then reflects a CDI of 189 (12.9%/6.8% × 100). Knowing this piece of information puts a whole different spin on Barton Springs's potential in the market. Even though consumption of Barton Springs is about average in New York, it is not nearly as strong as the category, which means that there is a lot of sales potential for this brand in this market.

With the BDI and CDI information in hand, you can create an analysis called a *brand opportunity index* (BOI). A BOI is computed by dividing the CDI by the BDI. You are actually indexing the indexes. In the example of Barton Springs in New York, the CDI is 189 and the BDI is 94. That would make for a BOI of 201. This tells us that there is some growth opportunity for Barton Springs in this market. Many media planners use a quadrant analysis with CDI as one axis and BDI as the other to visually represent this analysis. See Exhibit 7.1 for an example of this analysis tool.

Table 7.1

Geographic Analyses

Rank	Designated Market Area® (DMA)	TV households	% of U.S.	Bottled water category sales	% Sales	CDI	Barton Springs brand sales	% Sales	BDI
1	New York	7,282,320	6.829	36,411,600	12.90	189	5,825,856	6.43	94
2	Los Angeles	5,318,040	4.987	26,590,200	9.42	189	7,977,060	8.80	177
3	Chicago	3,351,330	3.143	13,405,320	4.75	151	3,016,197	3.33	106
4	Philadelphia	2,830,470	2.654	8,491,410	3.01	113	1,981,329	2.19	82
5	San Francisco-Oak-San Jose	2,436,220	2.284	12,181,100	4.32	189	3,654,330	4.03	177
6	Boston (Manchester)	2,353,500	2.207	9,414,000	3.34	151	1,882,800	2.08	94
7	Dallas-Ft. Worth	2,195,540	2.059	8,782,160	3.11	151	2,195,540	2.42	118
8	Washington, DC (Hagrstwn)	2,169,230	2.034	6,507,690	2.31	113	1,735,384	1.92	94
9	Atlanta	1,971,180	1.848	7,884,720	2.79	151	1,774,062	1.96	106
10	Detroit	1,899,910	1.782	3,039,856	1.08	60	1,139,946	1.26	71
11	Houston	1,814,140	1.701	5,442,420	1.93	113	2,721,210	3.00	177
12	Seattle-Tacoma	1,659,100	1.556	4,977,300	1.76	113	1,659,100	1.83	118
13	Tampa-St. Pete (Sarasota)	1,620,110	1.519	3,240,220	1.15	76	1,296,088	1.43	94
14	Minneapolis-St. Paul	1,594,740	1.495	2,551,584	0.90	60	1,275,792	1.41	94
15	Cleveland-Akron (Canton)	1,528,840	1.434	2,446,144	0.87	60	1,223,072	1.35	94
16	Phoenix	1,524,130	1.429	7,620,650	2.70	189	2,286,195	2.52	177
17	Miami-Ft. Lauderdale	1,486,860	1.394	4,460,580	1.58	113	2,230,290	2.46	177
18	Denver	1,366,250	1.281	5,465,000	1.94	151	1,366,250	1.51	118
19	Sacramento-Stktn-Modesto	1,227,600	1.151	3,682,800	1.30	113	1,227,600	1.35	118
20	Orlando-Daytona Bch-Melbrn	1,224,470	1.148	3,673,410	1.30	113	979,576	1.08	94
21	Pittsburgh	1,165,660	1.093	1,865,056	0.66	60	815,962	0.90	82
22	St. Louis	1,156,370	1.084	1,850,192	0.66	60	925,096	1.02	94
23	Portland, OR	1,061,080	0.995	3,183,240	1.13	113	954,972	1.05	106
24	Baltimore	1,060,450	0.994	2,120,900	0.75	76	742,315	0.82	82
25	Indianapolis	1,019,870	0.956	1,427,818	0.51	53	713,909	0.79	82
26	San Diego	1,004,220	0.942	4,016,880	1.42	151	1,004,220	1.11	118
27	Hartford & New Haven	980,410	0.919	1,568,656	0.56	60	784,328	0.87	94
28	Charlotte	962,540	0.903	2,887,620	1.02	113	962,540	1.06	118
29	Raleigh-Durham (Fayetteville)	929,460	0.872	2,788,380	0.99	113	743,568	0.82	94
30	Nashville	880,670	0.826	1,409,072	0.50	60	704,536	0.78	94
31	Milwaukee	860,350	0.807	1,204,490	0.43	53	602,245	0.66	82
32	Cincinnati	854,250	0.801	1,195,950	0.42	53	597,975	0.66	82
33	Kansas City	852,510	0.799	1,534,518	0.54	68	596,757	0.66	82
34	Columbus, OH	835,780	0.784	1,170,092	0.41	53	585,046	0.65	82
35	Greenvll-Spart-Ashevll-And	792,110	0.743	1,901,064	0.67	91	475,266	0.52	71
36	Salt Lake City	769,230	0.721	2,307,690	0.82	113	461,538	0.51	71
37	San Antonio	718,730	0.674	2,156,190	0.76	113	1,078,095	1.19	177
38	Grand Rapids-Kalmzoo-B.Crk	713,800	0.669	999,320	0.35	53	499,660	0.55	82

Rank	Market								
39	West Palm Beach-Ft. Pierce	700,850	0.657	1,401,700	0.50	76	700,850	0.77	118
40	Birmingham (Ann and Tusc)	690,030	0.647	1,380,060	0.49	76	690,030	0.76	118
41	Norfolk-Portsmth-Newpt Nws	677,610	0.635	1,355,220	0.48	76	677,610	0.75	118
42	New Orleans	658,830	0.618	1,054,128	0.37	60	527,064	0.58	94
43	Memphis	653,840	0.613	1,569,216	0.56	91	653,840	0.72	118
44	Buffalo	639,190	0.599	767,028	0.27	45	383,514	0.42	71
45	Oklahoma City	636,970	0.597	1,273,940	0.45	76	636,970	0.70	118
46	Greensboro-H.Point-W.Salem	634,140	0.595	1,268,280	0.45	76	634,140	0.70	118
47	Harrisburg-Lncstr-Leb-York	626,660	0.588	877,324	0.31	53	438,662	0.48	82
48	Providence-New Bedford	624,020	0.585	748,824	0.27	45	374,412	0.41	71
49	Albuquerque-Santa Fe	620,230	0.582	1,860,690	0.66	113	620,230	0.68	118
50	Louisville	612,300	0.574	1,102,140	0.39	68	551,070	0.61	106
51	Jacksonville, Brunswick	587,200	0.551	1,056,960	0.37	68	528,480	0.58	106
52	Las Vegas	585,440	0.549	2,341,760	0.83	151	585,440	0.65	118
53	Wilkes Barre-Scranton	580,290	0.544	812,406	0.29	53	406,203	0.45	82
54	Austin	552,060	0.518	2,208,240	0.78	151	552,060	0.61	118
55	Albany-Schenectady-Troy	532,520	0.499	745,528	0.26	53	372,764	0.41	82
56	Little Rock-Pine Bluff	523,810	0.491	942,858	0.33	68	471,429	0.52	106
57	Fresno-Visalia	519,330	0.487	934,794	0.33	68	467,397	0.52	106
58	Dayton	506,240	0.475	708,736	0.25	53	354,368	0.39	82
59	Richmond-Petersburg	505,370	0.474	1,010,740	0.36	76	404,296	0.45	94
60	Tulsa	496,880	0.466	795,008	0.28	60	397,504	0.44	94
61	Charleston-Huntington	495,320	0.464	693,448	0.25	53	396,256	0.44	94
62	Mobile-Pensacola (Ft Walt)	490,590	0.46	981,180	0.35	76	392,472	0.43	94
63	Knoxville	489,710	0.459	783,536	0.28	60	391,768	0.43	94
64	Flint-Saginaw-Bay City	466,510	0.437	559,812	0.20	45	373,208	0.41	94
65	Lexington	454,440	0.426	817,992	0.29	68	363,552	0.40	94
66	Wichita-Hutchinson Plus	445,220	0.418	712,400	0.25	60	356,200	0.39	94
67	Roanoke-Lynchburg	445,000	0.417	623,000	0.22	53	311,500	0.34	82
68	Toledo	432,770	0.406	519,324	0.18	45	259,662	0.29	71
69	Green Bay-Appleton	418,580	0.393	502,296	0.18	45	251,148	0.28	71
70	Ft. Myers-Naples	413,730	0.388	827,460	0.29	76	330,984	0.37	94
71	Honolulu	401,330	0.376	1,203,990	0.43	113	401,330	0.44	118
72	Des Moines-Ames	400,830	0.376	561,162	0.20	53	280,581	0.31	82
73	Springfield, MO	400,390	0.375	480,468	0.17	45	240,234	0.27	71
74	Tucson (Sierra Vista)	399,800	0.375	1,599,200	0.57	151	399,800	0.44	118
75	Paducah-C.Girardeau-Harrisbg-Mt Vernon	395,190	0.371	474,228	0.17	45	256,874	0.28	76
76	Portland-Auburn	391,930	0.368	470,316	0.17	45	254,755	0.28	76
77	Rochester, NY	388,600	0.364	466,320	0.17	45	252,590	0.28	77
78	Omaha	386,600	0.363	695,880	0.25	68	251,290	0.28	76
79	Spokane	381,130	0.357	762,260	0.27	76	247,735	0.27	77
80	Syracuse	375,880	0.352	676,584	0.24	68	244,322	0.27	77
81	Shreveport	372,950	0.35	596,720	0.21	60	242,418	0.27	76
82	Champaign&Sprngfld-Decatur	371,240	0.348	519,736	0.18	53	241,306	0.27	77

(continued)

Table 7.1 (continued)

Rank	Designated Market Area® (DMA)	TV households	% of U.S.	Bottled water category sales	% Sales	CDI	Barton Springs brand sales	% Sales	BDI
83	Huntsville-Decatur (Flor)	359,260	0.337	646,668	0.23	68	233,519	0.26	76
84	Columbia, SC	357,810	0.336	715,620	0.25	75	232,577	0.26	76
85	Chattanooga	351,610	0.33	421,932	0.15	45	228,547	0.25	76
86	Madison	348,590	0.327	418,308	0.15	45	226,584	0.25	76
87	South Bend-Elkhart	326,470	0.306	587,646	0.21	68	212,206	0.23	77
88	Cedar Rapids-Wtrlo-IWC&Dub	323,810	0.304	453,334	0.16	53	210,477	0.23	76
89	Jackson, MS	320,260	0.3	448,364	0.16	53	208,169	0.23	77
90	Tri-Cities, TN-VA	318,390	0.299	382,068	0.14	45	206,954	0.23	76
91	Burlington-Plattsburgh	317,700	0.298	508,320	0.18	60	206,505	0.23	76
92	Davenport-R.Island-Moline	306,450	0.287	367,740	0.13	45	199,193	0.22	77
93	Waco-Temple-Bryan	303,560	0.285	607,120	0.22	75	197,314	0.22	76
94	Colorado Springs-Pueblo	302,750	0.284	908,250	0.32	113	196,788	0.22	76
95	Baton Rouge	295,790	0.277	591,580	0.21	76	192,264	0.21	77
96	Johnstown-Altoona	294,450	0.276	353,340	0.13	45	191,393	0.21	77
97	Harlingen-Wslco-Brnsvl-McA	287,230	0.269	631,906	0.22	83	287,230	0.32	118
98	Savannah	284,160	0.266	454,656	0.16	61	184,704	0.20	77
99	Evansville	280,860	0.263	393,204	0.14	53	182,559	0.20	77
100	Youngstown	277,760	0.26	388,864	0.14	53	180,544	0.20	77
101	El Paso	276,330	0.259	552,660	0.20	76	276,330	0.30	118
102	Lincoln & Hstngs-Krny Plus	266,890	0.25	533,780	0.19	76	173,479	0.19	77
103	Greenville-N.Bern-Washngtn	266,390	0.25	346,307	0.12	49	173,154	0.19	76
104	Ft. Wayne	264,140	0.248	316,968	0.11	45	158,484	0.17	71
105	Charleston, SC	262,560	0.246	341,328	0.12	49	170,664	0.19	77
106	Springfield-Holyoke	258,330	0.242	361,662	0.13	53	170,664	0.19	82
107	Tallahassee-Thomasville	255,980	0.24	460,764	0.16	68	230,382	0.20	82
108	Ft. Smith-Fay-Sprngdl-Rgrs	255,390	0.239	255,390	0.09	38	127,695	0.25	106
109	Tyler-Longview (Lfkn&Ncgd)	254,780	0.239	305,736	0.11	45	152,868	0.14	59
110	Florence-Myrtle Beach	253,630	0.238	304,356	0.11	45	152,178	0.17	71
111	Lansing	248,250	0.233	446,850	0.16	68	148,950	0.17	71
112	Sioux Falls (Mitchell)	244,310	0.229	244,310	0.09	38	146,586	0.16	71
113	Traverse City-Cadillac	243,870	0.229	219,483	0.08	34	146,322	0.16	71
114	Reno	241,660	0.227	483,320	0.17	75	144,996	0.16	71
115	Augusta	240,710	0.226	288,852	0.10	45	144,426	0.16	71
116	Montgomery (Selma)	240,290	0.225	240,290	0.09	38	144,174	0.16	71
117	Peoria-Bloomington	236,810	0.222	473,620	0.17	76	142,086	0.16	71
118	Fargo-Valley City	231,530	0.217	208,377	0.07	34	138,918	0.15	71
119	SantaBarbra-SanMar-SanLuOb	230,250	0.216	552,600	0.20	91	207,225	0.23	106
120	Monterey-Salinas	228,290	0.214	547,896	0.19	91	205,461	0.23	106
121	Eugene	223,630	0.21	447,260	0.16	75	156,541	0.17	82
122	Macon	221,300	0.208	309,820	0.11	53	154,910	0.17	82
123	La Crosse-Eau Claire	217,930	0.204	261,516	0.09	45	130,758	0.14	71
124	Boise	216,960	0.203	260,352	0.09	45	130,176	0.14	71
125	Lafayette, LA	213,380	0.2	256,056	0.09	45	128,028	0.14	71
126	Columbus, GA	203,510	0.191	244,212	0.09	45	122,106	0.13	71

127	Yakima-Pasco-Rchlnd-Knnwck	199,120	0.187	278,768	0.10	53	139,384	0.15	82
128	Corpus Christi	191,280	0.179	267,792	0.09	53	153,024	0.17	94
129	Amarillo	189,880	0.178	227,856	0.08	45	151,904	0.17	94
130	Bakersfield	186,400	0.175	447,360	0.16	91	149,120	0.16	94
131	Columbus-Tupelo-West Point	186,100	0.175	223,320	0.08	45	111,660	0.12	70
132	Chico-Redding	184,280	0.173	331,704	0.12	68	165,852	0.18	106
133	Monroe-El Dorado	177,700	0.167	177,700	0.06	38	106,620	0.12	70
134	Wausau-Rhinelander	175,790	0.165	175,790	0.06	38	105,474	0.12	71
135	Rockford	175,560	0.165	175,560	0.06	38	105,336	0.12	70
136	Duluth-Superior	172,250	0.162	172,250	0.06	38	103,350	0.11	70
137	Beaumont-Port Arthur	170,560	0.16	170,560	0.06	38	102,336	0.11	71
138	Topeka	168,390	0.158	168,390	0.06	38	101,034	0.11	71
139	Columbia-Jefferson City	164,200	0.154	164,200	0.06	38	98,520	0.11	71
140	Sioux City	157,860	0.148	157,860	0.06	38	94,716	0.10	71
141	Medford-Klamath Falls	157,500	0.148	157,500	0.06	38	94,500	0.10	70
142	Wichita Falls & Lawton	157,410	0.148	125,928	0.04	30	94,446	0.10	70
143	Erie	157,070	0.147	157,070	0.06	38	94,242	0.10	71
144	Wilmington	155,350	0.146	155,350	0.06	38	93,210	0.10	70
145	Joplin-Pittsburg	152,980	0.143	122,384	0.04	30	91,788	0.10	71
146	Terre Haute	151,180	0.142	241,888	0.09	60	90,708	0.10	71
147	Lubbock	149,990	0.141	299,980	0.11	75	89,994	0.10	70
148	Albany, GA	149,180	0.14	298,360	0.11	76	89,508	0.10	71
149	Bluefield-Beckley-Oak Hill	143,230	0.134	114,584	0.04	30	57,292	0.06	47
150	Wheeling-Steubenville	141,790	0.133	113,432	0.04	30	56,716	0.06	47
151	Salisbury	141,590	0.133	113,272	0.04	30	56,636	0.06	47
152	Rochestr-Mason City-Austin	139,060	0.13	111,248	0.04	30	55,624	0.06	47
153	Bangor	137,830	0.129	110,264	0.04	30	55,132	0.06	47
154	Binghamton	136,670	0.128	109,336	0.04	30	54,668	0.06	47
155	Minot-Bismarck-Dickinson	133,070	0.125	106,456	0.04	30	53,228	0.06	47
156	Anchorage	132,740	0.124	106,192	0.04	30	53,096	0.06	47
157	Biloxi-Gulfport	132,200	0.124	105,760	0.04	30	52,880	0.06	47
158	Odessa-Midland	131,800	0.124	105,440	0.04	30	52,720	0.06	47
159	Panama City	130,660	0.123	104,528	0.04	30	52,264	0.06	47
160	Sherman, TX-Ada, OK	120,770	0.113	96,616	0.03	30	48,308	0.05	47
161	Palm Springs	119,010	0.112	238,020	0.08	75	23,802	0.03	23
162	Gainesville	116,380	0.109	232,760	0.08	76	23,276	0.03	24
163	Abilene-Sweetwater	114,660	0.108	183,456	0.07	60	22,932	0.03	23
164	Quincy-Hannibal-Keokuk	110,250	0.103	88,200	0.03	30	22,050	0.02	24
165	Idaho Falls-Pocatello	108,400	0.102	86,720	0.03	30	21,680	0.02	23
166	Clarksburg-Weston	105,640	0.099	84,512	0.03	30	21,128	0.02	24
167	Utica	103,450	0.097	82,760	0.03	30	20,690	0.02	23
168	Hattiesburg-Laurel	100,910	0.095	80,728	0.03	30	20,182	0.02	23
169	Missoula	98,380	0.092	78,704	0.03	30	19,676	0.02	24
170	Billings	98,150	0.092	78,520	0.03	30	19,630	0.02	24

(continued)

Table 7.1 (continued)

Rank	Designated Market Area® (DMA)	TV households	% of U.S.	Bottled water category sales	% Sales	CDI	Barton Springs brand sales	% Sales	BDI
171	Dothan	97,520	0.091	156,032	0.06	61	19,504	0.02	24
172	Yuma-El Centro	96,400	0.09	250,640	0.09	99	19,280	0.02	24
173	Elmira	95,760	0.09	76,608	0.03	30	19,152	0.02	23
174	Lake Charles	92,680	0.087	111,216	0.04	45	18,536	0.02	24
175	Rapid City	91,720	0.086	110,064	0.04	45	18,344	0.02	24
176	Watertown	89,580	0.084	89,580	0.03	38	17,916	0.02	24
177	Marquette	88,040	0.083	140,864	0.05	60	17,608	0.02	23
178	Harrisonburg	86,320	0.081	103,584	0.04	45	17,264	0.02	24
179	Alexandria, LA	85,540	0.08	102,648	0.04	45	17,108	0.02	24
180	Bowling Green	81,790	0.077	98,148	0.03	45	16,358	0.02	23
181	Jonesboro	81,580	0.076	81,580	0.03	38	16,316	0.02	24
182	Greenwood-Greenville	79,750	0.075	79,750	0.03	38	15,950	0.02	23
183	Jackson, TN	79,570	0.075	79,570	0.03	38	15,914	0.02	23
184	Grand Junction-Montrose	72,010	0.068	72,010	0.03	38	14,402	0.02	23
185	Meridian	70,670	0.066	56,536	0.02	30	14,134	0.02	24
186	Charlottesville	67,490	0.063	121,482	0.04	68	13,498	0.01	24
187	Great Falls	64,110	0.06	64,110	0.02	38	12,822	0.01	24
188	Parkersburg	63,580	0.06	50,864	0.02	30	12,716	0.01	23
189	Lafayette, IN	59,160	0.055	106,488	0.04	69	11,832	0.01	24
190	Eureka	59,130	0.055	94,608	0.03	61	11,826	0.01	24
191	Twin Falls	58,470	0.055	58,470	0.02	38	11,694	0.01	23
192	Laredo	57,940	0.054	57,940	0.02	38	11,588	0.01	24
193	St. Joseph	57,840	0.054	57,840	0.02	38	11,568	0.01	24
194	Lima	57,560	0.054	57,560	0.02	38	11,512	0.01	24
195	Butte-Bozeman, MT	56,400	0.053	56,400	0.02	38	11,280	0.01	23
196	San Angelo	53,660	0.05	53,660	0.02	38	10,732	0.01	24
197	Cheyenne, WY-Scottsbluff	51,870	0.049	82,992	0.03	60	10,374	0.01	23
198	Ottumwa-Kirksville	51,570	0.048	51,570	0.02	38	10,314	0.01	24
199	Mankato	50,970	0.048	50,970	0.02	38	10,194	0.01	23
200	Casper-Riverton	50,010	0.047	50,010	0.02	38	10,002	0.01	23
201	Bend, OR	47,410	0.044	47,410	0.02	38	9,482	0.01	24
202	Zanesville	32,280	0.03	25,824	0.01	30	6,456	0.01	24
203	Fairbanks	31,860	0.03	25,488	0.01	30	6,372	0.01	23
204	Victoria	30,400	0.028	36,480	0.01	46	6,080	0.01	24
205	Presque Isle	29,300	0.027	29,300	0.01	38	5,860	0.01	24
206	Juneau, AK	25,270	0.024	25,270	0.01	37	5,054	0.01	23
207	Helena	24,380	0.023	24,380	0.01	38	4,876	0.01	23
208	Alpena	17,960	0.017	14,368	0.01	30	3,592	0.01	23
209	North Platte	15,670	0.015	12,536	0.00	30	3,134	0.00	23
210	Glendive	4,960	0.005	3,968	0.00	28	992	0.00	22
Total		106,641,910	100	282,238,765			90,601,242		

Source: Nielsen DMA Populations.

Exhibit 7.1   **Geographic Quadrant Anslysis**

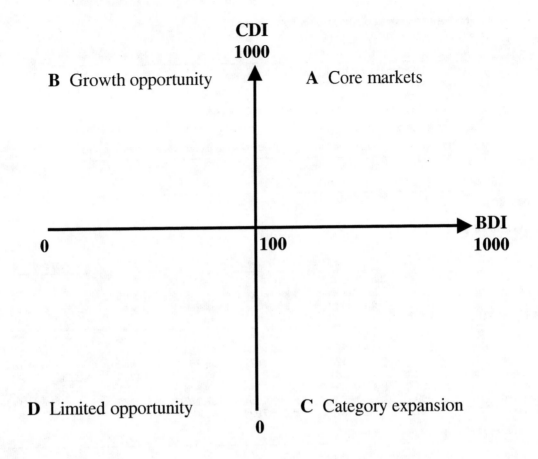

One other analysis that is computed through geographic analysis is the point where it might make more sense to purchase media on a national basis compared with buying it on a market-by-market basis. This is called a national-to-local media breakeven point. It does vary considerably from medium to medium (see Table 7.2). For example, the rule of thumb for purchasing network prime-time television is when your brand is in 66 percent of American homes. But your brand needs to be in only 25 percent of the United States before it would make more economic sense to purchase national cable rather than buying each individual system in every market. By calculating the BDIs for your brand, you can determine if the preponderance of sales are in a few markets or if you may need to have a broader base of advertising support.

Survey of Buying Power

On an annual basis, the magazine *Sales and Marketing Management* publishes a guide called the *Survey of Buying Power* (see Table 7.3). This guide holds a wealth of market information provided largely by Claritas, Inc. The guide is organized by state and by metropolitan area or SMSA (Standard Metropolitan Statistical Area) and by county. The statistics for each SMSA include some basic demographic data such as age, ethnicity, and income profiles. There is also some good category sales information printed in this issue. Some of the items include

Table 7.2

National-to-Local Media Breakeven Points

Media	Breakeven %[1]
Network TV to spot TV (prime)	66
Network radio (:30) to spot radio (:60)	33
National cable to local cable	25
National magazines to local edition of national magazine	33

Source: FKM Agency estimates.

[1]Percent of U.S. where national media becomes more cost efficient than local media.

Table 7.3

Survey of Buying Power

Metro market	TTL POP (000)	Retail sales (000)		Median HH/ EBI $	Buying power index	5-year projection	
		Furniture, home furnishings & electrical appliances	Motor vehicle & parts dealers			% change	% change retail sales
Austin	1,398.1	1,961,632	5,370,208	47,220	0.6656	40.2	37.5
Cincinnati	1,675.5	919,884	5,942,330	40,435	0.6166	21.5	13.2
Milwaukee	1,512.4	1,333,121	5,407,767	39,267	0.5555	18.1	19.3
Raleigh/Durham	1,272.1	1,176,681	4,332,749	43,648	0.4864	28.4	23.6
Portland, OR	2,013.0	1,428,392	6,544,621	41,226	0.7231	24.2	15.1
Providence, RI	989.7	435,736	2,094,085	37,072	0.3170	17.5	11.8
San Jose, CA	1,741.7	5,276,315	6,255,792	62,725	0.7981	22.6	31.0

Source: 2003 *Survey of Buying Power.*

total food sales by market, food sales by grocery versus eating out, automotive sales, and retail and apparel sales. All of this information could be used as a basis for calculating the CDI for the market we discussed earlier.

There are two statistics that are unique to this source. The first is *effective buying income,* or EBI. Effective buying income is a measurement of disposable income. The second is a computation called a *buying power index,* or BPI. Buying power index is a measure of spending power by market that takes population, EBI, and retail sales into account to determine a market's ability to buy goods. Obviously, the higher the index, the more likely a market has the financial ability to buy your product.

The *Survey of Buying Power* also forecasts their data for the next 5 and 10 years, so you can use this information to determine if a market has long-term growth potential. These forecasts are also good to measure how your brand is growing relative to the forecast growth in a given market. The *Survey of Buying Power* is a good tool to use if there is little or no category information readily available for the brand that you happen to be working on. Even if you have proprietary category information, the *Survey of Buying Power* can be another resource to validate your geographic approach and to see the long-term viability of certain markets.

Unit 7 Exercises
Working with Geographic Marketing Information

1. What are the top ten category development index (CDI) markets for bottled water? How much category volume do they account for?

2. Which market offers the best brand opportunity index (BOI) for Barton Springs—Miami or Phoenix?

3. What are the best markets to cover 50 percent of sales for Barton Springs based on brand development index (BDI)?

4. Barton Springs added more distribution to New York and now has increased its sales by $5 million. What is the impact on New York's BDI based on this increase in sales?

5. Find the sales per household of Barton Springs brand in Juneau, Alaska.

6. Barton Springs just ran a promotion in Reno, Nevada, that increased household consumption of Barton Springs by 25 percent. How does this increase in consumption change this market's sales and BDI?

7. Barton Springs wants to schedule advertising in their top markets that represent 70 percent of brand sales. By doing this, is the brand at a national breakeven point to begin to use network television?

8. What is the market with the highest per capita sales of furniture?

9. What will be the best market for automotive sales based on the five-year growth rate forecast?

Unit 8
Working with Seasonality Marketing Information

Working with media involves working closely with marketing information. Media plans are built around achieving the goals outlined in the marketing plan. A media planner must have a solid understanding of what marketing information is available and needs to do a thorough job in developing a sound media plan.

One of the key media objectives that require specific marketing information is when to advertise. This requires knowledge of the seasonality of sales for both the brand you are advertising and the category it competes in.

Seasonality Indices

Seasonality indices are important tools to develop and use when deciding on the best time to advertise. An index sets the standard value against which other values can be compared. For example, if every month of the year had the same sales index of 100, then each month would contain 8.3 percent of sales. Dividing 100 percent of sales by twelve months gives you an average monthly sales figure of 8.3 percent.

So, if you have a retail brand where 20 percent of its sales are in December, then you would have a seasonal index of 241 (20/8.3 × 100) for that month. Obviously, that might be a pretty important time for you to schedule your advertising. The higher the index, the more important that month is for consideration of advertising.

Another analysis of seasonality would be to compare how your brand does in a certain time frame with how the category as a whole performs during that same time frame (see Exhibit 8.1). For example, if you are working with a brand of bottled water that has sales of 8.6 percent in April, but that category has 10.4 percent of its sales in the same month, you may conclude that April could be a month where you could boost your sales.

Consumers are buying a lot of bottled water during April, with an index of 120, yet your brand has a seasonal sales index of 90.

If you were only evaluating your brand's seasonality index for April, you may decide not to put much advertising support behind that month because the seasonality index is 90. Yet, if you take into account the category consumption for the same time frame, you

Exhibit 8.1   **Seasonality Sales for Annual Water Consumption, 2000**

- - - - Barton Springs Brand   ———— Bottled Water Category

may conclude that it might be a good time to advertise because the category seasonality index is 120.

Developing a seasonality sales index requires having proprietary sales information from your client. The seasonality index is typically developed on a monthly basis, but you can construct an index on a quarterly or even daily basis if that best suits the type of brand for which you are developing a media plan.

Brand Purchase Dynamics

Seasonality of sales will tell you what months are stronger than others for your brand's sales. It is an important component of understanding when to advertise. The other component of when to advertise is the understanding of the purchase dynamics of the brand.

For example, while auto sales may be higher at the end of the year, someone may be in the market for a new car for months before the actual purchase. So, in this case, whereas the sales data may tell you one thing, the actual time in the market considering the purchase may be another.

So, understanding the awareness of the brand, the consideration time for purchase, and the purchase dynamics plays a significant role in how you allocate your advertising dollars. The type of brand you are marketing greatly impacts the length of time you advertise. We mentioned auto purchases, which are a high-ticket item. These are typically well thought out, planned purchases. Buying a lottery ticket, on the other hand, may be a spur-of-the-moment decision driven by whether or not you are feeling lucky that day. Each type of purchase dictates how you allocate your dollars.

Another facet of seasonality is the timing of the actual purchase of the brand. If you are advertising to send dinnertime traffic to a fast-food restaurant, you may want to advertise heavily from 3 P.M. to 7 P.M., when most dinner decisions are made. Or if you know that most retail sales occur from Thursday through Saturday, you may elect to advertise only on those days.

Seasonality is more than just looking at the sales index. It should be an exercise in understanding consumer behavior.

Unit 8 Exercises
Working with Seasonality Marketing Information

1. Using the graph in Exhibit 8.1, calculate the index for the three best bottled water category sales months. Give the month, the percent of sales, and the index.

2. Compare the three strongest sales months for the bottled water category versus the Barton Springs brand. How do they compare on an index basis?

3. When do you think consumers are thinking about buying bottled water? How would that knowledge play into when you might advertise?

4. Research the purchase dynamics of buying a refrigerator. How long does it take for someone to make this type of purchase? How often does one buy a refrigerator? How does this impact your scheduling of media?

Unit 9

Working with a Communication Budget

All communication plans begin and end with an accounting of the communication budget. The amount of dollars allocated to the communications task will largely dictate the type of communication channels and tactics that are possible. For example, if your communications budget is $1.0 million, you won't be scheduling a national Super Bowl commercial for $3.0 million. The budget puts a parameter around what can be done.

Companies develop their communication budgets in a variety of ways. Some develop the budget based on the task or objective. Others update their budget based on last year's efforts. Other companies develop their budget based on the competition. There is no right or wrong way to develop the communication budget. It is up to the company and the rigor with which they can tie communication dollars to a specific marketing and business outcome.

Communication Budget as a Percentage of Sales

Regardless of the method of developing the communication budget, it will undergo scrutiny from the senior management. Every budget is put into the context of the total sales or revenue of the company. The marketing or advertising manager will be asking senior management for money, as will the managers of other departments such as information technologies, human resources, and operations. No company has unlimited resources, and CEOs must ultimately decide what percentage of their companys' sales will be devoted to marketing and to communications.

Table 9.1 is a hypothetical example of four companies that compete in the life insurance category. Each brand is detailed in terms of how much it allocates to communications (its budget), its total sales, and the percentage it allocates to communications.

For example, Boston Life allocates $5 million to communications. They have total annual revenue or sales of $125 million. The percentage that they allocate to communications is 4 percent of their total sales. This is calculated by dividing $5 million by $125 million

$$(\frac{5}{125} \times 100 = 4.0\%).$$

Table 9.1

Communication Budget as a Percent of Sales

Brand	Communication budget ($ millions)	Total sales ($ millions)	Percentage
Boston Life	5.0	125.0	4.0
American Life	7.5	250.0	3.0
Great Lakes	15.0	250.0	6.0
Sierra Madre	20.0	1,000.0	2.0
Total	47.5	1,625.0	2.9

You can tell from this simple analysis (see Table 9.1) that the average spent on communications among the four brands is approximately 3 percent of total revenue. The range is from a low of 2 percent for Sierra Madre to a high of 6 percent for Great Lakes.

A CEO would request this type of analysis to understand the context in which the competition is allocating their resources as compared with his brand. Based on such an analysis, the CEO may adjust the overall amount of dollars allocated to communications either up or down.

Categories of Communication Dollars

Once an overall communication budget has been determined, there are four broad categories that the marketing director or advertising manager reviews. The four categories are as follows:

1. Working Dollars

Working dollars are allocated to programs that will impact the market. It can be paid media, promotions, publicity, or digital initiatives. It is any activity that is directed outward or is impacting the marketplace.

2. Nonworking Dollars

Nonworking dollars are allocated to the creation of the programs. It can be production of the creative message, talent cost for a spokesperson or celebrity, or other items that facilitate the activity. The nonworking costs, which are necessary to activate programs, cannot impact the marketplace on their own.

3. Contingency Dollars

Contingency dollars are dollars that are set aside for a variety of situations. It can be to provide a cushion for potential cost overruns. Or it can be a fund to purchase opportunistic media properties or programs that may arise during the course of the year.

Table 9.2

Communication Budget Allocation by Brand

Brand	Total comm. budget ($ millions)	Agency compensation	Production	Contingency	Media	Promo	PR	Digital
				% Allocation				
Boston Life	5.0	15	20	—	40	—	5	20
American Life	7.5	10	15	—	35	—	10	30
Great Lakes	15.0	10	10	—	40	10	10	20
Sierra Madre	20.0	5	10	5	50	10	5	15

4. Agency Compensation

Agency compensation refers to the dollars that are allocated to compensate the agency or agencies for their work. This can be a fee or a commission or a hybrid of methods. The budget item is how much the advertiser will compensate his or her agency partners for their work in devising and activating the programs.

The goal of the marketing director or advertising manager is to optimize the working percentage of the communication budget. More working dollars leads to greater market success. These four areas become discussion items in management meetings on the overall use of the communication dollars.

Communication Allocation

The challenge of the communication planner is to allocate the dollars to the appropriate channels. The communication budget may include agency compensation and contingency or it may exclude those items. Regardless, the task is to allocate the dollars across the channels.

At this stage of the process, the communication budget is allocated in broad terms to working areas such as paid media or advertising, promotions, public relations, and digital areas. It is also allocated to nonworking areas such as production. Once allocation is established, then each area is responsible for developing strategies and tactics from their specific part of the overall budget.

Table 9.2 provides an example of the communication budget allocation for each of the four hypothetical insurance companies. As you can see, each brand has a slightly different weighting of the communication channels. For example, Sierra Madre allocates 50 percent of their budget to paid media but American Life allocates just 35 percent. Great Lakes and Sierra Madre allocate resources to promotions whereas the other two do not.

There is no right or wrong way to allocate communication dollars. The allocation is driven by each brand's marketing and communication objectives. As we will review in the competitive media unit (Chapter 42), communication planners do review how budgets are allocated in a competitive context, just as the CEO reviews overall budgets within a competitive context.

In summary, allocating the communication budget is the key strategic item in meeting the overall communication objective. The overall budget is reviewed by the CEO and the specific allocation of resources is then reviewed by the marketing or advertising manager. The communication planner is responsible for the overall strategy of the budget and works with the marketing and/or advertising director to determine the overall budget.

Unit 9 Exercises
Working with a Communication Budget

1. What are the communication budget, total sales, and percentage of sales for the Great Lakes brand in Table 9.1?

2. What would the percentage of sales be for the Great Lakes communication budget if the budget was reduced by $5 million?

3. What is the difference between working and nonworking dollars?

4. What is the percentage of the communication budget that American Life is allocating to digital communications based on Table 9.2?

5. What is the agency compensation for Boston Life as compared with Sierra Madre? Which brand do you feel is getting more for their money?

Part II
Media Objectives and Strategies

Unit 10
Working to Define Media Objectives

Media objectives define what you want to accomplish with your media plan. Many students and professionals confuse media objectives and media strategies. A media objective is not the actual use of media. That is a strategy. A media objective is how you plan on directing the media strategy. It is not unlike how a conductor has a plan to direct his orchestra. He directs who, when, where, and how much each instrument plays. The same is true for media objectives. They form the foundation of the media plan. There are four key media objectives for any media plan.

1. Target market (who)
2. Seasonality or timing (when)
3. Geography (where)
4. Reach and frequency (how much)

A media objective has the same characteristics of any objective. It should have clarity, that is, it should be measurable and it should state an action. For example, your objective is to answer 100 percent of the workbook questions correctly. That is a clear objective. You should practice gaining this type of clarity for each of the four key media objectives. Let's take a look at each one.

Target Market

The target market is whom you are going to direct your media plan to reach. You may have a primary and secondary target market. Your target may be defined in a variety of ways: demographically, behaviorally, or by need states. Regardless, a media objective for a target market might look something like this:

> To target heavy-category fast-food eaters who represent 75 percent
> of fast-food consumption.

The target definition should be as specific as possible. It should also be one that the media team can use in preparing its media strategy. In this case, heavy, medium, and light usage is a common method of segmenting target markets. Segmenting target markets is a form of media research a planner can use to determine the best media to reach this audience.

Seasonality, or Timing

Seasonality, or timing, is when you plan to direct your message to the target market. You may elect to advertise all the time or to emphasize certain periods of time. Those are the objectives that form the seasonality objective. Here is an example of a seasonality objective:

> To provide 50 percent additional weight (coverage) in order to introduce the product in the three-month launch phase, to be followed by coverage continuity of 75 percent of the weeks that make up the balance of the year.

This objective directs the media team as to when they should emphasize a period of time with more media. It then directs them to provide media coverage for the rest of the year.

Geography

The geographic objective is the "where." Where is the media to be placed? Will it be a national plan or a local plan? Or will it be a national plan with specific markets for additional support? This directs the media team where to place the media support. Here is an example of a geographic objective:

> To provide national support with an emphasis in ten key markets that have greater than 150 BDI and represent 25 percent of brand sales.

This objective is clear and measurable. It directs the media strategy team where to schedule the appropriate media support.

Reach and Frequency

Reach and frequency objectives help the media strategy team to understand how much media weight they must provide in a given period of time. Typically, reach and frequency goals have specific time goals. Most of these time goals correspond to a brand's purchase cycle. The following is an example of reach and frequency goals.

> To reach 90 percent of the target market an average of four times within the brand's four-week purchase cycle.

Reach and frequency tie into the target market and the seasonality objectives. And you may have different reach and frequency objectives for different geography. This is especially true when you have placed an emphasis on a certain group of markets.

Those are the Big Four media objectives. Sometimes there is a need to write a specific objective that emphasizes the need for the media to tie in to the overall communication idea or strategy. The following is an example of such an objective based on a hypothetical target of fast-food eaters:

> To use media that demonstrate the appetite appeal of the brand of
> the fast food.

This specific objective directs the media strategy team to select visual media. In this case, the objective may go without stating, particularly if it is already in the communication brief. If there are any doubts, though, about the role of media in the advertising program, this is a good way to reinforce this specific objective.

Media objectives are the direction of the media plan. They are not the selection of the type of media. Always use "to" as the beginning word of an objective. Make sure your objectives are measurable.

Unit 10 Exercises
Working to Define Media Objectives

1. What is the difference between an objective and a strategy?

2. What are the four key media objectives?

3. Is the statement "to schedule commercials on CNN" a media objective? If "yes," why? If "no," why not?

Unit 11
Working with Reach

This chapter introduces you to actual terms that are used in advertising media planning and buying.

Reach

Reach is a vital concept in advertising media because it refers to how well you communicate with your audience.

There are two basic kinds of reach: *numerical reach* and *percentage reach*. Numerical reach expresses reach as a number. For example, your advertising might reach 100 million adult men and women, or you might reach 1,200 business majors on a college campus, or, in a metropolitan area, you may be able to reach 560,000 heads of households who are women. Many times we concentrate our reach on units of people instead of on individual persons; thus, you may reach 150,550 households in a city.

The percentage reach is measured as the percentage of a population with which your advertising communicates. You may be able to reach 62 percent of adults in the United States, or you might reach 85 percent of the business majors on a college campus, or your advertising may reach 75 percent of women in a city.

Using units other than individual persons, you may reach 46 percent of households in a certain area. Or you may be able to reach 68 percent of television households in a region; television households are the households that have one or more operating television sets, which would be of great interest to television advertisers.

Similarly, broadcast advertisers are interested in the reach coverage of radio households. And print advertisers are interested in the reach coverage of newspaper households.

Because, in surveying our audiences, we often use samples that are small, we can estimate the percentage reach first and then calculate the numerical reach based on that percentage. For example, suppose you survey 2,000 television households and find that 60 percent of them watch television on Monday evenings. You can then easily calculate that 1,200 of those households are in the Monday-evening viewing audience.

$$2,000 \times 0.6 = 1,200.$$

(Remember that 60% = 0.60 or 0.6.)

Reach is often abbreviated as *Rch.* or simply as *R*.

Total Audience Impressions

The term *audience impression* is used to describe each time a person sees or hears your advertisement. It does not matter whether the person has been exposed to the advertising before; each exposure counts as an audience impression.

Say that a television viewer sees your television commercial six times. There would be six audience impressions for that member of the audience.

More than one person will be exposed to an advertisement, and each exposure is an audience impression. If you count all the exposures for all the audience members, you have the *total audience impressions* (TAI). By the way, *audience* is often abbreviated as *aud* and *impressions* is often abbreviated as *imps.*

To make this concept easier to understand, imagine that there are three members in the audience. Andy is exposed to the advertisement three times, Beth is exposed twice, and Chet is exposed four times. You simply add them to get the total audience impressions.

Audience member	Audience impressions
A	3
B	2
C	4
Total aud imps (TAI)	9

Of course, most of the time there will be more than a single advertisement in an advertising campaign, and there may be advertisements on a variety of media and in a variety of vehicles within each media type. Thus, you may be running television advertising on two networks, magazine advertising in five different magazines, and newspaper advertising in 440 different newspapers. Still, to calculate total audience impressions, you simply count how many times each audience member is exposed to any of the advertisements in your advertising campaign, and then add them up.

Audience member	Audience impressions		
	Television	Magazine	Newspaper
A	3	4	2
B	2	3	5
C	4	0	3
Aud imps per medium	9	7	10

So there would be 26 TAI in this case.

Television aud imps	9
Magazine aud imps	7
Newspaper aud imps	10
Total aud imps (TAI)	26

Sometimes, total audience impressions are called gross impressions. The concept for calculating gross impressions is the same: simply add each exposure or audience impression and get the total.

Notice that TAI are the result of both the reach and the frequency figures; frequency is explained in units 5 and 6 of this book.

Unit 11 Exercises
Working with Reach

1. A television ratings survey shows that 8 percent of the television audience in Localville watches the evening news. If the population of Localville is 550,000, what is the projected audience (i.e., the numerical reach)?

2. The Localville newspaper has 110,000 readers on an average day. What is the reach in percent?

3. Bartertown has a radio listening population of 450,000. Using the percentage reach figures given, figure the projected audience (i.e., the numerical reach) for each of the following programs. The programs total either more or less than 100 percent because audience members listen to more than one program.

	Audience % reach	Numerical reach
All Talk Radio	12	_____
News	17	_____
Sports Call-in	9	_____
Weather Update	4	_____
Entertainment Express	22	_____
Kids' Korner	7	_____

Unit 12
Working with Combinations of Media

Many advertising campaigns, if not most of them, use more than one advertising medium to reach an audience. It only makes sense: different types of media reach different kinds of people, so using a combination of media can add to the reach achieved by the campaign. And because most audience members pay attention to more than one media type, a combination of media may also offer increased frequency of exposure.

Advertising media calculations get a little bit more complicated when combinations of the media are used, but the concepts are still relatively easy to understand and use.

Dealing with frequency is fairly simple. If you have six advertising insertions a week on radio and three insertions a week in newspapers, you have a total of nine insertions a week from this combination of media (6 + 3 = 9). The insertion frequency is simply the sum of all the advertising insertions.

Calculating effective frequency (i.e., frequency of exposure) is a little more difficult but no more so than when using a single advertising medium. Multiple media are simply combined and then entered into a software program such as Telmar's reach and frequency module to develop a frequency distribution. (The next unit defines frequency more fully.)

Nevertheless, calculating the reach of combined media cannot be done by simple addition. Think for a minute about an advertising campaign that uses two different media, television and Sunday supplements. If you reach 62 percent of your target group through television and you reach 51 percent through Sunday supplements, you cannot add them together and assume that you have achieved a reach level of 113 percent. Obviously, you cannot reach more than 100 percent of your audience—and it is likely that you cannot really come close to 100 percent; reaching, say, 65 percent or 75 percent may be all that can be achieved.

So how do you figure the combined reach?

The easiest way is to use a table for calculating cumulative audiences (see Table 12.1).

Suppose you reach 20 percent of your target audience with Medium A and 21 percent with Medium B. As Table 12.1 indicates, you are likely reaching 36 percent (where the 20 percent row meets the 21 percent column) of your target audience, not the 41 percent that would result from simple addition. The reason is that there is some overlap or duplication; some audience members will see your advertising in both media.

Table 12.1

Table for Calculating Cumulative Audiences

Medium A Reach	\ Medium B Reach →																																										
	5	7	9	11	13	15	17	19	21	23	25	27	29	31	33	35	37	39	41	43	45	47	49	51	53	55	57	59	61	63	65	67	69	71	73	75	77	79	81	83	85	87	89
10	14	16	18	20	21	23	25	27	28	30	32	34	36	37	39	41	43	44	46	48	50	51	53	55	58	59	60	62	64	66	67	69	71	73	75	77	78	80	82	84	86	88	90
12	16	18	20	21	23	25	27	28	30	32	33	35	37	39	40	42	44	45	47	49	51	52	54	56	58	60	62	64	65	67	69	70	72	74	76	78	79	81	83	85	87	88	90
14	18	20	21	23	25	26	28	30	31	33	35	37	38	40	41	43	44	46	48	50	51	53	55	57	58	60	62	64	65	67	69	70	72	74	76	78	79	81	83	85	87	88	90
16	20	22	23	25	27	28	30	31	33	35	36	38	39	41	43	44	46	47	49	50	52	54	56	58	60	62	63	64	66	68	69	71	72	74	76	77	80	81	83	85	87	89	91
18	22	23	25	27	28	30	31	33	34	36	38	39	41	42	44	45	47	48	50	52	53	55	56	58	60	62	63	64	66	67	69	71	72	75	77	78	80	82	84	85	87	89	91
20	24	25	27	28	30	31	33	34	36	38	39	41	42	44	45	47	48	50	52	53	54	56	58	60	61	63	64	66	67	68	70	72	73	75	77	79	80	82	84	86	88	89	91
22	26	27	29	30	32	33	35	36	38	39	40	42	43	45	47	48	49	51	52	54	55	57	59	60	62	63	65	66	68	69	71	72	74	75	79	81	81	83	85	86	88	90	91
24	28	29	30	32	33	34	36	38	39	41	42	43	45	46	48	49	50	52	54	55	56	58	59	61	62	64	66	67	68	70	72	73	75	76	78	80	81	83	85	86	88	90	91
26	29	3	32	34	35	37	38	40	41	42	43	45	46	47	49	50	52	53	55	56	57	59	61	62	63	65	67	68	69	71	72	74	75	77	79	80	82	83	85	86	88	90	91
28	31	33	34	35	37	38	40	41	42	44	45	46	47	49	50	52	53	54	56	57	58	60	61	63	64	65	67	68	70	71	72	74	75	77	79	80	82	83	85	86	88	90	91
30	33	34	36	37	38	40	41	42	44	45	46	47	49	50	51	53	54	55	57	58	60	61	62	64	66	67	68	69	70	72	73	75	76	78	79	80	82	83	85	87	89	90	91
32	35	36	38	39	41	42	43	45	46	47	49	50	52	53	54	56	57	58	59	60	61	63	65	66	67	69	70	72	73	74	76	77	78	80	81	83	84	86	87	89	90	91	92
34	37	38	39	41	42	43	44	46	47	48	49	51	52	53	55	56	57	59	60	61	62	64	65	66	68	69	71	72	74	75	76	77	79	80	81	83	84	86	87	89	90	91	92
36	39	40	41	42	44	45	46	47	49	50	51	52	54	55	56	57	59	60	61	62	63	65	66	67	69	70	71	73	74	75	76	78	79	81	82	83	85	86	88	89	90	91	92
38	41	42	43	44	46	47	48	49	50	51	52	53	55	56	57	58	59	60	61	62	63	64	65	67	68	69	71	72	73	74	75	77	78	80	81	82	84	85	86	88	89	91	92
40	43	44	45	46	48	48	50	51	52	53	54	56	57	58	59	60	61	62	64	65	66	67	68	69	70	72	73	74	75	76	78	79	80	81	82	84	85	86	88	89	90	92	92
42	44	45	46	47	49	50	51	52	53	55	56	57	58	59	60	61	63	64	65	66	67	68	69	70	71	73	74	75	76	76	77	79	80	82	83	84	85	87	88	89	91	92	92
44	46	47	48	49	50	51	52	54	55	56	57	58	59	60	61	62	63	64	66	67	68	69	70	71	72	74	75	76	77	78	79	81	82	83	84	85	86	88	89	90	91	92	92
46	48	49	50	51	52	53	54	55	56	57	58	59	60	61	62	63	64	65	66	68	69	70	71	72	73	75	76	77	78	79	80	81	83	84	85	85	87	88	89	90	91	92	92
48	50	51	52	53	53	54	55	56	57	58	59	60	61	62	63	64	67	68	69	71	72	73	74	75	76	77	78	79	80	81	82	83	84	85	86	87	88	89	90	91	92	93	
50	51	53	54	55	56	57	58	59	60	61	62	63	64	65	66	67	68	69	70	71	72	73	75	76	77	77	78	79	80	80	81	82	83	84	85	86	87	88	89	90	91	93	
52	52	54	55	56	57	58	59	60	61	62	63	64	65	66	67	68	69	70	71	72	73	74	75	76	77	78	79	80	81	82	83	84	85	86	87	88	89	90	91	92	93		
54	54	55	56	57	58	59	60	61	62	63	64	65	66	67	68	69	70	71	72	73	74	75	76	77	78	79	80	81	82	83	84	85	86	87	88	89	90	91	92	93	93		
56	56	57	58	59	60	61	61	62	63	64	65	66	67	68	69	70	71	72	73	74	75	76	77	77	78	79	80	81	82	83	84	85	86	87	88	88	89	90	91	92	93		
58	58	59	59	60	61	62	63	64	65	66	67	68	69	69	70	71	72	73	74	75	76	77	77	78	79	80	81	82	83	83	84	85	86	87	88	89	90	90	91	92	93		
60	60	61	61	62	63	64	64	65	66	67	68	69	69	70	71	72	73	74	75	76	77	78	78	79	80	81	82	82	83	84	85	86	87	87	88	89	90	90	91	92	93	94	
62	62	63	63	64	65	66	66	67	68	69	70	71	71	72	73	74	75	76	77	78	79	79	80	81	82	83	83	84	85	86	87	87	88	89	89	90	91	91	92	93	94		
64	64	65	65	66	67	67	68	69	70	71	72	72	73	74	75	76	77	78	79	79	80	81	82	83	84	85	85	86	87	88	88	89	90	90	91	92	93	94					
66	65	66	67	67	68	69	70	71	72	73	73	74	75	76	77	78	80	81	82	82	83	84	85	86	86	87	88	89	89	90	91	91	92	93	93	94							
68	67	68	68	69	70	71	72	73	74	75	76	77	78	79	80	81	82	83	83	84	85	86	87	88	88	89	90	91	91	92	93	93	94										
70	69	70	70	71	72	73	73	74	75	76	77	77	78	79	80	80	81	82	83	84	84	85	86	87	88	88	89	89	90	91	91	92	93	93	94								
72	71	72	72	73	73	74	75	76	76	77	78	78	79	80	80	81	82	83	83	84	85	85	86	87	87	88	89	89	90	91	91	92	93	93	94								
74	73	74	74	75	75	76	76	77	78	79	79	80	81	81	82	83	83	84	85	85	86	87	87	88	89	89	90	90	91	92	92	93	93	94	95								
76	75	75	76	76	77	77	78	79	79	80	80	81	82	82	83	84	84	85	86	86	87	88	88	89	90	90	91	91	92	93	93	94	94	95									
78	77	77	78	78	89	89	89	80	80	81	82	82	83	84	84	85	85	86	86	87	88	88	89	89	90	90	91	91	92	92	93	93	94	94	95								
80	79	79	80	80	81	82	82	83	83	84	84	85	86	86	87	87	88	88	89	89	90	90	91	91	92	92	93	93	94	94	95											
82	81	81	82	82	83	84	84	85	85	86	86	87	87	88	88	89	89	90	90	91	91	92	92	93	93	94	94	95	95													
84	83	83	84	84	85	85	86	86	87	87	88	88	89	89	90	90	91	91	92	92	93	93	94	94	95	95																
86	85	85	86	86	87	87	88	88	89	89	90	90	91	91	92	92	93	93	94	94	95																					
88	87	87	88	88	89	89	90	90	91	91	92	92	93	93	94	94	95																									
90	89	91	91	92	92	93	93	94	94	95	95																															

If you wanted to combine more than two media, you can simply look up each succeeding pair of reach percentages. Say you have three media with these reach percentages.

Medium	% Reach
A	20
B	21
C	15

First, look up the combined reach for Medium A and Medium B. You'll get 36 percent, just as we did earlier. Then combine that result, 36 percent, with the reach percentage for Medium C, 15 percent. The combined reach is 45 percent for all three media.

These combination figures are derived from standard statistical probability tables, which means they do not apply to your specific situation. It also means that there may be a small error in the combination figures, and the more media types you combine, the larger that error can get. So, the combined figures for only two types of media will be more accurate than the figures for four or five or more combinations of media. That is why media professionals rely on sophisticated software systems that calculate multimedia reach and frequency.

You can also use these combination tables for two or more vehicles from the same medium. If you use two magazines, one reaching 20 percent of the target and the other reaching 21 percent, the combination would still be 36 percent, just as it was for two combined media types.

As already noted, because these combination figures come from standard probability tables, they may not apply to your specific situation. For that reason, try to get specific combination figures for your combined media; they will be more accurate. If you can get the actual figures, use them; if you cannot, use the combination tables.

There may be a time when you do not have such a table readily available. In that situation, you can calculate the combined reach on your own. There is a formula for estimating the combined unduplicated reach.

$$[(A \text{ reach}) + (B \text{ reach})] - [(A \text{ reach}) \times (B \text{ reach})]$$

In this formula, enter the reach figures as decimals (i.e., 22 percent reach is entered as 0.22). So, if one medium or vehicle reaches 14 percent of the target group and another reaches 13 percent, enter those figures in the formula.

$$[(0.14) + (0.13)] - [(0.14) \times (0.13)] =$$
$$[0.27] - [0.0182] = 0.2518$$
(or about 25 percent combined reach).

Go back to Table 12.1 and check on how this figure compares with the one from that chart.

Again, this formula can be used for combined reach of multiple vehicles in a single medium, or for the combined reach of a combination of media types. Also, the formula can be applied repeatedly, just as the table was, to estimate the combined reach of more than two vehicles or media types. You simply apply the formula in a series of two vehicle steps. Once you get the answer from the first two vehicles, you then use that answer to combine with the next vehicle. You can repeat the process indefinitely. Remember these are only estimates, so the more media vehicles or the more media types that are combined, the less reliable the resulting combined reach figure will be.

Unit 12 Exercises
Working with Combinations of Media

1. Use Table 12.1 (Table for Calculating Cumulative Audiences) to arrive at the correct figures.

    a. You are advertising on two television programs that achieve the reach percentages listed. What is their combined reach?

Program	Reach (%)
Diving for Dollars	13
Guess the Costs	10

    b. You are advertising on three local radio stations. Each of them achieves the reach level shown. What is their total reach?

Station	Reach (%)
WDZZ	9
WFAM	14
WBTC	16

c. You are advertising in four magazines with the respective reach figures shown below. What is the combined reach of all four magazines?

Magazine	Reach (%)
Around the House	11
The Fixer Upper	14
Feathering the Nest	20
Handyman Specials	26

2. Now use the formula for combined reach shown previously in Unit 12 to solve the following problems. To prove you have used the formula, enter the formula in the spaces provided, fill in the appropriate numbers, and show your resulting calculations.

a. You are advertising in two local newspapers with the reach percentages given below. What is the combined reach of these two newspapers? Remember to show your work.

Newspaper	Reach (%)
The Gazette	31
The Press	21

b. You are advertising on three television networks. Each achieves the reach level indicated. Calculate the combined reach of all three networks. Remember to show your work.

Network	Reach (%)
ABS	17
CNC	11
NBB	18

Unit 13
Working with Frequency

Even if your advertising has extensive reach, it may not be effective unless you place the advertising often enough and the intended audience is exposed to it a sufficient number of times. Reaching an audience a single time is seldom effective. In fact, many advertising media experts consider *frequency* as more essential than reach. Frequency is abbreviated *Freq.* or simply *F.*

How often the advertising appears is called frequency, and there are two kinds of frequency, just as there are two kinds of reach.

Insertion

First, there is the *frequency of insertion,* which is how many times the advertising is run. If your advertisement appears every day in a daily newspaper, you would have a frequency of insertion of seven times per week.

Exposure

However, few if any audience members will see or hear your advertising every time it appears. If you run the advertising seven times a week in a newspaper, the average audience member may read the advertisement only two or three times. So the *frequency of exposure* is how many times, on average, that the audience members see or hear your advertising. Obviously, the frequency of exposure will be a smaller number than the frequency of insertion.

The frequency of exposure is also known in the advertising industry as *effective frequency,* because no matter how many times you run your advertising, what matters is how many times it reaches its audience.

One method media planners use to analyze advertising frequency is called frequency distribution. It tells them what percentage of their audience was reached, say, only once, what percentage was reached twice, what percentage was reached three times, and so on.* Obviously, it is preferable for a sizable portion of the target audience to be reached as many times as possible.

When you work in advertising, you may see what is called a frequency table. A weekly frequency table for an Internet advertising site may look like this.

---

*For more information on frequency distributions, see Larry D. Kelley and Donald W. Jugenheimer, *Advertising Media Planning: A Brand Management Approach.* 3d ed. (Armonk, NY: M.E. Sharpe, 2012), esp. pp. 94–95 for a definition, and p. 82 for an example.

Frequency	Reach (%)
3+	40
5+	15
7+	3

In this case, the table indicates that 40 percent of the Internet site visitors looked at the website three or more times during the week, 15 percent visited the site five or more times a week, and 3 percent visited seven or more times a week. Note that the frequency table also includes information on reach: The figures 3+, 5+, and 7+ refer to frequency and the percentages refer to reach.

The 3+, 5+, and 7+ frequency levels are often used in advertising because many media practitioners feel that an advertising campaign is not effective unless it reaches the target audience at least three times, or five times, or seven times—or even more often.

Turn back to Unit 3 and review the explanation of total audience impressions (TAI). If you take the numerical reach and multiply it by the frequency, the result will be your TAI.

Audience member	Audience impressions
1	3
2	2
3	3
4	4

In this case, there is a numerical reach of 4 and there are 12 total audience impressions. The average frequency is 3. So the numerical reach [R(#)] multiplied by the frequency [F] gives you the total audience impressions [TAI].

$$R(\#) \times F = TAI$$

$$4R \times 3F = 12\ TAI$$

Unit 13 Exercises
Working with Frequency

1. An advertising campaign in the *Daily Gazette* reaches 30,500 persons who see the advertising a total of 92,400 times. What is the average frequency?

2. An advertising campaign on KLMN radio reaches 20,900 persons who hear the advertising a total of 121,700 times. What is the average frequency? Is it frequency of insertion or frequency of exposure?

3. An advertising campaign directed toward 2,100,000 persons achieves 15,600,000 total audience impressions. What is the average frequency?

4. Another advertising campaign that achieves 101,500,000 total audience impressions also achieves an average frequency of 5.6 times. What is the reach?

5. If an advertising campaign has an average frequency of 6.6 to an audience of 11,000,000 persons, what is the number of total audience impressions?

Unit 14
Working with Frequency Levels

Earlier, we discussed advertising frequency, including effective frequency and frequency distributions. Now that you also understand ratings and *gross rating points* (GRPs), we can add more to our understanding of advertising frequency and getting enough frequency to make advertising effective yet efficient.

Frequency is an important consideration in advertising media. As you can imagine, running an advertisement only once may not work. For one thing, the audience members may not be exposed to that particular advertising insertion; they may be doing other things when that advertisement appears. And even if the audience members are exposed to the single advertisement, they may not react to it. It often takes time to catch the audience's attention, build their interest, and convince them that they should buy a certain product or service. Even then, it may require repeat exposures to get the audience to act—to go to the store, make a telephone call, order online, or take some other action in response to your advertising message.

So, how much advertising frequency is enough? There is no easy answer to that question. New items require more time to inform the audience about product or service features and benefits. Complicated items need more time for explanation. Replacement items require time to induce customers to give up their old purchase habits and then, if possible, convince them to try your product or service. Expensive items may require more effort to convince the customers to try this item instead of spending their dollars on something else.

No matter what may complicate the selling situation, one possible solution is increasing the frequency of advertising. Also, remember the difference between the insertion frequency and the exposure frequency (or effective frequency). Just because you place an advertisement several times does not mean that the audience members will see or hear it every time. An advertising campaign usually has much higher insertion frequency than exposure frequency.

For all these reasons, most experienced advertisers run frequent advertising. Even more important, of course, is the effective frequency: how many times the average audience member is actually exposed to the advertising message.

The key levels are usually 3+, 5+, 7+, or even higher, meaning that audience members need to be exposed to the advertising campaign at least three or more times, or five or more times, or seven or more times, and so on. This exposure frequency needs to occur within a limited time frame; obviously, seeing or hearing an advertisement three times within a week is more effective than three times in a month or three times in an entire year.

Gross Rating Points

From our discussion, you will remember that advertising frequency is one of the contributing factors in GRPs. Gross rating points are the sum of the ratings for a certain time period, usually one week, but because a single week may not be entirely representative (i.e., the figures may be higher or lower than normal), we often measure the rating points over a four-week period and then divide by four to find the weekly average.

Since we are adding the ratings points, we are automatically including frequency because there is one advertising insertion for each ratings figure. Thus, reach (as a percentage) multiplied by frequency gives us GRPs, or

$$R\ (\%) \times F = GRP$$

For example, reaching 40 percent of the audience 5 times each would provide 200 GRPs.

$$40\% \ Rch. \times 5 \ Freq. = 200 \ GRPs, \ or$$
$$40\% \ R \times 5 \ F = 200 \ GRPs$$

Target rating points (TRP) may be more significant because they are the GRP for the message that actually reaches our intended target audience. GRPs include the reach and frequency to all audience members, whether they are prospects or not. TRPs should be higher figures than GRPs because we should be doing a better job of reaching a higher percentage of our target group than we would for all audience members, just as we should be achieving higher frequency for the target group than for the entire audience.

Effective Rating Points

An advertising campaign is most efficient if it reaches the right audience members the correct number of times, not too many and not too few. We need to achieve optimal levels of frequency, again, not too high and not too low.

Some advertisers might consider it effective to reach some percentage of the target audience at least once; the assumption is that 1+ is effective reach. Most experienced advertisers aim for a higher level of reach, such as 3+, 5+, or higher levels of frequency.

The *effective rating points* (ERPs) are a measure of how much advertising is needed during some certain period of time to accomplish the campaign's reach and frequency objectives.

Effective rating points may be expressed as a range rather than a minimal level. Just aiming for 3+ reach sets no upper-end limit, so some audience members might be exposed dozens if not hundreds of times, even though the minimal effective level is likely to be much less.

Advertisers must take into account the problem of irritation caused by overloaded frequency on a small audience group. Thus, the range for ERP might be 3–10 times, which means the target group is exposed at least three times but fewer than 11 times in a time frame such as four weeks. So ERP might be 3–10 exposures in a certain time period.

Another way to consider ERPs is a reduction from the total number of GRPs or the total number of gross impressions (or total audience impressions, expressed as TAI). Total gross impressions minus ineffective exposures would equal effective rating points.

If effective reach is those persons reached at least three times, or at least five times or whatever level is desired, then we must realize that the term "effective reach" really refers to frequency rather than to reach.

Notice how the formula changes slightly from

$$R \times F = GRP$$

to

$$ER \times F = ERP$$

where *ER* is effective reach.

Using Frequency Distributions

A table that shows various levels of frequency distributions can be very useful to an advertising media planner. As is often the case, such a chart shows both reach and frequency levels. Table 14.1 is an example of a frequency distribution table for radio and television.

At the top of the table are the various levels of GRPs that might be achieved. Along the left side of the chart is a range of frequency levels from 1 to 12; note that these figures are for exposure frequencies, not insertion frequencies. Then, under each level of GRPs, there are percentage reach figures for both radio and television. Two kinds of reach percentages are shown: one for reaching *at least* that frequency level and another for reaching *exactly* that frequency level and no higher. You may also notice that these figures happen to be for reaching a target of women ages 25–54 and for certain periods of the daily broadcast schedule; if you wanted other media or other targets or other schedules, you would use a different chart.

Look at the first column for the frequency level 5. Under the "200 GRPs" heading, for radio, there are two percentage reach levels provided: 14.8 and 3.3. These figures mean that when you buy 200 GRPs, you can expect to reach 14.8 percent of the targeted women *at least* five times and 3.3 percent of the targeted women *exactly* five times. For television, the percentage reach figures are 8.1 and 3.6, meaning that using 200 GRPs will likely cause you to reach 8.1 percent of the targeted women five or more times and 3.6 percent exactly five times.

So, even though this kind of table is called a frequency distribution, it really gives information about *both* reach and frequency.

Table 14.1

Frequency Distribution for Radio and Television

Target reached (%)

	200 GRPs				400 GRPs				600 GRPs			
	Radio		Television		Radio		Television		Radio		Television	
Exposures	At least	Only	At least	Only	At least	Only	At least	Only	At least	Only	At least	Only
(x)	(x+)	(x)	(x+)	(x)	(x+)	(x)	(x+)	(x)	(x+)	(x)	(x+)	(x)
1	50.4	15.8	64.6	22.4	50.4	15.8	64.6	22.4	59.7	11.3	84.3	8.6
2	34.6	9.2	42.2	16.9	34.6	9.2	42.2	16.9	48.4	7.0	75.7	9.7
3	25.4	6.2	25.3	10.8	25.4	6.2	25.3	10.8	41.4	5.1	66.0	9.9
4	19.2	4.4	14.5	6.4	19.2	4.4	14.5	6.4	36.3	4.0	56.1	9.4
5	14.8	3.3	8.1	3.6	14.8	3.3	8.1	3.6	32.3	3.3	46.7	8.5
6	11.5	2.5	4.5	1.9	11.5	2.5	4.5	1.9	29.0	2.8	38.2	7.3
7	9.0	1.9	2.6	1.1	9.0	1.9	2.6	1.1	26.2	2.4	30.9	6.2
8	7.1	1.4	1.5	0.7	7.1	1.4	1.5	0.7	23.8	2.0	24.7	5.1
9	5.7	1.2	0.8	0.3	5.7	1.2	0.8	0.3	21.8	1.9	19.6	4.1
10	4.5	0.9	0.5	0.2	4.5	0.9	0.5	0.2	19.9	1.6	15.5	3.3
11	3.6	0.7	0.3	0.1	3.6	0.7	0.3	0.1	18.3	1.5	12.2	2.6
12	2.9	0.6	0.2	0.1	2.9	0.6	0.2	0.1	16.8	1.3	9.6	2.0
Average frequency	4.0		3.1		4.0		3.1		10.1		7.1	

Source: Telmar.

Notes: Target = women ages 25–54. Dayparts = radio: Monday–Saturday 6 A.M.–7 A.M. (using five stations); and television: average mix of early morning/daytime/prime time/late night with 20 percent cable programming.

Unit 14 Exercises
Working with Frequency Levels

1. Use the frequency distribution chart (Table 14.1) to answer the following questions.

   a. At 400 GRPs, what is the "at least" percentage reach for television at an effective frequency level of 8?

   b. What is the "only" percentage reach for television at the same frequency level?

   c. For radio, and still using the same frequency level, what is the "at least" percentage of reach?

   d. Again, using the same level of advertising, what is the "only" percentage reach for radio?

2. Use the 4 level of effective frequency at an advertising level of 600 GRPs in television.

   a. What are the two reach numbers given at that advertising level?

   b. In your own words, explain what the "at least" figure means.

   c. Again in your own words, explain what the "only" figure means.

3. If you wish to reach about 20 percent of the target group at least ten times using radio, what advertising level would you use?

4. If you wish to reach at least 20 percent of the target group at least ten times using television, what advertising level would you use?

5. As discussed in this chapter/unit, we know that the TRP level should be higher than the GRP level. Should the ERP level be higher or lower than the GRP level? Why?

Unit 15
Working with Emotional versus Rational Appeals

Working with the Creative Team

A media plan is not constructed in isolation. It is a part of an overall marketing and advertising strategy. To best execute the advertising strategy and remain true to the brand's personality, media must work in concert with the creative execution.

Within the advertising process, the media and the creative unit have typically come at the advertising problem from very different points of view. The media department has been driven by efficiency and the creative department has been driven by impact. In today's more fragmented and complex media landscape, the creative and media teams are working more in concert to achieve some level of consumer engagement. Engagement is where the creative execution meshes nicely with the media context in which it is shown.

As a media planner, there are three areas of qualitative judgment that should be considered within any media plan. These are the brand's personality, the advertising message strategy, and the creative execution.

Type of Brand

The type of brand you are advertising can dictate what types of media are most appropriate for the advertising message. For example, if you are advertising golf clubs, you are likely to look to golf magazines, broadcast, and online properties to place your ads. If you actually looked to reach the most golfers, however, you would find that broader media outlets such as *Sports Illustrated* or *Monday Night Football* would reach more of the golf audience.

So, the questions media professionals ask themselves are, Does the media make sense for the brand? Is it within the context of what consumers would expect? For example, you wouldn't expect to see an ad for Wal-Mart's clothes in *Vogue* magazine, even though some *Vogue* readers do shop at Wal-Mart. On the other side of the coin, if Wal-Mart had some very fashionable merchandise to market, an unexpected ad in *Vogue* could generate some consumer buzz.

The other issue with matching media to the brand is to look at the brand's assets. Does the brand have certain visual or verbal distinct brand assets that would play into the media plan? For example, Intel has used an audio pneumonic device in its ads, so it is important to take that into account when planning media. On the other hand, Absolut Vodka is a totally visual-driven brand. A plan for this brand should focus on its unique visual elements. These brand nuances could lead the creative group to decide that certain colors or a certain emotional tone is critical.

If you look at the brand as the consumer, you can begin to frame what types of media best convey its strengths.

Brand Message Strategy

The type of message is going to largely dictate the media strategy. A "one day sale," for instance, is very different from convincing consumers your brand is worth a premium price.

The message strategy is the driving force behind the media and the creative executions. There are certain media that are best for conveying a price message. The newspaper is the cornerstone of sale events. In fact, if your brand is scheduling a short-term sale, then you have no chance of success if you use either outdoor media or magazines, which are monthly media with long lead times for advertising placement. If the cost for producing a television commercial is more than the media budget for the one-day sale, then television may not make sense either.

On the other hand, if your message is to convey quality or portray an emotional feel, you're dealing with a whole other set of criteria. Television advertising, cinema advertising, or even rich media can convey messages that are more emotional than other types of media. But suppose you need to tell the consumer a more detailed product story; then, you need to look to media that can provide more details. In this case, you may look to print or to driving consumers to a website where they can review as much information as possible about the brand.

Creative Units

Once the media mix has been determined, then it is up to the media and creative groups to determine the best media unit for the plan. This can be a real source of tension between the two groups since it is a trade-off between efficiency and impact.

Media professionals evaluate media units based on their ability to generate advertising recall. For some media such as the Internet, media groups can determine how various units perform on a click-through or cost-per-sale basis. Media professionals use research indicating how different units perform and apply these to media planning. For example, a 15-second commercial on network cable costs about half that of a 30-second commercial, yet research shows that advertising recall of the former is 75 percent of the latter. This type of analysis would indicate that a 15-second commercial is a good value if the creative group can execute their message within this time limit. Depending on the makeup of the creative group, this can be a source of tension between both groups.

Some creative messages can be delivered in a variety of units. For example, an ad that says there is a sale tomorrow can be produced quickly, or it can be lengthened to show more emotion or more merchandise. In these cases, the media challenge is how to best use all the available creative units for the greatest impact.

Unit 15 Exercises
Working with Emotional versus Rational Appeals

1. You are doing a media plan for the Milk Board. What brand matching would you have to take into account for this brand and how might it affect your media selection?

2. What are the message strategy strengths and weaknesses of using radio as a medium?

3. Your client suggests that the best way to convey his quality steak is to put it on a billboard. Do you agree with his advice?

4. If a full-page 4-color ad in *Woman's Day* costs $100,000, and a 3/4-page 4-color ad costs $70,000, which ad size do you think would have the greatest advertising recall? Why?

5. Your online media budget is only $3,000. You can buy 30 full banners for this amount, or you can buy four interstitials. (Interstitials are online ads that load before a content page.) Which would give you the most for the money, in your opinion? Explain your decision.

6. The media group recommends that a client use a mix of 50 percent 30-second ads and 50 percent 15-second ads for their network cable television campaign. The creative group wants to use only30-second ads. How much impact would the brand gain or lose by using 30-second ads exclusively if a 30-second ad costs twice as much as a 15-second ad?

Unit 16
Working with Test Cities and Standards

Test Cities and Standards

Testing advertising before the actual campaign helps determine whether the advertisements themselves are effective, whether the media combination is apt, and what kind of customer response can be anticipated.

Three major factors determine the selection of cities or markets for advertising tests: representativeness, media offered, and appropriate size.

Representativeness

So that test results are fairly accurate, the test-market population needs to resemble the population as a whole. Usually, this aspect is measured by comparing the test market's population demographics with the demographics of the total U.S. population.

Of course, test cities and markets must reflect the results that would be derived from much larger areas, so the actual numbers will not match those of the total country, yet if the percentages of those in certain demographic categories are relatively similar, the test will likely be a better predictor of the audience reaction to the eventual advertising campaign.

Media Offerings

Another important factor in the selection of test-market locations is whether the local media offer a wide enough selection of media types, so that all aspects of the advertising campaign can be tried in the test markets. For example, if television will be used in the campaign, then the availability of television stations will be a critical factor in selecting test markets. Most markets have a local newspaper and local radio stations.

In major markets, most if not all types of advertising media are available, even including city or regional editions of national magazines as well as local magazines. In smaller markets, though, some media types are not available. Only very large markets tend to have city editions of major magazines, other large markets are likely to have local magazines, but small markets are unlikely to have their own magazines and may not even have local television stations.

Market Size

We generally do not conduct market tests in the entire country because it would be too expensive and because it would constitute an entire campaign rather than a test. Most often, test cities and markets are selected because they are affordable. The advertising media in major cities will be expensive, especially for a test, so medium-sized markets are used. These markets are of a size to offer relatively inexpensive testing.

Other Factors

Because we seek test markets that are representative, that have most types of media, and that are of a manageable size, there are some cities that are most often used for test marketing and advertising. It is also important that the available media not be too widespread in order to cover areas far outside the test. In addition, the test markets should be somewhat isolated to prevent interference by media from other markets. Wichita, Kansas, Peoria, Illinois, and Fort Wayne, Indiana, are common test markets because they meet all these factors and because their mid-country location reflects common media-audience habits.

Many times, marketing and advertising tests make use of multiple markets. A single test market may not be entirely reliable, and some unforeseen occurrence could upset the test. Using multiple test locations also permits the use of experimental versus control groups to compare the test-campaign results with the existing (i.e., the older unchanged) campaign.

Sometimes, competitors attempt to upset marketing tests, so widespread publicity about testing is usually not desirable. Such interference is another reason to use multiple markets and cities for testing. In multiple-market testing, it is unlikely that more than one location would suffer from competitor interference.

Unit 16 Exercises
Working with Test Cities and Standards

1. Find relevant demographic information for the city in which you live and compare it with the demographics of the total U.S. population. Use the table below to enter your findings.

Demographic Data	Your City	Total U.S.
Total population	_____	_____
% population ages 18–34	_____	_____
% population ages 35–49	_____	_____
% population ages 50+	_____	_____
Median household income	_____	_____
Median individual income	_____	_____
Median age	_____	_____
% with four-year college education	_____	_____
% with high school diploma	_____	_____
% employed full-time	_____	_____
% employed part-time	_____	_____
% not employed	_____	_____
% males	_____	_____
% females	_____	_____

2. Now conduct some research to find the local advertising media available for your city. Use the table below to enter your information. If your market has many media vehicles, you may need to expand the table.

Name of City or Market	Media Vehicle Names
Daily newspaper(s)	_____
Weekly newspaper(s)	_____
Radio stations	_____
Television stations	_____
Cable television system(s)	_____
Local magazine(s)	_____
Outdoor advertising operator(s)	_____
Telephone directory companies	_____
Online display opportunities	_____

3. Now assess the suitability of your city or market for use as a test-market area.

   a. Overall, how well does your city or market population match the U.S. demographics?

   b. In which demographic categories is your city or market closest to the U.S. averages for those categories?

c. In which demographic categories does your city or market's average differ most from the U.S. average in the same categories?

d. Does your city or market offer a wide enough variety of media that might be used for advertising tests? How much variety does it offer?

e. In which media categories does your city or market offer the best advertising test opportunities?

f. In which media categories does your city or market fail to offer strong advertising test opportunities?

g. Finally, what is your overall assessment of your city or market as a possible test market for advertising?

Unit 17
Working with Quintiles

Advertisers often variously group prospective customers in order to reach enough types of audiences efficiently and effectively. Some of these groupings make use of *quintiles*.

The basic target groupings are referred to as *market segments*. Segmentation can be done in many ways:

- Geographics
- Demographics
- Psychographics
- Sociographics
- Media graphics (types of media used and amounts of usage)
- Lifestyles (sometimes referred to as "values and lifestyles")
- Geodemographics (a combination of demographics and geographics)
- Product usage (heavy, medium, light, and so on)
- Benefits

Using quintiles is a way of resegmenting the market segments of similar customers. Specific groups are subdivided into more groups, in order to create more potential customers.

Percentiles

It may be easier to understand quintiles if we begin with *percentiles*. Because most people have some experience with percentiles, they are often used in analyzing the results of standardized tests.

In using percentiles, we divide all the results (or persons) into 100 equal categories, from highest rated to lowest rated. Say a student takes a standardized test and is placed in the 78th percentile. Seventy-seven percent (and therefore 77 segments) are below this student's percentile placement and 22 percent (and thus 22 segments) are above. The remaining 1 percent falls within the student's segment.

Similarly, a score in the 44th percentile means that 43 percent of the scores are lower, 56 percent are higher, and 1 percent is in the same grouping.

Deciles

Deciles are similar to percentiles, except that the scores or the persons are divided into 10 equal groupings instead of 100.

For example, a person whose income is in the 7th decile has 6 deciles (60 percent) in lower-income groups and 3 deciles (30 percent) in higher-income groups. The remaining decile (10 percent) is part of the 7th decile.

Quintiles

With *quintiles,* we divide the persons or scores into five equal-sized groups. Using five groups instead of ten (as with deciles) or 100 (as with percentiles) makes the data easier to handle and analyze. If all the market segments were redivided into 100 additional groups, the amount of information would be overwhelming. Moreover, there is not much difference between the 54th percentile and the 55th percentile—yet there is a meaningful difference between the top quintile (top 20 percent), or Quintile I, and the second-best 20 percent quintile (Quintile II).

Ideally, the five quintiles would be of exactly the same size. (For example, out of a population of one million, 200,000 people (20 percent) would be in each quintile group. Instead, each quintile will only be approximately, but not exactly, 20 percent of the total.

Quintile	Percent of total	Number of people
I	20	199,500
II	20	199,500
III	20	200,750
IV	20	201,250
V	20	199,000
	100	1,000,000

As noted above, we usually begin with Quintile I, then go down through the other quintiles in order. If we use quintiles to describe how much television people might watch each week, Quintile I would be those who view television the most (the "heavy" users)—and on down through the quintiles until Quintile V, which would be the lightest users of television and those who do not watch television at all.

Quintile	TV viewers
I	Heaviest users
II	Next heaviest
III	Moderate users
IV	Light users
V	Lightest users and nonusers

As we noted earlier, quintiles are often used to divide up user groups into additional groups. Suppose we are advertising disposable razors to adult males, and we are considering using radio to reach them. Table 17.1 shows what the quintiles for radio listening might look like for heavy users of disposable razors (i.e., at least three days a week).

Quintile	Number of users	Percent (%)
I	5,422	21.1
II	5,062	19.7
III	5,375	20.9
IV	5,123	19.9
V	4,801	18.5

Pay special attention to the number of users in each group. As the heading indicates, the figures are rounded off to the nearest 1,000. Thus, the number of men in Quintile I is 5,422,000, not 5,422. Each figure must be multiplied by 1,000 to get the correct value. This rounding is used merely to save space.

The quintiles refer to the level of radio usage from highest level (Quintile I) to the lowest level (or nonuser) of radio (Quintile V). So Quintile II refers to the men who are heavy users of disposable razors and who listen to a lot of radio, but not as much radio as do those in Quintile I. Quintile IV refers to the men who are heavy users of disposable razors but who are light users of radio. This kind of information provides a good idea of whether radio is a good advertising medium for reaching those men who are the heaviest users of disposable razors.

Terciles

There are some cases where a market segment is divided into only three groups, called terciles. Terciles may be used instead of quintiles when there are relatively small target groups, because five groupings (quintiles) may be too specific or might result in uneven sizes of groupings.

Look at the table on terciles. The table displays terciles for women who use medicated skin creams and who also read the Sunday papers.

Tercile	Number (000)	Percent (%)
I	5,270	35.1
II	4,663	31.0
III	5,092	33.9

In this example, all the persons are adult females who use medicated skin creams and read the Sunday papers. Tercile I comprises only women who are heavy readers of the Sunday papers, while Tercile III comprises those women who read the Sunday papers only infrequently or not at all.

Using Quintiles

Quintiles may have the most significant impact when one part of the usage pattern is so heavy or so light that it simply does not fit into 20 percent of the total audience. In this situation, one or more quintiles may be larger or smaller than the expected 20 percent. The table on quintiles provides data about magazine use among adult female heavy users of home hair coloring. Quintile I is the heavy users of magazines and Quintile V is the light users and nonusers of magazines.

Quintile	Number (000)	% Down	% Across	Index
I	1,075	24.7	5.4	124
II	950	21.9	4.8	109
III	767	17.6	3.9	88
IV	749	17.3	3.8	86
V	810	18.5	4.1	93

By reviewing the actual number of women in each group, or by comparing the percentages in the "% down" column or comparing the index figures, we can see that magazines appear to be a good medium for reaching heavy users of home hair coloring.

If we then compare the heaviest users (Quintile I) of magazines with the corresponding heavy users of each of the other major mass media, we can get an even clearer comparison. The Quintile I figures (heaviest users) for each of the major mass media used by adult female heavy users of home hair coloring is given in the accompanying table. Note that the figures in the "% down" column do not necessarily total to 100 percent because these figures are drawn from five different datasets, one for each medium listed.

Medium (Quintile I)	Number (000)	% Down	% Across	Index
Magazines	1,075	24.7	5.4	124
Newspapers	958	22.0	4.8	110
Television	1,036	23.9	5.2	119
Radio	907	20.8	4.6	104
Outdoor	960	22.1	4.8	110

Now we can see even more clearly that magazines are the strongest of these mass media for reaching adult female heavy users of home hair coloring products. The next most effective medium appears to be television, followed by newspapers and outdoor (which are almost tied).

As you can see, quintiles (along with deciles and terciles) are very useful classifications because they clearly differentiate the various levels of media consumption by the groups under consideration.

Table 17.1 is an example of actual quintile data. Be sure you understand the meaning of the topic headings and that you can use the data provided. The first column are samples of actual quintile research findings; is the remaining columns are the explanation of how the quintile data are gathered and compiled by Mediamark Research Inc. (MRI). You will also use this example for some of the exercises that follow.

Notice that the sizes of the quintile groups are not exactly equal, although the goal is to have five equal-sized groups of 20 percent each. The unweighted ("Unwgtd") data show the actual numbers. The next row are the projected national figures; each of these figures must be multiplied by 1,000 to bring it up to accurate size. (Percentages may not total 100 percent because not all brands and consumption data are covered.) Data for some media will not total 100 percent because not everyone in the survey utilized that particular medium; for example, the vertical percentages in the Internet data total far less than 100 percent because

Table 17.1

Actual Quintile Data

		All	Total beer/ale: Budweiser all users	Budweiser heavy users	Total beer/ale: Miller Lite all users	Miller Lite heavy users
All	Unwgtd	51,774	6,271	1,413	3,040	592
	(000)	205,368	24,847	5,898	10,492	2,002
	Horz %	100	12.1	2.9	5.1	1.0
	Vert %	100	100	100	100	100
	Index	100	100	100	100	100
Internet Quintile I	Unwgtd	7085	874	140	568	94
	(000)	23,836	2,890	448	1,825	290
	Horz %	100	12.1	1.9	7.7	1.2
	Vert %	11.61	11.6	7.6	17.4	14.5
	Index	100	100	65	150	125
Internet Quintile II	Unwgtd	6,833	848	162	481	91
	(000)	23,658	2,857	570	1,636	315
	Horz %	100	12.1	2.4	6.9	1.3
	Vert %	11.52	11.5	9.7	15.6	15.7
	Index	100	100	84	135	137
Internet Quintile III	Unwgtd	6,601	852	155	473	97
	(000)	23,889	3,039	528	1,409	279
	Horz %	100	12.7	2.2	5.9	1.2
	Vert %	11.63	12.2	9.0	13.4	14.0
	Index	100	105	77	115	120
Internet Quintile IV	Unwgtd	6,266	787	172	484	99
	(000)	23,907	2,853	656	1,657	314
	Horz %	100	11.9	2.7	6.9	1.3
	Vert %	11.64	11.5	11.1	15.8	15.7
	Index	100	99	95	136	135
Internet Quintile V	Unwgtd	5,844	768	196	356	66
	(000)	23,774	3,178	821	1,337	229
	Horz %	100	13.4	3.5	5.6	1.0
	Vert %	11.58	12.8	13.9	12.8	11.4
	Index	100	110	120	110	99
Magazine Quintile I (heavy)	Unwgtd	10,790	1,532	327	738	133
	(000)	40,999	5,940	1,329	2,558	506
	Horz %	100	14.5	3.2	6.2	1.2
	Vert %	19.96	23.9	22.5	24.4	25.3
	Index	100	120	113	122	127
Magazine Quintile II	Unwgtd	11,160	1,407	309	702	124
	(000)	41,045	5,218	1,210	2,144	400
	Horz %	100	12.7	3.0	5.2	1.0
	Vert %	19.99	21.0	20.5	20.4	20.0
	Index	100	105	103	102	100
Magazine Quintile III	Unwgtd	10,736	1,293	281	675	136
	(000)	41,039	4,917	1,267	2,282	385
	Horz %	100	12.0	3.1	5.6	0.9
	Vert %	19.98	19.8	21.5	21.8	19.2
	Index	100	99	108	109	96
Magazine Quintile IV	Unwgtd	10,156	1,095	265	555	119
	(000)	41,163	4,529	1,031	2,016	384
	Horz %	100	11.0	2.5	4.9	0.9
	Vert %	20.04	18.2	17.5	19.2	19.2
	Index	100	91	87	96	96

(continued)

Table 17.1 *(continued)*

		All	Total beer/ale: Budweiser all users	Budweiser heavy users	Total beer/ale: Miller Lite all users	Miller Lite heavy users
Magazine Quintile V (light)	Unwgtd	8,932	944	231	370	80
	(000)	41,121	4,243	1,060	1,491	326
	Horz %	100	10.3	2.6	3.6	0.8
	Vert %	20.02	17.1	18.0	14.2	16.3
	Index	100	85	90	71	81
Newspaper Quintile I	Unwgtd	12,021	1,537	313	771	147
	(000)	41,129	5,306	1,120	2,334	483
	Horz %	100	12.9	2.7	5.7	1.2
	Vert %	20.03	21.4	19.0	22.2	24.1
	Index	100	107	95	111	120
Newspaper Quintile II	Unwgtd	11,151	1,242	279	665	120
	(000)	40,947	4,290	1,065	2,113	350
	Horz %	100	10.5	2.6	5.2	0.9
	Vert %	19.94	17.3	18.1	20.1	17.5
	Index	100	87	91	101	88
Newspaper Quintile III	Unwgtd	9,977	1,264	297	611	118
	(000)	41,048	5,350	1,366	2,192	379
	Horz %	100	13.0	3.3	5.3	0.9
	Vert %	19.99	21.5	23.2	20.9	19.0
	Index	100	108	116	105	95
Newspaper Quintile IV	Unwgtd	9,845	1,204	267	578	103
	(000)	41,158	5,181	1,153	2,208	358
	Horz %	100	12.6	2.8	5.4	0.9
	Vert %	20.04	20.9	19.6	21.0	17.9
	Index	100	104	98	105	89
Newspaper Quintile V	Unwgtd	8,780	1,024	257	415	104
	(000)	41,086	4,721	1,194	1,645	431
	Horz %	100	11.5	2.9	4.0	1.1
	Vert %	20.01	19.0	20.2	15.7	21.6
	Index	100	95	101	78	108
Outdoor Quintile I	Unwgtd	10,358	1,286	272	732	151
	(000)	40,974	4,922	1,110	2,644	562
	Horz %	100	12.0	2.7	6.5	1.4
	Vert %	19.95	19.8	18.8	25.2	28.1
	Index	100	99	94	126	141
Outdoor Quintile II	Unwgtd	10,598	1,341	309	692	125
	(000)	41,018	4,845	1,228	2,263	383
	Horz %	100	11.8	3.0	5.5	0.9
	Vert %	19.97	19.5	20.8	21.6	19.1
	Index	100	98	104	108	96
Outdoor Quintile III	Unwgtd	10,933	1,373	289	662	128
	(000)	40,878	5,329	1,146	2,097	394
	Horz %	100	13.0	2.8	5.1	1.0
	Vert %	19.9	21.5	19.4	20.0	19.7
	Index	100	108	98	100	99
Outdoor Quintile IV	Unwgtd	10,410	1,196	283	562	105
	(000)	40,989	4,698	1,166	2,031	370
	Horz %	100	11.5	2.8	5.0	0.9
	Vert %	19.96	18.9	19.8	19.4	18.5
	Index	100	95	99	97	93
Outdoor Quintile V	Unwgtd	9,475	1,075	260	392	83
	(000)	41,509	5,054	1,249	1,457	292
	Horz %	100	12.2	3.0	3.5	0.7
	Vert %	20.21	20.3	21.2	13.9	14.6
	Index	100	101	105	69	72

		All	Total beer/ale: Budweiser all users	Budweiser heavy users	Total beer/ale: Miller Lite all users	Miller Lite heavy users
Radio Quintile I	Unwgtd	9,813	1,334	332	605	137
	(000)	40,913	5,933	1,467	2,330	482
	Horz %	100	14.5	3.6	5.7	1.2
	Vert %	19.92	23.9	24.9	22.2	24.1
	Index	100	120	125	111	121
Radio Quintile II	Unwgtd	10,628	1,396	333	650	131
	(000)	41,166	5,439	1,309	2,207	408
	Horz %	100	13.2	3.2	5.4	1.0
	Vert %	20.04	21.9	22.2	21.0	20.4
	Index	100	109	111	105	102
Radio Quintile III	Unwgtd	11,111	1,350	276	745	139
	(000)	41,258	5,078	1,095	2,518	453
	Horz %	100	12.3	2.7	6.1	1.1
	Vert %	20.09	20.4	18.6	24.0	22.6
	Index	100	102	92	119	113
Radio Quintile IV	Unwgtd	10,726	1,262	258	629	121
	(000)	41,019	4,556	1,079	2,040	407
	Horz %	100	11.1	2.6	5.0	1.0
	Vert %	19.97	18.3	18.3	19.4	20.3
	Index	100	92	92	97	102
Radio Quintile V	Unwgtd	9,496	929	214	411	64
	(000)	41,013	3,842	948	1,397	252
	Horz %	100	9.4	2.3	3.4	0.6
	Vert %	19.97	15.5	16.1	13.3	12.6
	Index	100	77	80	67	63
TV (total) Quintile I	Unwgtd	9,413	1,105	285	408	79
	(000)	41,077	4,874	1,283	1,446	248
	Horz %	100	11.9	3.1	3.5	0.6
	Vert %	20	19.6	21.8	13.8	12.4
	Index	100	98	109	69	62
TV (total) Quintile II	Unwgtd	10,338	1,341	298	641	134
	(000)	41,030	5,188	1,278	2,161	472
	Horz %	100	12.6	3.1	5.3	1.2
	Vert %	19.98	20.9	21.7	20.6	23.6
	Index	100	105	108	103	118
TV (total) Quintile III	Unwgtd	10,655	1,334	271	708	140
	(000)	41,007	5,061	1,068	2,398	483
	Horz %	100	12.3	2.6	5.9	1.2
	Vert %	19.97	20.4	18.1	22.9	24.1
	Index	100	102	91	114	121
TV (total) Quintile IV	Unwgtd	10,667	1,317	281	655	128
	(000)	41,006	5,266	1,242	2,181	444
	Horz %	100	12.8	3.0	5.3	1.1
	Vert %	19.97	21.2	21.1	20.8	22.2
	Index	100	106	105	104	111
TV (total) Quintile V	Unwgtd	10,701	1,174	278	628	111
	(000)	41,248	4,457	1,027	2,307	354
	Horz %	100	10.8	2.5	5.6	0.9
	Vert %	20.09	17.9	17.4	22.0	17.7
	Index	100	89	87	109	88
TV (prime time) Quintile I	Unwgtd	10,107	1,246	280	545	101
	(000)	40,930	4,947	1,134	1,710	300
	Horz %	100	12.1	2.8	4.2	0.7
	Vert %	19.93	19.9	19.2	16.3	15.0
	Index	100	100	96	82	75

(continued)

Table 17.1 *(continued)*

		All	Total beer/ale: Budweiser all users	Budweiser heavy users	Total beer/ale: Miller Lite all users	Miller Lite heavy users
TV (prime time) Quintile II	Unwgtd	10,581	1,311	269	675	146
	(000)	41,097	4,830	1,003	2,270	466
	Horz %	100	11.8	2.4	5.5	1.1
	Vert %	20.01	19.4	17.0	21.6	23.3
	Index	100	97	85	108	116
TV (prime time) Quintile III	Unwgtd	10,581	1,317	294	644	118
	(000)	41,200	5,235	1,354	2,261	471
	Horz %	100	12.7	3.3	5.5	1.1
	Vert %	20.06	21.1	23.0	21.6	23.5
	Index	100	105	114	107	117
TV (prime time) Quintile IV	Unwgtd	10,495	1,288	292	641	122
	(000)	41,032	5,190	1,323	2,275	430
	Horz %	100	12.7	3.2	5.6	1.1
	Vert %	19.98	20.9	22.4	21.7	21.5
	Index	100	105	112	109	108
TV (prime time) Quintile V	Unwgtd	10,010	1,109	278	535	105
	(000)	41,108	4,645	1,085	1,975	334
	Horz %	100	113	2.6	4.8	0.8
	Vert %	20.02	18.7	18.4	18.8	16.7
	Index	100	93	92	94	83
TV (day time) Tercile I	Unwgtd	4,319	472	131	177	36
	(000)	20,264	2,414	683	737	135
	Horz %	100	11.9	3.4	3.6	0.7
	Vert %	9.87	9.7	11.6	7.0	6.7
	Index	100	98	117	71	68
TV (day time) Tercile II	Unwgtd	4,561	466	101	208	37
	(000)	20,393	2,141	469	750	136
	Horz %	100	10.5	2.3	3.7	0.7
	Vert %	9.93	8.6	8.0	7.1	6.8
	Index	100	87	80	72	69
TV (day time) Tercile III	Unwgtd	4,860	510	120	228	37
	(000)	20,475	2,120	530	795	128
	Horz %	100	10.4	2.6	3.9	0.6
	Vert %	9.97	8.5	9.0	7.6	6.4
	Index	100	86	90	76	64
Yellow Pages Tercile I	Unwgtd	8,240	1,034	244	536	104
	(000)	3,3049	4,254	1,057	2,047	401
	Horz %	100	12.9	3.2	6.2	1.2
	Vert %	16.09	17.1	17.9	19.5	20.0
	Index	100	106	111	121	124
Yellow Pages Tercile II	Unwgtd	8,691	1,020	225	585	118
	(000)	33,051	3,809	925	1,948	399
	Horz %	100	11.5	2.8	5.9	1.2
	Vert %	16.09	15.3	15.7	18.6	19.9
	Index	100	95	97	115	124
Yellow Pages Tercile III	Unwgtd	8,441	989	208	553	93
	(000)	32,915	3,836	824	1,900	327
	Horz %	100	111	2.5	5.8	1.0
	Vert %	16.03	15.4	14.0	18.1	16.3
	Index	100	96	87	113	102

Source: Doublebase Mediamark Research Inc.

Notes: weighted population (1,000).

Projections relatively unstable. Use with caution. Base: All.

All users = drank in last 6 months; heavy users = 6+ glasses past 7 days.

Table 17.2

Broadcast Media

Quintile	TV	Cable	Radio
I	40+	30+	10+
II	20 to 40	17 to 30	5 to 10
III	7 to 20	7 to 7	2.5 to 5
IV	1 to 7	1 to 7	1.0 to 2.5
V	0 to 1	0 to 1	0 to 1

only slightly more than half the respondents used the Internet during the survey period. Nevertheless, the percentages are still similar to one another (all about 11–12 percent) because they are equal-sized groups. By comparison, the vertical percentages for the magazine data total 100 percent (actually, 99.99 percent because of rounding).

The Media Meaning of a Quintile

Now that you know that Quintile I is the heaviest consumption group and that Quintile V is the lightest consumption group, let's put some media definitions to these sometimes abstract concepts.

The table listing media shows the number of hours of weekly usage for television (including cable) and radio. As you review the table, you can see how much time heavy users spend watching television.

As you can see from Table 17.2, someone who is in Quintile I for television usage is watching more than 40 hours of television per week. That is more than 5.5 hours of viewing per day. Contrast that to someone in Quintile V, who is watching one hour or less per day. From a strategy perspective, you could advertise on just about any program and be able to reach the viewer in Quintile I, but you would have to find just the right program to reach that selected viewer in Quintile V.

Print and online dimensions are different from those of broadcast. Tables 17.3 and 17.4 show newspaper, magazine, and online quintile definitions.

For newspaper, the quintile is based on the frequency of reading a daily newspaper. If you read all the issues, you are in Quintile I, or if you only read one issue, then you fall into Quintile V. Magazines are based on the depth of reading rather than the frequency. The more magazines you read in a month, the higher you fall in the quintile range. If you read seven or more magazines per month, then you are considered a heavy reader, while if you read one magazine per month, you are considered a very light reader. Online quintiles are still being fine-tuned. For now, they are based on the number of times you log on and use the Internet. A heavy user is someone who is using the Internet 85+ times per month or is logging on three times per day. A light user is someone who does not use the Internet at all.

It is important to put the quintile usage numbers in context when you are looking at the indices to understand what media your target market consumes. An average viewer of television may spend more time with this medium than the heaviest listener of radio. Quintiles tell an interesting media story. Remember how to read them and always keep in mind what the meaning behind the numbers is.

Table 17.3

Print Media

Quintile	Newspaper (read issues of daily)	Magazines (# per month read)
I	7 of 7	7+
II	4 to 7 of 7	4 to 7
III	2.5 to 4 of 7	2.5 to 4
IV	1.25 to 2.5 of 7	1.25 to 2.5
V	0 to 1.25 of 7	0 to 1.25

Table 17.4

Online Media

Quintile	# of times used in a month
I	85+
II	29–84
III	2–28
IV	1
V	0

Unit 17 Exercises
Working with Quintiles

1. Below are the gross income figures for several research respondents. Group the figures into quintiles.

$36,566

$42,769

$77,340 —

$97,213

$33,334

$41,789

$56,783

$62,944

$72,888 —

$70,143 —

$60,046

$39,576

$49,428

$30,322

$21,583

$84.228

$24,732

$38,589

$29,485

$41,568

20

2. Using the quintile data provided in Table 17.1, answer the following questions:

   a. In Magazine Quintile II, what does the number 1,210 mean in the data for heavy users of Budweiser beer?

   b. In that same set of data, what does the figure 103 mean?

   c. Again using the same dataset, what does the figure 3.0 mean?

   d. Using that same set of findings, what does the figure 309 mean?

   e. Finally, using the same data, what does the figure 20.5 mean?

3. What advertising medium would you recommend to advertise Lite Beer from Miller? Explain your reasoning.

4. Why are weekly magazines weighted by 4 while monthly magazines are weighted by only 1, as shown in Table 17.1?

5. Use Table 17.1 to answer the following questions.

   a. Which medium has the most unevenly sized quintile groups? Why do you think there is unevenness in these group sizes for this particular medium?

   b. Which medium has the most evenly sized quintile groups? Why do you think there is evenness in these group sizes for this particular medium?

Unit 18
Working to Define Media Strategies

If media objectives are the "what," then media strategies are the "how." Media strategies are inexplicably linked to media objectives. Media strategies are the answer to how you would achieve the objective.

In other words, objectives are simply "*doing* something" while strategies mean "*by* doing something." Media strategies, then, are the overall use of media to achieve the media objectives. Media strategies take two overall forms. The first is the media mix. The media mix is the combination of media you recommend to achieve the outlined objectives. The second is media scheduling. Scheduling is when you recommend deploying the various media types to meet the objectives.

Media Strategy versus Media Tactics

Media strategy is often confused with media tactics. Media strategy is the broad strategy of using media while tactics are the specific media vehicles. For example, a media objective may be to reach 80 percent of female homemakers. The strategy to accomplish this objective is to use a combination of cable television, magazines, and online display. The tactics would be to use Lifetime cable network, *Good Housekeeping* magazine, and Yahoo for online display.

Media strategies typically use categories of media while media tactics are the specific media vehicles. The only time this is not the case is when there is no broader umbrella for the category. A sponsorship of the Super Bowl would be an example of this.

Media Strategy Examples

Media strategies should match specifically to media objectives. You shouldn't devise a media strategy in a vacuum. The best way to organize media strategies is to match them to the four overall media objectives that we covered in Unit 10. They are target, geography, seasonality/timing, and reach/frequency. The table shows examples of media strategies for each of these objectives.

Objective	Strategy
1. To reach 90 percent of teenage boys	By using a mix of television, print, online, and gaming
2. To provide support for all four-week product purchase cycles	By providing continual support with magazines and by flighting the television schedule
3. To provide national support with emphasis on the top ten DMAs	By using national cable and magazines and by using radio and in-store media within the top ten DMAs

Media strategies follow media objectives. They are the action plan for your recommendations for allocating the budget. Some media planners use allocation percentages as a part of their media strategies. For example, if the objective is to provide national brand support; a strategy statement could be "By allocating 80 percent of the available dollars to national print and television."

Strategy Alternatives

There is more than one way to meet the objectives outlined. A method many media planners use when developing a media plan is to review alternative strategies rather than the recommended one. For example, if the overall goal of the plan is to reach 90 percent of the target an average of four times per month, the media planner may develop three or more alternative plans for review. These plans would have different combinations of media or different weighting of the same medium. One might be a television-only plan. A second plan might be a combination of television and print. And a third plan might be a combination of television, print, online, and radio. Regardless of what the alternatives were, they would be analyzed in terms of how they met the overall media objectives. This is a routine method that media planners use to justify their specific recommendations.

Summary

Media strategies should answer the objectives outlined in the media plan. To provide a strong media plan, you should align your strategies specifically with the objectives. If you find that you have strategies that do not match an objective, then you should reconsider those strategies. Once you provide a recommended strategy, consider alternative plans in order to make sure your plan is the best path to take to meet the objectives.

Unit 18 Exercises
Working to Define
Media Strategies

1. How would you define a media strategy?

2. What are the two general types of media strategies?

3. What is the difference between a media strategy and a media tactic?

4. How would you craft a media strategy to meet the following media objective: "To generate buzz?"

Unit 19
Effectiveness, Engagement, and Commoditization

We like to think that our advertising works, but we also know that not every advertising message is effective, that different advertising messages do not work equally well, and that no advertising message works with every customer. In fact, judging the effectiveness of our advertising is one of the biggest dilemmas facing advertisers. As the founder of the Wanamaker's Department Store in Philadelphia, John Wanamaker, was quoted as saying, "I know that half of my advertising is wasted. The problem is I don't know which half."

We also must realize that most consumers do not think they react to advertising, or at least they don't think they react very often. As you work in advertising, you will hear people say, "Advertising doesn't work on me at all" and "I don't know why advertisers spend so much on advertising that doesn't work."

So our problem is to determine whether our advertising is working and just what effect it brings to the marketplace. Even if you know that your advertising is working, how can you determine what effect is brought about by the media effort, as opposed to the message or the research or the product-placement or public-relations phase of a campaign?

It may be helpful to look at the advertising process as a model or diagram. Exhibit 19.1 shows a diagram of the advertising media process designed by the Advertising Research Foundation (ARF). The vertical axis shows reach, the number of persons affected; the horizontal axis shows frequency, the number of times that audience members are affected. Prospects are above the horizontal line and nonprospects are below it. The process moves from left to right through six stages, from vehicle distribution (Stage I) all the way to sales response (Stage VI). It may be easiest to imagine this diagram as an advertisement appearing in a print magazine: Stage I is the distribution of copies of the magazine (vehicle) itself, Stage II is audience exposure to the magazine, Stage III is exposure to the actual advertisement, Stage IV is perceiving the advertisement, Stage V is being communicated to by the advertisement, and Stage VI is buying the advertised product or service.

There are five trends that are currently popular in analyzing advertising: convergence, interactivity, engagement, commoditization, and cadence. Let's look at a couple of them in more detail.

Exhibit 19.1   **The ARF Model for Evaluating Media Effectiveness**

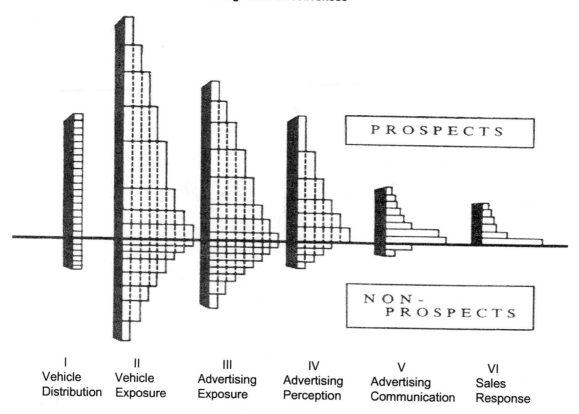

I	II	III	IV	V	VI
Vehicle Distribution	Vehicle Exposure	Advertising Exposure	Advertising Perception	Advertising Communication	Sales Response

Source: Copyright © 1961 and 1983 Advertising Research Foundation (ARF). Used by permission.

Engagement

Today's consumers have an opportunity to be engaged with advertising messages almost all the time. There is more communication available through mobile media such as mobile telephones, mobile music players, mobile laptop computers, and mobile Internet access.

Engaging potential customers is highly relevant for modern advertising as competing media continue to fragment audiences, as digital communications change the advertising environment, and as the competition increases for consumers' attention. It is no longer enough to "count eyeballs," as older advertising research has often been referred to when it involved adding up the number of readers or viewers; instead, it is important to engage individual customers.

The Internet obviously has an inherent advantage in engaging customers, because customers go to the Internet for purposeful searches and pay close attention to what they find there. However, other media also provide engagement; in fact, the magazine industry says that magazines engage audiences best because readers are actively involved with their favorite magazine, and magazines can build strong personal relationships with their audiences.

Even the Internet may not be as powerful in providing engagement as one might first think, because research shows that online conversion to buying behavior occurs in the same (original) online session only 1 percent of the time, with another 7 percent coming with later online sessions, and as much as 92 percent of the buying decisions occurring offline, after the Internet session.

Media may be the most important advertising aspect affecting engagement. The media placement controls whether the audience sees or reads the advertising, which is necessary for audience response. The media themselves may be engaging, and smart advertising media planners will use that facet to maximize audience engagement with their advertisements.

Some advertising practitioners differentiate between *media engagement,* which is due only to the media themselves, and *advertising engagement,* which would involve other factors (such as message strategies) in addition to media.

Commoditization

Commoditization occurs when a product or service becomes indistinguishable from others like it. For example, if all the banks in a community offer the same services, are open the same hours, and have multiple convenient locations, then banking in that town is like a commodity. When commoditization does occur, consumers tend to make buying decisions on price alone, rather than on other features. Commoditization (sometimes called *commodification*) can be done purposely or it can be an unintentional outcome that no marketer was trying to achieve.

In term of economics, this process moves the market closer to a pure-competition or perfect-competition situation. Consumers usually benefit from commoditization, because competition only on a price basis tends to lead, of course, to lower prices. However, advertising may suffer because it is more difficult to advertise a service or item when there are no actual differences, that is, no product differentiation.

Unit 19 Exercises

Effectiveness, Engagement, and Commoditization

1. Look again at the ARF Model in Exhibit 19.1 and at the explanation provided there. Why is there more horizontal breadth in all the stages following Stage I than in Stage I itself?

2. Again looking at the ARF Model in Exhibit 19.1, why are there no consumers below the horizontal line in Stage VI?

Exhibit 19.2 **400 GRP Level**

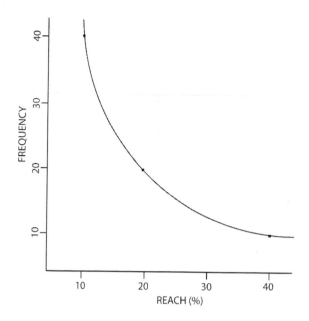

3. Look at Exhibit 19.2.

   With a goal of 10 percent reach, how many advertising insertions per week would you need to achieve 400 GRP per week?

4. Again look at Exhibit 19.2. Buying 400 GRP per week, what reach level would you achieve if you placed 20 advertisements per week?

5. What media techniques might you use to achieve more engagement with an advertising campaign?

6. What message techniques might you use to achieve more engagement with an advertising campaign?

7. Some advertising media practitioners differentiate between *media engagement* and *advertising engagement*. Which of the two is likely to be stronger than the other? Why?

8. How does branding relate to commoditization? Does branding work toward commoditization or against it?

9. What are other methods (in addition to branding) by which a commoditized product, service, or idea might be differentiated?

Part III
Media Tactics

Unit 20
Working to Define Media Tactics

Media objectives outline where you want to go. Media strategies outline how to get there. Media tactics provide the specific details on how to get there. So, if your objective is to get to Dallas and your strategy is to fly there, the tactic is to take Southwest Flight #9 that departs Tuesday at 2 P.M., arrives at 4 P.M., and costs $99.

Media tactics, then, are the details of your media plan. Tactics become the actual plan. You can't implement strategies without tactics. Media tactics include four components; description, cost, impressions, and the rationale.

Description

The description details what you are recommending. In the case of print, it would be the specific publications, the creative unit placed, and the purchase frequency. For example, if your strategy is to schedule women's magazines, a tactic would be to schedule six full-page four-color ads in *Good Housekeeping*.

Descriptions vary by the medium chosen. So, in the case of broadcast, a tactic written in a media plan would include the types of stations, the dayparts to be purchased, and the creative unit to be used. It may or may not include the specific programs at this juncture since they have yet to be negotiated. This is done once the plan is approved. However, it could be done simultaneously, if the marketer has bought off on the broad direction of the media strategies.

Outdoor media would include the type of unit, the number to be purchased, and the general locations. The specific details would be conveyed upon the final purchase.

Online display would contain the sites, the creative unit, and the dayparts to be purchased. Search engine marketing would include the pool of keywords to be tested and the geography of the test.

Cost

All tactics include costs. Costs are provided at the category level and at the tactic level. For example, you may allocate a budget of $4 million to national magazines. The plan would itemize each publication's cost that would then be added together to reach the $4 million magazine budget.

The cost for each element in the media plan should reflect the agency compensation agreement. If the agency is working on a commission basis, then the media should contain the appropriate commission. If the agency is working on a fee basis, then the media should be shown in net dollars. At the tactics level, the marketer will want to understand the specific costs that he or she will be billed. The tactical cost aspect of the plan becomes the financial road map for the marketer in working with his internal accounting.

Impressions

All tactics will include the amount of the target reached. This can be done a number of ways. It can be shown by GRPs or it can be shown by impressions or both. As more communication plans contain a variety of elements from paid media to digital media to promotions and more, the planner is moving toward impressions as the standard for reach measurement for tactics. This is the simplest form of showing reach and the easiest to use across any form of communication.

For example, you would show that *Good Housekeeping* cost $750,000 for three ads and generated 9 million impressions based on a target of women ages 25 to 54. The key to showing impressions in the media plan for each tactic is to help the marketer understand the target for which impressions are calculated. That provides a frame of reference for the client to understand the strength of each element.

Rationale

There are a number of ways of executing a media strategy. Therefore, the tactics you recommend should contain a detailed rationale. The rationale for a media tactic revolves around how the tactic reaches the target, how cost efficient it is, and how it may benefit the brand through association.

For example, your rationale for selecting *Good Housekeeping* might be as follows:

- *Good Housekeeping* has the highest coverage of our target.
- *Good Housekeeping*'s CPM is 12 percent below average for the women's service group.
- *Good Housekeeping* will endorse our brand through the use of the *Good Housekeeping* seal of approval.

This is a strong rationale for why *Good Housekeeping* should be a part of the magazine plan. Each media tactic should have a similar rationale. Not all tactics will have all of these components. The important part of a rationale is to answer the question of why this specific vehicle instead of another.

Media tactics are the backbone of the media plan. It is what the marketer wants to understand since it is the specifics of what will be in the marketplace. Each tactic should contain a detailed description. It should include the cost, the number of impressions, and a detailed rationale for why it was selected.

Unit 20 Exercises
Working to Define Media Tactics

1. How would you define a media tactic?

2. What are the key components of media tactics?

3. What is the cost and audience guarantee for *Time* magazine in the United States for a full-page ad run of book? Please review the tactics as if they were a part of a plan.

4. What is different about writing tactics for promotional recommendations?

5. If you have access to SRDS, provide the tactical plan for the following:

a. A magazine plan using women's service publications based on an annual budget of $1 million using a creative unit of a full-page four-color bleed.

b. An outdoor plan for Houston and Dallas/Fort Worth based on an annual budget of $500,000 using 14 × 48 bulletins.

c. A national cable plan based on an annual budget of $2 million using a 30-second creative unit.

Unit 21
Working with Media Cost Comparisons

It makes sense that advertisers want to use the most efficient media they can so they can control their advertising costs. It should also make sense that media vehicles with larger audiences will usually charge more than will vehicles with smaller audiences.

Problems arise, however, in trying to determine which vehicle or vehicles are the best buy in a certain advertising situation. Trying to be cost efficient is not necessarily the same as using the least expensive or most economical media. An advertising media vehicle can be most efficient even though it is higher in cost than other vehicles.

For example, there are two newspapers in Gothamville: the *Banner* and the *Herald*. The *Banner* has a circulation of 320,000 and charges $2.45 per column-inch for advertising. The *Herald* has a circulation of 640,000 and charges $4.15 per column-inch of advertising space. The *Herald* has 100 percent more circulation but it charges only 70 percent more. Obviously, the *Banner* is cheaper, but the *Herald* is more efficient.

Comparing advertising rates is easy in this situation because one vehicle has exactly twice the circulation of the other. But that is rarely the case, so we need a quick and easy way to compare the cost efficiencies of two or more advertising vehicles.

The only fair approach to comparing the cost efficiencies of two or more vehicles is on the basis of equal audience size. Because both advertising costs and media audience sizes vary considerably from one media vehicle to another, you must hold one of those items constant while you consider the other.

Cost per Thousand

One such approach is using *cost per thousand,* which is abbreviated as CPM in the advertising business (m = *mille,* which means 1,000 in Latin).

To use CPM, we consider each of the media vehicles as if they had equal-sized audiences, an audience of 1,000 for each (hence the term "cost per thousand"). We then take either the audience size or the circulation and reduce it in size to the figure 1,000.

The CPM formula for print media normally uses the circulation of the publications under consideration.

$$\text{CPM} = \frac{\$\,\text{Advertisement insertion cost}}{\text{Circulation}} \times 1,000$$

Dividing by the circulation takes the value down to the equivalent of distributing only one copy of the publication, and then multiplying by 1,000 takes the value up to the level equivalent to a circulation of 1,000. In effect, you are asking, If all the media vehicles had a circulation of 1,000, what would their advertising rates be?

The figure of 1,000 is used because it gives a solid dollar-and-cents result, which is easy to comprehend and easy to work with. Let's look at a comparison where we reduce a publication to a circulation of only one, versus a circulation of 1,000.

If the circulation were one copy, the cost comparison would work this way for a publication where an advertisement costs $100,000 and the circulation is 245,000.

$$\frac{\$\,\text{Advertisement insertion cost}}{\text{Circulation}} = \frac{\$100,000}{245,000} = \$0.4082$$

The result, $0.4082, is a bit tricky to work with. But taking the circulation to 1,000 would result in this:

$$\frac{\$\,\text{Advertisement insertion cost}}{\text{Circulation}} \times 1,000 = \frac{\$100,000}{245,000} \times 1,000 = \$408.16$$

The resulting $408.16 makes more sense and is easier to work with as dollars and cents. We usually take CPM calculations out to two decimal places, that is, to the nearest cent, just as we do with most costs in U.S. money.

If you don't know what size advertisement you might like to use in a certain medium, you can still make the CPM comparison between two or more vehicles by simply using a standard-size advertisement insertion cost. For example, in comparing two magazines, it is common to use the advertising page rate (the cost of buying a full page of advertising in each magazine) as the estimated advertising insertion cost.

For broadcast and other media, we don't really have suitable circulation figures; the term *circulation* means something very different (and quite technical) in the broadcast media, so instead of dividing the advertising rate by circulation, we commonly divide by the audience size. Thus, for broadcast and other nonprint vehicles, we use a slightly different CPM formula.

$$\text{CPM} = \frac{\$\,\text{Advertisement insertion cost}}{\text{Audience size}} \times 1,000$$

Of course, the size of the audience would be larger than the size of the circulation, so using an audience figure in the denominator of the formula will give us a smaller CPM figure. Thus, CPM figures for broadcast media are usually quite a bit cheaper than for print media—not because the broadcast media are necessarily more efficient but because we are using a larger (audience) number in the denominator.

You also need to keep in mind that it is not sensible to calculate the CPM for a single media vehicle. The CPM calculation is used to compare cost efficiencies of at least two (and often many more) vehicles, so you need to calculate the CPM for each one.

If one vehicle has a CPM of $12.36 and another has a CPM of $11.74, the second one has the lower cost per thousand and is thus more efficient at reaching a thousand audience members or a thousand households, and so on.

Cost per Point

Another way to compare the cost efficiencies of two or more media vehicles is by using *cost per point* (CPP). The full name of this process is cost per rating point, so some practitioners abbreviate the term as "CPRP" or "CPR" or "C/RP," but the most common acronym is "CPP."

Because a rating is basically measuring reach as a percentage, using CPP compares the media vehicle cost efficiency on the basis of reaching 1 percent of the audience. In essence, you are asking, If each media vehicle reached 1 percent of the audience, what would it cost?

The formula for cost per point is quite easy to state and to remember.

$$CPP = \frac{Cost}{Points}$$

The formula, stated a bit more completely, would look like this:

$$CPP = \frac{\$\ Advertisement\ insertion\ cost}{Number\ of\ rating\ points}$$

Or like this:

$$CPP = \frac{\$\ Advertisement\ insertion\ cost}{Rating}$$

Using CPP is just as easy as the formula indicates. If you place an advertisement with a radio station at a cost of $2,500 and the rating for the station at that hour is 2.2 percent the cost per point is calculated this way:

$$CPP = \frac{\$2,500}{2.2\%\ Rtg.} = \$1,136.36\ per\ rating\ point\ [or,\ \$1,136.36/Rtg.\ Pt.]$$

As we do with CPM, we usually take CPP calculations out to two decimal places, that is, to the nearest cent, just as we do with most costs in U.S. money. As with CPM, CPP is used to compare the cost efficiency of two or more media vehicles, so the calculations are made for each of the vehicles. If one vehicle has a CPP of $212.55 and another vehicle has a CPP of $220.10, the first one has the lower CPP and is thus more efficient at reaching one percent of the audience.

Table 21.1

Adult CPM Comparison Weighted by Impact

Medium	Unit	CPM ($)	Impact score	WTD CPM ($)
Television	:30	6.00	100	6.00
Cable	:30	7.00	90	7.78
Radio	:60	4.50	75	6.00
Newspaper	½ pg B&W	15.00	70	21.43
Magazine	Full pg 4/c	8.50	80	10.63
Outdoor	30 sheet poster	3.00	30	10.00
Internet	Banner	10.00	40	25.00

Source: FKM Agency estimates.

Weighted CPM and CPP

An experienced media planner or buyer may place extra weight or value on the costs of certain kinds of media or on certain kinds of media buys. It is important to realize that this kind of media "weighting" requires making some decisions about what kind of media placement is more valuable for the particular situation in which it is being used. There is no hard-and-fast rule that everyone in the advertising media business uses for every situation.

Table 21.1 shows adult CPM comparison weighted by impact. For the seven media types listed, there is a standard unit listed for each. Of course, you may be using other sizes or lengths of advertising units, but these are the units being considered in this situation. Then comes the CPM in this particular case for each of the media, followed by an *impact score;* based on research and intuition, the media analysts have judged how much impact there is on the audience for each medium, with 100 being the maximum impact.

The final weighted cost-per-thousand (WTD CPM) figures are derived by considering the original CPM in combination with the impact scores. For television, the weighted CPM has been calculated this way:

$$\frac{\$6.00 \text{ CPM}}{\text{Impact score}} = \$6.00 \text{ WTD CPM}$$

And for these newspapers, the calculations look like this:

$$\frac{\$15.00 \text{ CPM}}{0.70 \text{ impact score}} = \$21.43 \text{ WTD CPM}$$

You can see that the percentage impact scores are used as decimals, so 70 is expressed as 0.70. You will also see that by dividing the original CPM figures by the impact scores, the higher impact scores will result in higher WTD CPM figures (higher in value because they cost less) and the lower impact scores will result in lower WTD CPM figures (lower in value because they cost more).

Keep in mind that making intermedia comparisons can be tricky and requires a good deal of experience. For example, no one can be certain whether one television commercial is worth three radio commercials, say, or five newspaper advertisements.*

---

*For a more complete discussion of the problems of making intermedia comparisons, see Larry D. Kelley, Donald W. Jugenheimer, and Kim Bartel Sheehan, *Advertising Media Planning: A Brand Management Approach,* 3d ed. (Armonk, NY: M.E. Sharpe, 2012).

Table 21.2

San Antonio TV Daypart CPP Comparison by Average Rating Research (Adults 18–49)

Daypart	Avg CPP ($)	Avg rating	Avg rating index	WTD CPP ($)
Early morning	104	2.0	68	153
Early fringe	139	1.3	44	316
Early news	148	2.7	91	163
Prime access	198	3.1	105	189
Prime	256	4.2	142	180
Late news	215	5.1	172	125
Late fringe	89	2.3	78	114
Average	164	3.0	100	164

Source: SQAD, Inc.

Similar calculations can provide weighted cost per point (WTD CPP) figures. In Table 21.2 there are seven categories of television advertising times with an average cost row at the bottom. An Average Rating Index figure indicates how effective the media planner considers each of these television dayparts to be. Again, the original CPP figures are combined with the Average Rating Index figures to provide a WTD CPP. For prime time, the weighted CPP was calculated this way:

$$\frac{\$256 \text{ CPP}}{1.42 \text{ Avg. Rating Index}} = \$180 \text{ WTD CPP}$$

And for this example, in early news, the calculations look like this:

$$\frac{\$148 \text{ CPP}}{0.91 \text{ Avg. Rating Index}} = \$163 \text{ WTD CPP}$$

As before, the percentage index figures are applied as decimals, so 91 is expressed as 0.91. You will see again that when dividing the original CPP figures by the Average Rating Index figures, the higher index scores will result in higher WTD CPP figures (higher in value because they cost less), and the lower index scores will result in lower WTD CPP figures (again, lower in value because they cost more).

Keep in mind that the impact and index scores provided in these tables apply only to the marketing, advertising, and media situation for which they were derived, and that these weight adjustments may not apply to every situation.

Unit 21 Exercises
Working with Media Cost Comparisons

1. You are considering placing advertising on one of the three radio stations shown below, but you can only afford to advertise on one of the stations. Using the CPM for each station, decide which station would be more economical. Show your calculations.

Station	TVHH listening	Cost per :30 commercial
WAAA	20,000	$204
WBBB	12,000	136
WCCC	8,000	90

2. You are considering advertising in magazines, but you need to know which one is most efficient. Use CPMs to rank these magazines from most cost efficient to least cost efficient. Show your calculations.

Magazine	Accumulative audience	Cost of full-page B&W insertion
Modern Fishing	160,000	$2,000
Hunting & Trapping	86,000	$1,550
Hikes & Bikes	190,750	$2,790
Woods & Home	225,450	$4,100

3. You want to use television advertising to reach the population of Plainville, but you can likely afford to use only one of the three television stations in that market. Use CPPs to decide which station is most efficient. Show your calculations.

Station	Rating	Cost per :30 ad
KMTV	6.8	$200
KUDD	12.9	400
KRUD	10.1	285

4. Poortown has a population of about 200,000 and also has two newspapers, but you can afford to use only one of them. Compare the relative efficiency of these two newspapers for a 72-column-inch advertisement placement. Here are their advertising and audience figures.

The Times	The Tribune
$1.40 per column-inch	$1.50 per column-inch
Audience = 80,000	Audience = 90,000

a. First, compare the two newspapers on cost per thousand. Show your work.

   Times   *Tribune*

b. Now compare the two newspapers on cost per rating point. Show your work.

   Times   *Tribune*

c. Which paper would you use, and why?

5. Refer to Table 21.1 to rank the seven media according to their cost efficiencies, starting with the most efficient.

_____

_____

_____

_____

_____

_____

6. Refer to Table 21.2 to rank the seven television dayparts according to their cost efficiencies, starting with the least effective.

_____

_____

_____

_____

_____

_____

Unit 22
Working with Estimating

Estimating saves time. It prevents wasted work. It helps media planners and buyers meet deadlines. It permits easier budgeting. It also permits trial-and-error approaches without the investment of too much time, money, or effort.

Estimating in advertising media work usually involves two of three topic areas:

> Audience size
> Budget amount
> Media that are affordable

Using one of these three variables can help estimate one of the others:

- Knowing audience size, you can estimate the needed budget or you can estimate the number of media needed to reach that audience.
- Knowing the budgeted amount, you can estimate the size of audience that you can afford to reach or you can estimate the media that you can afford to use.
- Knowing the media that you wish to use, you can estimate the audience that you can reach using those media or you can estimate the budget that you will need to purchase those media.

Advertising media estimating guides are available from syndicated research services and publishers and sometimes from the media themselves; large advertising agencies may even prepare their own estimating guides.

Knowing only an estimate may be good enough for early work on an advertising media plan. If you have a budget and you want to know how many people you can afford to reach and how many times you can afford to reach them, an estimate will provide very close (although not exact) information. You'll be spared the need to go through an entire media buying effort only to find out that you don't have enough money in your budget or that you could have afforded more media weight. Similarly, you can use your budget to estimate the amount of advertising you can afford to purchase, but without the necessity of actually contacting all the media outlets that you might use.

For example, if you know that you have a budget of $10,000 a week for radio advertising and that, on the radio station that you are considering, each radio commercial spot costs about $1,500, then you can estimate that you can afford to purchase 6 or 7 spots each week on that radio station [$10,000 / $1,500 = 6.67]. You cannot, of course, purchase 6 and 2/3 spots; you must buy either 6 or 7 spots. But because this is an estimate, the figure of 6 or 7 is close enough; now at least you have a rough idea of the advertising frequency you can buy. Knowing this figure will help you decide if the budget for that station is adequate, or if you need more money, or if you should consider cheaper radio stations, or if you might be able to get by with a lower budget, or if you could buy on more stations.

Similarly, if you know that a television rating point averages $225 in a certain market and that you want to purchase 75 GRP (gross rating points) per week, then you know that you need about $16,875 a week for that television advertising ($225 × 75 = $16,875). And if the campaign will run for 39 weeks, you can estimate that you need a total television budget for that market of approximately $658,125 ($16,875 × 39 = $658,125).

If a local radio station has an average morning-drive-time rating of 3.9 percent and an average advertisement placement during that time segment costs $85, then you can estimate that the approximate CPP (cost per rating point) during that time slot costs about $22 ($85 / 3.9 = $21.79, which you can round to $22). Remember, your figures do not need to be exact because, after all, you are just looking for an estimate.

Unit 22 Exercises
Working with Estimating

1. A table of reach estimates for late evening spot television indicates that it requires 50 late evening GRP per week to achieve a 60 percent reach in an average market. SRDS Media Solutions™ indicates that the average cost of a late evening 30-second spot television announcement in Des Moines, Iowa, is $150, and the average late evening station rating is 3.0 during late evening in that city. Estimate the cost of using late evening spot television to achieve a 60 percent reach of Des Moines television homes for a 26-week period.

2. You have been given a $4,500,000 advertising budget by your client for consumer media advertising expenditures. You estimate that your overall CPM for all media will be $15 for the year. Approximately how many TAI could be purchased with this budget?

3. Using the information from the previous questions, if your target audience contains 60,000,000 adult females, how many times (frequency) will each person be exposed to your commercial messages during the year?

4. You know that there are about 300 million persons living in the United States. Your market target is adult males ages 18–49 who earn $15,000 and more (household incomes) and who have attended or graduated from college. Data from Simmons Market Research Bureau (SMRB) indicate that:

   adults are 66% of the total U.S. population;

   males are 42% of all adults;

   persons 18–49 are 40% of all adults;

   persons earning $15,000+ household incomes are 63% of the adults; and

   45% of adults have attended or graduated college.

   Estimate the approximate size of your target group in the United States. Show your work.

5. A table of reach estimates for daytime and spot television indicates that it requires 45 daytime GRPs per week to achieve a 50 percent reach in an average market. SRDS indicates that the average cost of a daytime 30-second spot television announcement in Philadelphia is $200, and the average daytime television station rating is 4.0 during daytime in that city. Estimate the cost of using daytime television to achieve a 50 percent reach of Philadelphia television homes for a 13-week period.

6. You are buying 100 GRPs per week over a four-week spot radio schedule on three stations. Use the chart below to help you calculate the estimated average frequency of exposure for the four-week total. Show your calculations.

Market	Number of Stations Used per Adult Rating			
Points per week	1	2	3	4
25	20*	30*	—	—
50	25*	40*	45*	55*
100	30*	45*	52*	60*

*% adults exposed

7. You need to estimate the cost of using television in the largest 20 markets during late news, with a goal of 50 gross rating points per market. Use the information below, and show your calculations.

ADI Mkts	Cost per rating point		
	Prime	Late news	Daytime
Top 10	$1,750	$1,200	$ 515
Top 20	3,200	2,100	930
Top 30	3,950	2,700	1,350

8. You are the advertising director for a medium-sized retail store located in Kansas City, Missouri, and much of your work concerns the advertising media that are used in your promotions. Your store's selling efforts are directed at a total of six market areas.

Market	Number of households
Kansas City, MO (& suburbs)	902,000
Kansas City, KS (& suburbs)	65,000
St. Joseph, MO	32,000
Topeka, KS	57,000
Lawrence, KS	22,000
Johnson County, KS (Kansas City suburbs)	87,000
Total	1,165,000 HH

Assume that all the households have television sets (i.e., there is 100 percent penetration of television) and also assume that there are 2.25 viewers per household on the average. Your annual advertising budget for the store is $94,250 per year. Your cost-per-thousand (CPM) goal is $7.50. Your advertising is placed directly; you do not use an advertising agency. The advertising budget does not have to cover production costs—you have separate funds for that, and some media outlets also help with production.

a. Assuming that newspapers are available in all six of your market areas, allocate $50,000 of your total budget to newspapers in each market, based on the size of each market. Show your work.

b. There are four major commercial television stations serving the Kansas City market on which you have been running some advertising. The average number of households tuned to each station is given below. Calculate each station's rating, share, and projected audience for the entire six-market selling area. Then calculate the households using television (HUT) and the projected audience for all four stations together. Show your calculations.

Households	Rating	Share	Projected audience
KCTV	256,300	_____	_____
KMBC-TV	209,700	_____	_____
KSHB	81,550	_____	_____
WDAF-TV	163,100	_____	_____

Households using television (HUT):   _____

Projected audience for all four stations: _____

c. What is the number of total audience impressions (TAI) that you can afford during a year of advertising? Show your work.

d. Your assistant has figures on your spot television advertising in the St. Joseph market. The figures indicate that you are reaching 28 percent of the St. Joseph market by using four spots per week on KQTV (Ch. 2 in St. Joseph). You look up the ratings for the station and you find that each of your spots has the following ratings:

Spot A	6 rtg.
Spot B	9 rtg.
Spot C	5 rtg.
Spot D	8 rtg.

Are you reaching 28 percent of that market? Why or why not?

e. Kansas City is the 27th largest market in the United States. You have on hand the following information for average quarter-hour audience ratings for selected dayparts in spot radio.

ADI mkts.	Morning Drive Weekdays 6–10 A.M.			Late Afternoon Drive Weekdays 3–8 P.M.		
	Men	Women	Teens	Men	Women	Teens
Top 10	0.9	1.1	1.9	0.7	0.8	4.3
Top 20	1.0	1.3	2.0	0.8	0.9	4.5
Top 30	1.1	1.4	2.2	0.9	1.0	5.0

Use these figures to calculate the approximate number of spot radio announcements that you would need per week in Kansas City to generate a monthly level of 100 GRP among adult males (1 month = 4 weeks, approximately) for the time periods indicated below. Show your calculations.

In morning drive time:

In late afternoon drive time:

f. You have a goal of reaching an average household 14 times during the year's advertising. Calculate the feasible percentage and amount of reach. Show your work. (Base your calculations on the entire six-market area.)

Reach in percent:

Reach in projected number of households:

Unit 23
Working with a Media Calendar and Flowcharts

Calendars and Flowcharts

Every media plan contains a schedule of the media to be used in the plan. Most media plans are done on some form of either calendar or fiscal year. Some are done monthly, or quarterly, or on an annual basis. Regardless of the time frame, media planners use a distinctive media calendar.

Media Calendars

The media calendar is not like a typical monthly calendar. The standard form used for a media calendar is generally the one used by the broadcast media, which always begins on a Monday and spans the full week.

For example, the 2012 broadcast calendar (see Table 23.1) for January contains five weeks and begins on December 26, 2012. A regular monthly calendar would begin with the month of December, and the first broadcast week would contain only one day in January.

Media calendars are used for media planning because the media that are purchased bill the advertiser based on the media calendar; therefore, a bill for January media would cover activity during the last week of December of the prior year.

Advertisers using a regular calendar for the accounting of a media schedule may get a rude awakening when the media bills do not conform to their regular calendar. So, unless there is a special provision made by the media, all bills will follow this broadcast media standard.

Media Flowcharts

Once a media plan is completed, the planner uses a media flowchart to summarize when the activity is to be scheduled. Scheduling media is the basis for the media flowchart. However, flowcharts come in all shapes and sizes. Many media planners use the flowchart to convey budget information, reach and frequency metrics, and even estimated campaign metrics such as advertising or brand awareness.

RADIO ADVERTISING BUREAU

2010-2012
Broadcast Calendar

Member Response Hotline
800.232.3131

Member Response Email
member_response@rab.com

Website
www.rab.com

Address
1320 Greenway Dr.,
Ste. 500
Irving, TX 75038

2010

January
	M	T	W	T	F	S	S
1	28	29	30	31	1	2	3
2	4	5	6	7	8	9	10
3	11	12	13	14	15	16	17
4	18	19	20	21	22	23	24
5	25	26	27	28	29	30	31

February
6	1	2	3	4	5	6	7
7	8	9	10	11	12	13	14
8	15	16	17	18	19	20	21
9	22	23	24	25	26	27	28

March
10	1	2	3	4	5	6	7
11	8	9	10	11	12	13	14
12	15	16	17	18	19	20	21
13	22	23	24	25	26	27	28

April
14	29	30	31	1	2	3	4
15	5	6	7	8	9	10	11
16	12	13	14	15	16	17	18
17	19	20	21	22	23	24	25

May
18	26	27	28	29	30	1	2
19	3	4	5	6	7	8	9
20	10	11	12	13	14	15	16
21	17	18	19	20	21	22	23
22	24	25	26	27	28	29	30

June
23	31	1	2	3	4	5	6
24	7	8	9	10	11	12	13
25	14	15	16	17	18	19	20
26	21	22	23	24	25	26	27

July
27	28	29	30	1	2	3	4
28	5	6	7	8	9	10	11
29	12	13	14	15	16	17	18
30	19	20	21	22	23	24	25

August
31	26	27	28	29	30	31	1
32	2	3	4	5	6	7	8
33	9	10	11	12	13	14	15
34	16	17	18	19	20	21	22
35	23	24	25	26	27	28	29

September
36	30	31	1	2	3	4	5
37	6	7	8	9	10	11	12
38	13	14	15	16	17	18	19
39	20	21	22	23	24	25	26

October
40	27	28	29	30	1	2	3
41	4	5	6	7	8	9	10
42	11	12	13	14	15	16	17
43	18	19	20	21	22	23	24
44	25	26	27	28	29	30	31

November
45	1	2	3	4	5	6	7
46	8	9	10	11	12	13	14
47	15	16	17	18	19	20	21
48	22	23	24	25	26	27	28

December
49	29	30	1	2	3	4	5
50	6	7	8	9	10	11	12
51	13	14	15	16	17	18	19
52	20	21	22	23	24	25	26

2011

January
	M	T	W	T	F	S	S
1	27	28	29	30	31	1	2
2	3	4	5	6	7	8	9
3	10	11	12	13	14	15	16
4	17	18	19	20	21	22	23
5	24	25	26	27	28	29	30

February
6	31	1	2	3	4	5	6
7	7	8	9	10	11	12	13
8	14	15	16	17	18	19	20
9	21	22	23	24	25	26	27

March
10	28	1	2	3	4	5	6
11	7	8	9	10	11	12	13
12	14	15	16	17	18	19	20
13	21	22	23	24	25	26	27

April
14	28	29	30	31	1	2	3
15	4	5	6	7	8	9	10
16	11	12	13	14	15	16	17
17	18	19	20	21	22	23	24

May
18	25	26	27	28	29	30	1
19	2	3	4	5	6	7	8
20	9	10	11	12	13	14	15
21	16	17	18	19	20	21	22
22	23	24	25	26	27	28	29

June
23	30	31	1	2	3	4	5
24	6	7	8	9	10	11	12
25	13	14	15	16	17	18	19
26	20	21	22	23	24	25	26

July
27	27	28	29	30	1	2	3
28	4	5	6	7	8	9	10
29	11	12	13	14	15	16	17
30	18	19	20	21	22	23	24
31	25	26	27	28	29	30	31

August
32	1	2	3	4	5	6	7
33	8	9	10	11	12	13	14
34	15	16	17	18	19	20	21
35	22	23	24	25	26	27	28

September
36	29	30	31	1	2	3	4
37	5	6	7	8	9	10	11
38	12	13	14	15	16	17	18
39	19	20	21	22	23	24	25

October
40	26	27	28	29	30	1	2
41	3	4	5	6	7	8	9
42	10	11	12	13	14	15	16
43	17	18	19	20	21	22	23
44	24	25	26	27	28	29	30

November
45	31	1	2	3	4	5	6
46	7	8	9	10	11	12	13
47	14	15	16	17	18	19	20
48	21	22	23	24	25	26	27

December
49	28	29	30	1	2	3	4
50	5	6	7	8	9	10	11
51	12	13	14	15	16	17	18
52	19	20	21	22	23	24	25

2012

January
	M	T	W	T	F	S	S
1	26	27	28	29	30	31	1
2	2	3	4	5	6	7	8
3	9	10	11	12	13	14	15
4	16	17	18	19	20	21	22
5	23	24	25	26	27	28	29

February
6	30	31	1	2	3	4	5
7	6	7	8	9	10	11	12
8	13	14	15	16	17	18	19
9	20	21	22	23	24	25	26

March
10	27	28	29	1	2	3	4
11	5	6	7	8	9	10	11
12	12	13	14	15	16	17	18
13	19	20	21	22	23	24	25

April
14	26	27	28	29	30	31	1
15	2	3	4	5	6	7	8
16	9	10	11	12	13	14	15
17	16	17	18	19	20	21	22
18	23	24	25	26	27	28	29

May
19	30	1	2	3	4	5	6
20	7	8	9	10	11	12	13
21	14	15	16	17	18	19	20
22	21	22	23	24	25	26	27

June
23	28	29	30	31	1	2	3
24	4	5	6	7	8	9	10
25	11	12	13	14	15	16	17
26	18	19	20	21	22	23	24

July
27	25	26	27	28	29	30	1
28	2	3	4	5	6	7	8
29	9	10	11	12	13	14	15
30	16	17	18	19	20	21	22
31	23	24	25	26	27	28	29

August
32	30	31	1	2	3	4	5
33	6	7	8	9	10	11	12
34	13	14	15	16	17	18	19
35	20	21	22	23	24	25	26

September
36	27	28	29	30	31	1	2
37	3	4	5	6	7	8	9
38	10	11	12	13	14	15	16
39	17	18	19	20	21	22	23
40	24	25	26	27	28	29	30

October
41	1	2	3	4	5	6	7
42	8	9	10	11	12	13	14
43	15	16	17	18	19	20	21
44	22	23	24	25	26	27	28

November
45	29	30	31	1	2	3	4
46	5	6	7	8	9	10	11
47	12	13	14	15	16	17	18
48	19	20	21	22	23	24	25

December
49	26	27	28	29	30	1	2
50	3	4	5	6	7	8	9
51	10	11	12	13	14	15	16
52	17	18	19	20	21	22	23
53	24	25	26	27	28	29	30

Most flowcharts contain some basic information for the advertising campaign. Table 23.2 is an example of a media-planning flowchart. This flowchart contains the following information:

1. The column to the far left contains a summary of the media, an overview of the media vehicles, and the media units used in the campaign.
2. The column headings denote the broadcast calendar for the year.
3. At the far right are the budget summary for the year and the percentage of the total media spend for each medium (on the second page of the chart).
4. Across the bottom of the flowchart is some summary reach and frequency information for the advertising schedule.
5. You will also notice other details, such as when the flowchart was prepared. Many advertisers ask their media teams to continually update their flowcharts with actual dollars and delivery as the year progresses. In this case, the flowchart takes on a forecast for the year as well as a recap of past spending and delivery.

This is a standard media-planning calendar. Advertiser categories and brands may have different nuances, depending on their specific media-planning situation. The purpose of the flowchart is to give the advertiser a snapshot of the media schedule, which contains the most important metrics for that specific brand.

So, as you develop media plans, ask yourself what you think are the most important items you would like to see on a flowchart. Use the flowchart here as a template to make adjustments you believe would enhance the flowchart's value for your brand.

Table 23.2

Bob's Baked Beans: 2007 Media Flowchart, May 15, 2006

2007	January				February				March				April					May				June			
	1	8	15	22	29	5	12	19	26	5	12	19	26	2	9	16	23	30	7	14	21	28	4	11	18
	134	95	94	99	97	128	98	88	92	90	92	97	136	84	89	89	89	92	101	88	87	107	93	89	96
Holidays	New Year's Day				Super Bowl								Easter					Mother's Day				Memorial Day	Father's Day		
National TV								300 TRPs										300 TRPs							
National TV		75			75				75			75	75					75		75		75			
:30 commercials																									
20% Early Morning (GMA/TS)		15			15				15			15	15					15		15		15			
7-8 units/week																									
80% Cable		60			60				60			60	60					60		60		60			
Approximately 11 networks																									
17 Weeks																									
75 Women 25-54 TRPs/week																									
Total 1,275 TRPs																									
Magazines																									
Full Page 4-Color Insertions																									
Approx. 5 Magazines																									
Magazine A																									
Magazine B																									
Magazine C																									
Magazine D																									
Magazine E																									
Total																									

Note: All costs shown as client cost which factors in 9.38% commission. Integration fees are included in the network budget.

	July					August				September					October				November				December					Total TRPs	Est $ (000)
	25	2	9	16	23	30	6	13	23	27	3	10	17	24	1	8	15	22	29	5	12	19	26	3	10	17	24		
	92	115	98	87	86	85	92	90	87	89	105	93	88	88	89	91	90	89	91	93	97	139	148	87	104	131	212		
	4th of July									Labor Day									Thanksgiving				Christmas						
300 TRPs															375 TRPs													1275	$9,505.10
	75					75		75		75					75		75		75		75		75					1275	$9,505.10
	15					15		15		15					15		15		15		15		15					255	$3,386.20
	60					60		60		60					60		60		60		60		60					1020	$6,118.90
																												246	$1,724.00
																												1521	$11,229.10

=CPP

Table 23.2 (continued)

Bob's Baked Beans: 2007 Media Flowchart, May 15, 2012

Television Only—National Delivery

National	Total HH			Women 25–54			Working women 25–34 with kids			English domestic hispanic women 18–49		
	1st half	2nd half	Full year	1st half	2nd half	Full year	1st half	2nd half	Full year	1st half	2nd half	Full year
# weeks	8	9	17	8	9	17	8	9	17	8	9	17
TRPs	1007	1133	2141	600	675	1275	465	523	988	495	557	1053
Reach	75.6%	76.6%	80.7%	65.7%	66.9%	72.2%	66.6%	68.0%	73.6%	59.2%	60.4%	65.8%
Avg. Req.	13.3	14.8	26.5	9.1	10.1	17.7	7.0	7.7	13.5	8.4	9.2	16.0
3+ reach	60.4%	62.3%	71.1%	**47.4%**	**49.5%**	59.7%	44.3%	47.1%	60.6%	41.2%	43.2%	52.9%

Television plus Magazines—National Delivery

National	Women 25–54			Working women 25–34 with kids			English domestic hispanic women 18–49		
	1st half	2nd half	Full year	1st half	2nd half	Full year	1st half	2nd half	Full year
# weeks	8	9	17	8	9	17	8	9	17
TRPs	723	798	1521	568	626	1194	589	651	1242
Reach	82.8%	83.4%	88.3%	82.2%	82.9%	88.2%	75.8%	76.5%	82.5%
Avg. Req.	8.7	9.6	17.2	6.9	7.5	13.5	7.8	8.5	15.1
3+ reach	**59.6%**	**61.0%**	73.2%	56.4%	58.2%	71.6%	50.8%	52.3%	64.8%

Note: All costs shown as client cost which factors in 9.38% commission. Integration fees are included in the network budget.

Unit 23 Exercises
Working with Calendars and Flowcharts

1. How many broadcast weeks and months is a television flight that is scheduled from January 1, 2009, to February 28, 2012?

2. If you received a bill from a television station where you ran all the weeks in the April broadcast month, how many weeks of advertising might be on that bill?

3. Provide a media flowchart that schedules 12 weeks of television beginning May 1, 2012, on a consistent basis with 75 trips per week of support with half of the weight in daytime and the other half in late fringe. The target market is women ages 25–54. This is a national buy. The total dollars for the buy are $5.4 million.

4. Provide another media flowchart that adds a full-page, four-color bleed magazine schedule to the above national television schedule using three insertions each in *Woman's Day* and *Good Housekeeping*. The total cost for the print program is $900,000.

Part IV
Broadcast Media

Unit 24
Working with Broadcast Media Estimates

More dollars are spent in advertising on broadcast than on any other medium. Network television, cable, and radio—plus its local or spot cousins—are the media that advertisers have historically placed the most emphasis on within their respective advertising campaigns.

As we have seen in prior units in this book, broadcast audiences are measured largely by demographic ratings. As an advertiser or advertising agency purchases a schedule of television, cable, or radio, the combination of ratings from the various programs purchased forms the basis for reach and frequency analysis.

As we have also read in a prior unit, there are varying degrees of usage of each medium by different demographic groups. For example, men generally watch less television than women, so it takes more exposure to reach men on television than women. Therefore, one dimension that affects the outcome of broadcast audiences and its reach and frequency is the target audience that you have defined for your advertising schedule. Whether it is gender, age, income, or being married and having children in the household, each demographic variable will alter the course of reach and frequency to some degree.

There are also dimensions of how you purchase each medium that have an impact on the subsequent reach and frequency. In television, the number of different dayparts you schedule your commercials in has an impact on reach. If you place all your commercials in daytime, 9 A.M. to 4 P.M., Monday through Friday, there will be a ceiling on how many people you reach because less than 50 percent of the population watches this particular daypart. As a result, the majority of advertisers schedule their television advertising in more than one daypart to gain optimum reach. This is also true of the number of different programs you purchase. If you only purchase a few programs, for example *CBS News* and ABC's *Good Morning America,* your reach would be limited to just the pool of viewers who watch these two programs. Just as most advertisers schedule their advertising in multiple dayparts, they typically purchase a variety of programs to gain incremental reach.

Table 24.1 shows target reach based on an even distribution of television programming across a broad time frame, 6 A.M. to midnight. There is a section for men ages 18 and up and for women ages 18 and up.

As you can see, the first column consists of a running total of television rating points (GRPs) from a widely dispersed schedule. The second column is overall (or unduplicated) reach for the respective GRPs. The third column is the reach at a 3+ frequency level, and

Table 24.1

Percentage of Target Reached: Television

GRPs TV	Men 18+			Women 18+		
	Overall	3+	Frequency	Overall	3+	Frequency
50	29.5	5.3	1.7	32.1	4.1	1.6
100	43.8	17.0	2.3	47.9	16.5	2.1
150	49.7	24.9	3.0	55.2	25.1	2.7
200	54.6	32.6	3.7	60.7	34.3	3.3
250	58.0	39.3	4.3	65.3	41.4	3.8
300	60.9	44.4	4.9	67.0	46.3	4.5
350	63.1	48.6	5.5	70.4	51.8	5.0
400	65.5	52.7	6.1	72.6	56.4	5.5
450	67.0	55.4	6.7	74.2	59.7	6.1
500	68.5	58.1	7.3	74.9	62.2	6.7
550	69.6	60.2	7.9	76.8	65.2	7.2
600	71.0	62.6	8.5	78.1	67.7	7.7
650	72.0	64.2	9.0	78.9	69.5	8.2
700	73.0	65.9	9.6	79.7	71.1	8.8
750	74.0	67.4	10.1	80.3	72.5	9.3
800	74.8	68.7	10.7	81.3	74.3	9.8
850	74.8	69.2	11.4	82.0	75.6	10.4
900	76.3	70.9	11.8	82.4	76.4	10.9
950	76.8	71.7	12.4	83.0	77.5	11.4
1,000	77.4	72.6	12.9	83.5	78.3	12.0
1,050	77.9	73.2	13.5	84.0	79.2	12.5
1,100	78.5	74.1	14.0	84.6	80.0	13.0
1,150	78.9	74.8	14.6	85.0	80.7	13.5
1,200	79.4	75.4	15.1	85.6	81.5	14.0
1,250	79.8	76.0	15.7	85.8	81.9	14.6
1,300	80.2	76.5	16.2	86.2	82.6	15.1
1,350	80.5	77.0	16.8	86.5	83.0	15.6
1,400	80.9	77.5	17.3	87.0	83.6	16.1
1,450	81.2	78.0	17.9	87.2	84.0	16.6
1,500	81.5	78.4	18.4	87.5	84.4	17.1

Source: Telmar.

Note: Assumes an even distribution Monday–Sunday, 6 A.M.–midnight—over-the-air only.

the fourth and final column is the average frequency. The two sections for men and women show the disparity between their viewing patterns. A 600 GRP schedule reaches 71 percent of men ages 18 and up, but it reaches 78 percent of women in the same age range. As you review the table, notice the differences between the genders. These types of differences exist between younger and older viewers and more affluent and less affluent viewers as well.

Cable television has an inherent ceiling to its ability to generate reach since approximately 25 percent of the U.S. population do not subscribe to basic cable or to cable's competition, direct satellite broadcasting ("the dish"). So, as you review the reach and frequency of cable compared with that of over-the-air television, you would find that the reach is much lower at any given rating point level. For example, that same 600 rating point schedule that delivered 70 percent and over reach for traditional television only delivers 60 percent reach for cable. Table 24.2, which shows target reach for cable television, is set up the same as Table 24.1. The first column is overall rating points. The second column is the unduplicated reach, the third column is the 3+ reach, and the fourth column is the average frequency.

This example of cable delivery assumes a broad and even distribution of cable networks. Obviously, if you narrowed your selection of programming, dayparts, and networks, the

Table 24.2

Percentage of Target Reached: Cable

GRPs TV	Men 18+			Women 18+		
	Overall	3+	Frequency	Overall	3+	Frequency
50	25.7	5.8	1.9	25.8	5.8	1.9
100	35.9	13.3	2.8	36.0	13.3	2.8
150	41.9	19.2	3.6	42.2	19.2	3.6
200	46.1	23.7	4.3	46.4	23.8	4.3
250	49.3	27.4	5.1	49.5	27.5	5.0
300	51.7	30.4	5.8	52.0	30.5	5.8
350	53.8	33.0	6.5	54.1	33.1	6.5
400	55.5	35.2	7.2	55.8	35.3	7.2
450	57.0	37.1	7.9	57.3	37.3	7.9
500	58.2	38.8	8.6	58.6	39.0	8.5
550	59.4	40.3	9.3	59.7	40.5	9.2
600	60.4	41.7	9.9	60.7	41.9	9.9
650	61.3	43.0	10.6	61.6	43.2	10.5
700	62.1	44.1	11.3	62.5	44.3	11.2
750	62.9	45.1	11.9	63.2	45.4	11.9
800	63.6	46.1	12.6	63.9	46.4	12.5
850	64.2	47.0	13.2	6.6	47.3	13.2
900	64.8	47.9	13.9	65.2	48.1	13.8
950	65.4	48.7	14.5	65.7	48.9	14.5
1,000	65.9	49.4	15.2	66.3	49.7	15.1
1,050	66.4	50.1	15.8	66.8	50.4	15.7
1,100	66.9	50.7	16.4	67.2	51.0	16.4
1,150	67.3	51.4	17.1	67.7	51.7	17.0
1,200	67.7	52.0	17.7	68.1	52.3	17.6
1,250	68.1	52.5	18.4	68.5	52.8	18.3
1,300	68.5	53.1	19.0	68.8	53.4	18.9
1,350	68.8	53.6	19.6	69.2	53.9	19.5
1,400	69.2	54.0	20.2	69.5	54.4	20.1
1,450	69.5	54.5	20.9	69.8	54.8	20.8
1,500	69.8	55.0	21.5	70.2	55.3	21.4

Note: Assumes an even distribution generic cable only.

latter reach and frequency table would reflect a higher level of frequency with the ensuing level of rating points.

While there is a growing disparity in reach between men and women for traditional television, this relationship does not appear to be as strong with cable. Male viewership of cable programming is very strong and represents a disproportionate amount of their viewing. As a result, the reach and frequency for men and women are very similar at the varying stages of rating-point delivery.

Radio is not consumed in the same way as are television and cable. While people watch a wide number of television and cable programs that cover many networks, the average person listens to no more than three radio stations. This means that each radio station has a limited audience. The only way to increase reach is to continue to add radio stations to a buy. However, because radio is highly targeted, the more stations you add to a buy, typically, the less targeted they are to the specific audience you are seeking to reach. As a result, radio reach is not nearly as great as television as you continue to add rating points to a schedule.

Other dimensions that impact the reach of a schedule for radio are similar to television. Radio is purchased by dayparts: the morning drive time, midday, evening drive time, and

Table 24.3

Percentage of Target Reached: Radio

GRPs TV	Men 18+			Women 18+		
	Overall	3+	Frequency	Overall	3+	Frequency
50	29.0	5.1	1.7	30.9	4.5	1.6
100	37.9	13.6	2.6	40.8	13.7	2.5
150	42.2	19.5	3.6	45.5	20.2	3.3
200	44.7	23.5	4.5	48.3	24.8	4.1
250	46.4	26.4	5.4	50.1	28.1	5.0
300	47.6	28.6	6.3	51.4	30.5	5.8
350	57.3	35.1	6.1	61.8	37.6	5.7
400	58.3	37.0	6.9	62.8	39.8	6.4
450	59.0	38.6	7.6	63.6	41.6	7.1
500	59.7	39.9	8.4	64.3	43.1	7.8
550	60.2	41.1	9.1	64.9	44.4	8.5
600	60.6	42.0	9.9	65.4	45.5	9.2
650	61.0	42.9	10.7	65.8	46.5	9.9
700	61.3	43.7	11.4	66.1	47.3	10.6
750	61.6	44.3	12.2	66.4	48.1	11.3
800	61.9	44.9	12.9	66.7	48.8	12.0
850	62.1	45.5	13.7	66.9	49.4	12.7
900	62.3	46.0	14.4	67.2	49.9	13.4
950	62.5	46.4	15.2	67.4	50.5	14.1
1,000	62.6	46.8	16.0	67.5	50.9	14.8
1,050	62.8	47.2	16.7	67.7	51.4	15.5
1,100	62.9	47.6	17.5	67.8	51.8	16.2
1,150	63.0	47.9	18.3	68.0	21.1	16.9
1,200	63.1	48.2	19.0	68.1	52.5	17.6
1,250	63.2	48.5	19.8	68.2	52.8	18.3
1,300	63.3	48.8	20.5	68.3	53.1	19.0
1,350	63.4	49.0	21.3	68.4	53.4	19.7
1,400	63.5	49.3	22.0	68.5	53.6	20.4
1,450	63.6	49.5	22.8	68.6	53.9	21.1
1,500	63.7	49.7	23.5	68.7	54.1	21.8

evening are the standard weekday dayparts. Radio can also be limited to selected days of the week, which also impacts the reach potential of a schedule.

Table 24.3, showing percentage of target reached for radio, is similar to Tables 24.1 and 24.2. In this table, however, we are using a broad rotation of commercials from 6 A.M. to 7 P.M. on the weekday, which covers three of the four typical dayparts purchased for radio. Except for selected radio stations that have a large young-adult listenership, 80 percent and more of a station's listenership is confined to a 6 A.M. to 7 P.M. time frame. The radio example also utilizes a broad mix of radio stations, with six stations used for schedules above 300 rating points and four for schedules below 300 rating points.

Unit 24 Exercises
Working with Broadcast Media Estimates

Use Table 24.1 in Unit 24 to answer the following questions:

1. You are advertising to adult males by purchasing 200 gross rating points (GRPs) on network television.

    a. What percentage of the male audience can you expect to reach?

    b. How many times will you reach the average male audience member?

    c. What does the figure 32.6 in Table 24.1 mean?

2. You are advertising to adult females on network television.

   a. What GRP level would you need to reach 75 percent of your female target audience?

   b. What GRP level would you need to reach 75 percent of your target audience at least three times each?

   c. What GRP level would you need to reach the female audience an average of 10 times each?

   d. If there are 6,600,000 women in your target group, how many do you project that you can reach?

Use Table 24.2 in Unit 24 to answer the following questions:

3. You are advertising on cable television and purchasing 450 GRPs.

   a. What percentage of the cable audience can you expect to reach?

b. How many times will you reach the average audience member?

c. What does the figure 38.8 mean?

d. If there are 600,000 people in the target group, how many are you likely to reach?

4. You are using 300 GRPs on cable television to reach adult females.

   a. What percentage of the females can you expect to reach?

   b. How many times will you reach an average member of the target audience?

   c. What does the figure 30.5 mean?

Use Table 24.3 in Unit 24 to answer the following questions:

5. You are using radio advertising.

    a. What GRP level would you need to reach 50 percent of the audience?

    b. What GRP level would you need to reach 50 percent of the audience at least three times?

    c. What GRP level would you need to reach the audience an average of ten times each?

    d. If there are 355,000 households in your market with an average of 2.15 persons per household, how many households can you expect to reach?

    e. Using the figures from the previous question, how many people do you project that you can reach with your advertising?

6. You are advertising on cable television to reach adult males.

   a. What GRP level would you need to reach 55 percent of your male target audience?

   b. What GRP level would you need to reach 55 percent of your target audience at least three times each?

   c. What GRP level would you need to reach the male audience an average of seven times each?

7. Your target audience is composed of 70,000,000 persons who live in a total of 23,500,000 households. You are utilizing a prime-access broadcast television buy that achieves a rating of 9 and a share of 11. The households using television (HUT) at that hour is 37 percent. What is the percentage reach of this advertising buy?

Unit 25

Working with Broadcast Media Costs

As we have mentioned, the broadcast advertising marketplace is currently the largest area of advertising media investment in the United States. So, it follows that you are highly likely to be working with broadcast costs as you develop a media plan.

Regardless of the medium, the standard for developing media plans with broadcast costs is the *cost per point* (CPP). While media buyers will negotiate specific program or daypart rates as they work to attain their buying goals, these goals and the media plan's costs are based on CPP information. This information may be proprietary or historical data, or it may be planning information derived from *Spot Quotations and Data,* or SQAD. SQAD is a third-party source that compiles broadcast costs from submitting agencies and then prepares a report that allows media planners to forecast costs in the market. SQAD is the gold standard for broadcast cost estimates on both a national and local basis.

Regardless of the broadcast medium, there are some common factors that affect the CPP information. The first variable is *target audience.* As you can see from Table 25.3, there's a big difference in CPP between men and women. Other demographic variables such as age and income can also affect the CPP information.

The second variable is *geography.* Certain network (i.e., national) media are available in every market. Then there are spot (or local) media that are market specific. CPP information varies widely between network and spot media.

The third variable is the *creative unit.* For our purposes, we are using a 30-second (:30) television commercial and a 60-second (:60) radio commercial as the basis for the accompanying costs. In both television media and radio, the creative unit can impact costs greatly. For example, the cost of a 15-second (:15) commercial on network television is half the cost of a :30. However, it is typically 70 percent of the cost of a :30 on a spot or local basis. In network radio, a :30 commercial is half the cost of a :60 commercial, whereas in spot radio there is no difference in cost between a :30 and :60 unit.

The fourth variable is the *daypart(s)* you choose to schedule your advertising in. A daypart is a broad time frame for when you want to schedule your advertising. Dayparts are different for television and for radio. Tables 25.1 and 25.2 show standard dayparts for television and radio, respectively.

As you look at Table 25.3, you can see that costs vary widely by daypart. As a rule of thumb, costs increase as the audience increases. So, in television, prime time is where the

Table 25.1

Television Dayparts

Daypart	Days	Time frame EST
Morning	Mon.–Fri.	7:00 A.M.–9:00 A.M.
Daytime	Mon.–Fri.	10:00 A.M.–4:00 P.M.
Early fringe	Mon.–Fri.	4:00 P.M.–6:30 P.M.
Early news	Mon.–Fri.	6:30 P.M.–7:00 P.M.
Prime access	Mon.–Fri.	7:00 P.M.–8:00 P.M.
Prime time	Mon.–Sun.	8:00 P.M.–11:00 P.M.
Late news	Mon.–Sun.	11:00 P.M.–11:30 P.M.
Late fringe	Mon.–Fri.	11:30 A.M.–1:00 P.M.
Weekend	Sat.–Sun.	9:00 A.M.–5:00 P.M.

Table 25.2

Radio Dayparts

Daypart	Days	Time frame EST
Morning drive time	Mon.–Fri.	6:00 A.M.–10:00 A.M.
Midday	Mon.–Fri.	10:00 A.M.–3:00 P.M.
Evening drive time	Mon.–Fri.	3:00 P.M.–7:00 P.M.
Evening	Mon.–Sun.	7:00 P.M.–12:00 P.M.
Weekend	Sat.–Sun.	6:00 P.M.–7:00 P.M.

highest viewership is and it also has the highest cost. For radio, morning drive time has the highest listenership and, consequently, the highest cost. It is the media planner's job to balance cost efficiency with reach and frequency requirements. For the media planner, a trade-off exists between costs and delivery for every broadcast plan.

We will look first at network broadcast costs (Table 25.3). As a media planner, you have a wide array of options when planning network television. You can select from traditional networks, cable networks, or syndication. Syndicated programs are programs that are typically scheduled in fringe dayparts. *Wheel of Fortune* is a classic syndication staple. A syndicator is a company who produces and distributes the program and gains clearance for its property on different affiliated stations across the country.

There are also CPP estimates for network radio. In purchasing network radio there are a number of options—from demographic targeting to music targeting to specific "long form" programming. For example, *Rush Limbaugh* is an example of a specific radio program that can be purchased. Extended news analyses and financial advice programs are examples of long-form programs that are available on network radio.

In Table 25.3, Network Broadcast Cost Factors, there are two columns of CPP information. One is for men ages 18 and up and the other is for women ages 18 and up. All the information is based on :30 units for both television and radio. The costs are also based on a four-quarter average for the year. Broadcast costs do fluctuate from quarter to quarter. All of the latter costs are based either on a national schedule or on using the full network and not a specific geographic portion of it.

One final note on the network television costs before we move on to spot television and radio costs. Network television costs are based on participating in the *upfront market*. The network television marketplace traditionally is held in May, when advertisers purchase network programming on a fourth- through third-quarter cycle. This coincides with when the networks release their new prime-time programming for the fall sweep period. When

Table 25.3

Network Broadcast Cost Factors

Daypart	Cost per point ($)	
	Men 18+	Women 18+
Network TV		
Early morning	17,814	12,463
Daytime	—	6,156
News	13,407	11,263
Prime time	27,884	24,278
Late fringe	27,775	26,366
Cable TV		
Daytime	4,080	3,257
Early fringe	10,625	8,969
Prime time	10,239	10,473
Late fringe	7,407	7,952
Weekend	7,803	6,178
News	6,357	7,184
Syndication TV		
Daytime	—	4,955
Early fringe	13,675	11,295
Prime time	23,596	22,936
Late fringe	19,240	14,595
Network radio (6:00 A.M.–7:00 P.M.)	4,000	3,500

Sources: SQAD for television; FKM for network radio.

Note: Costs based on four-quarter average of final season.

Table 25.4

Seasonal Cost Index (in CPPs)

Quarter	Spot television	Spot radio
First	85	85
Second	110	107
Third	90	103
Fourth	115	105

advertisers purchase inventory in three of the four quarters, they get preferential pricing treatment and first choice of the specific programs they want to purchase. The second market is called the *scatter market,* in which network programming is purchased on a quarter-by-quarter basis. Historically, the scatter purchases have been, on average, 20 percent higher in costs than purchasing the same programming in the upfront market.

The same is true in network radio. The upfront market is typically in the fall after the television marketplace. Unlike network television, network radio purchases typically are made on a calendar year rather than a fourth-quarter through third-quarter network television upfront year.

Table 25.4 is an example of a seasonal index for spot television and radio costs. Spot broadcast costs are calculated on a market-by-market basis. Because each CPP is market specific, you can add the costs together to calculate multimarket situations. Spot broadcast costs fluctuate from quarter to quarter based on historical demand for station inventory. Television costs are usually higher in second and fourth quarters, when retail demand is highest. Radio costs are usually higher in the second quarter, with fourth and third next in order.

Table 25.5 is a television CPP chart from SQAD for fourth quarter 2011. The costs are for the top 100 television markets in the United States for both men and women ages 18–49.

Table 25.5

SQAD QuickView Report, TV

Target: Women 18–49

MARKET	RANK	POP	EM	DAY	EF	EN	PA	PR	LN	LF	CF
ABILENE-SWEETWATER	163	61,106	12	18	26	24	31	51	34	24	25
ALBANY, GA	145	94,337	21	23	29	42	43	114	63	66	48
ALBANY-SCHENECTADY-TROY	55	285,531	93	117	161	156	200	275	160	184	173
ALBUQUERQUE-SANTA FE	49	368,933	61	57	79	108	123	190	153	117	98
ALEXANDRIA, LA	176	53,976	18	13	18	37	33	45	41	25	22
ALPENA	208	8,282	13	9	26	18	18	31	26	19	23
AMARILLO	129	108,796	20	17	24	27	38	47	36	30	27
ANCHORAGE	155	88,130	25	22	35	50	32	52	49	29	32
ATLANTA	9	1,355,668	246	277	363	417	536	986	680	431	397
AUGUSTA	114	147,312	29	25	39	56	42	87	66	44	42
AUSTIN	54	376,280	133	98	134	181	166	244	243	138	136
BAKERSFIELD	130	132,799	52	35	53	61	76	120	77	56	55
BALTIMORE	23	645,315	185	163	250	269	347	568	329	274	262
BANGOR	153	73,794	21	26	26	36	31	41	44	34	30
BATON ROUGE	95	191,743	46	53	63	73	77	107	104	64	64
BEAUMONT-PORT ARTHUR	138	98,397	18	23	24	39	37	72	46	27	26
BEND, OR	199	27,684	17	23	29	36	17	30	24	25	27
BILLINGS	170	52,342	15	19	18	26	24	34	34	22	20
BILOXI-GULFPORT	156	80,820	35	35	58	58	65	133	50	65	62
BINGHAMTON	154	71,189	19	27	32	34	35	47	45	34	33
BIRMINGHAM (ANN AND TUSC)	40	395,422	48	52	87	111	122	199	135	59	73
BLUEFIELD-BECKLEY-OAK HIL	150	72,518	26	27	39	45	39	93	47	28	34
BOISE	123	135,147	43	33	46	52	48	74	66	49	48
BOSTON (MANCHESTER)	6	1,420,880	461	407	615	606	966	1727	1004	644	630
BOWLING GREEN	181	45,579	17	13	23	39	35	65	43	37	30
BUFFALO	44	348,241	74	65	119	118	135	201	175	128	124
BURLINGTON-PLATTSBURGH	89	178,595	41	42	63	81	90	122	98	68	66
BUTTE-BOZEMAN	194	31,177	21	18	22	29	27	32	31	20	21
CASPER-RIVERTON	200	26,851	11	20	19	29	19	22	27	13	16
CEDAR RAPIDS-WTRLO-IWC&DU	88	181,481	31	34	44	61	68	83	73	54	49
CHAMPAIGN&SPRNGFLD-DECATU	82	205,338	34	32	43	63	64	89	82	61	52
CHARLESTON, SC	104	161,408	27	30	40	44	41	82	44	43	42
CHARLESTON-HUNTINGTON	63	267,821	46	34	57	90	84	114	118	84	71
CHARLOTTE	28	585,022	108	91	109	154	145	287	197	113	111
CHARLOTTESVILLE	186	42,480	20	20	35	49	42	72	49	33	34
CHATTANOOGA	86	195,955	49	38	61	68	73	121	96	66	64
CHEYENNE-SCOTTSBLUF	196	27,851	19	21	20	45	29	48	38	25	23
CHICAGO	3	2,195,850	441	455	662	990	1018	2196	1256	551	607
CHICO-REDDING	132	99,438	19	17	19	33	34	40	33	26	23

Market											
CINCINNATI	32	510,735	93	119	132	170	165	339	210	151	142
CLARKSBURG-WESTON	165	54,231	22	20	34	33	29	51	35	30	32
CLEVELAND-AKRON (CANTON)	16	853,018	176	157	240	326	402	554	443	232	236
COLORADO SPRINGS-PUEBLO	93	181,666	47	33	47	59	66	97	85	54	51
COLUMBIA, SC	84	217,455	47	35	55	78	85	118	92	59	57
COLUMBIA-JEFFERSON CITY	139	94,909	20	21	25	31	30	41	35	27	26
COLUMBUS, GA	125	125,738	30	15	25	55	41	60	64	36	31
COLUMBUS, OH	34	500,119	128	106	152	230	246	420	295	171	162
COLUMBUS-TUPELO-WEST POIN	131	108,637	13	12	22	23	31	61	28	22	22
CORPUS CHRISTI	128	120,983	28	22	28	38	37	50	46	38	33
DALLAS-FT. WORTH	7	1,479,785	442	303	452	792	833	1371	979	385	419
DAVENPORT-R.ISLAND-MOLINE	94	160,804	59	50	45	85	77	96	108	79	62
DAYTON	59	277,240	63	85	99	122	120	140	158	118	109
DENVER	18	849,649	306	197	228	365	431	493	386	268	248
DES MOINES-AMES	73	219,291	41	40	50	66	73	85	87	72	61
DETROIT	10	1,149,274	200	196	352	306	464	690	548	268	310
DOTHAN	171	53,735	18	19	22	37	37	53	43	38	30
DULUTH-SUPERIOR	136	84,848	25	29	29	40	38	57	59	37	33
EL PASO (LAS CRUCES)	100	208,286	33	30	40	64	81	95	71	64	52
ELMIRA (CORNING)	173	51,287	21	19	35	46	43	56	49	43	39
ERIE	141	86,796	22	20	34	43	37	53	43	33	34
EUGENE	120	121,277	34	34	54	67	51	81	77	39	47
EUREKA	193	31,798	12	11	16	29	16	28	21	20	18
EVANSVILLE	99	153,241	42	36	48	81	107	115	100	60	54
FAIRBANKS	203	20,705	5	6	9	17	13	12	12	12	11
FARGO-VALLEY CITY	118	120,934	22	25	31	41	48	57	40	37	34
FLINT-SAGINAW-BAY CITY	64	267,813	55	51	85	108	76	115	130	74	80
FRESNO-VISALIA	57	368,127	74	65	104	140	169	192	156	150	127
FT. MYERS-NAPLES	70	169,984	86	57	65	106	97	129	113	79	72
FT. SMITH-FAY-SPRNGDL-RGR	108	148,717	28	29	40	57	62	90	74	37	39
FT. WAYNE	105	153,111	31	28	51	45	48	78	77	52	52
GAINESVILLE	162	73,276	35	44	61	67	49	106	94	62	62
GLENDIVE	210	2,274	11	9	13	11	10	14	12	18	16
GRAND JUNCTION-MONTROSE	190	32,660	20	18	27	32	26	33	35	22	25
GRAND RAPIDS-KALMZOO-B.CR	38	435,248	123	105	162	201	238	303	221	191	177
GREAT FALLS	188	33,090	9	12	14	19	15	22	23	15	15
GREEN BAY-APPLETON	68	235,235	41	37	51	74	90	98	82	82	67
GREENSBORO-H.POINT-W.SALE	46	361,066	43	45	79	106	109	210	139	84	82
GREENVILLE-N.BERN-WASHNGT	103	156,426	27	23	29	49	62	92	53	35	32
GREENVLL-SPART-ASHEVLL-AN	35	430,855	82	69	122	134	144	231	173	118	120
GREENWOOD-GREENVILLE	182	50,773	9	10	12	15	20	31	19	15	14
HARLINGEN-WSLCO-BRNSVL-MC	97	240,584	68	33	67	76	107	136	113	88	78
HARRISBURG-LNCSTR-LEB-YOR	47	359,046	108	82	151	156	166	252	209	176	164
HARRISONBURG	180	49,677	30	23	42	50	55	148	72	41	42
HARTFORD & NEW HAVEN	27	562,027	147	180	255	300	386	489	385	300	278

(continued)

Target: Women 18-49

MARKET	RANK	POP	EM	DAY	EF	EN	PA	PR	LN	LF	CF
HELENA	207	12,843	11	12	10	16	17	15	13	11	11
HONOLULU	72	264,003	48	42	51	86	88	100	99	57	54
HOUSTON	11	1,256,783	315	236	296	506	530	887	727	311	304
HUNTSVILLE-DECATUR (FLOR)	83	202,699	32	30	48	58	94	131	92	62	55
IDAHO FALLS-POCATELLO	164	70,616	15	15	19	24	32	41	27	20	20
INDIANAPOLIS	25	597,346	165	153	181	260	243	378	278	196	189
JACKSON, MS	90	201,399	26	29	43	40	53	109	72	41	42
JACKSON, TN	183	41,893	23	20	33	39	35	119	35	31	32
JACKSONVILLE	52	354,958	77	70	99	129	125	261	162	99	99
JOHNSTOWN-ALTOONA	96	157,564	28	30	52	47	54	82	59	50	51
JONESBORO	179	46,154	16	24	28	22	30	54	38	44	36
JOPLIN-PITTSBURG	146	82,259	17	14	18	29	34	44	34	31	25
JUNEAU	206	15,507	21	23	37	42	50	41	29	11	24
KANSAS CITY	31	512,580	97	92	149	159	204	272	249	141	145
KNOXVILLE	61	267,990	64	47	82	89	92	139	127	91	87
LA CROSSE-EAU CLAIRE	126	115,133	25	28	29	42	57	57	70	53	41
LAFAYETTE, IN	189	38,281	26	17	25	39	27	46	46	34	30
LAFAYETTE, LA	124	133,247	30	27	39	47	48	66	56	52	46
LAKE CHARLES	175	55,249	16	23	26	27	35	66	37	34	30
LANSING	110	148,805	39	43	58	80	65	91	86	57	58
LAREDO	191	52,910	36	25	34	40	39	67	37	40	37
LAS VEGAS	51	362,967	192	142	190	227	207	310	277	222	206
LEXINGTON	65	269,041	68	58	80	79	114	135	123	99	90
LIMA	185	39,119	13	17	14	36	40	45	25	22	18
LINCOLN & HASTINGS-KRNY	102	144,878	32	32	57	63	73	92	91	67	62
LITTLE ROCK-PINE BLUFF	56	288,167	54	55	66	91	106	138	100	68	67
LOS ANGELES	2	3,889,252	748	541	1077	1155	1592	3018	1306	1063	1070
LOUISVILLE	50	353,399	68	56	110	121	124	178	144	99	105
LUBBOCK	147	91,638	25	22	27	38	36	45	55	34	31
MACON	122	135,576	34	30	46	63	50	76	76	53	50
MADISON	85	203,115	58	55	72	98	110	121	97	97	85
MANKATO	198	28,250	33	24	32	52	48	64	49	44	38
MARQUETTE	178	43,437	10	12	18	28	29	40	35	14	16
MEDFORD-KLAMATH FALLS	140	78,915	19	20	32	36	40	49	33	18	25
MEMPHIS	43	406,434	58	57	91	112	141	209	147	84	88
MERIDIAN	184	40,308	15	12	21	25	20	39	33	26	24
MIAMI-FT. LAUDERDALE	17	946,972	267	245	320	478	530	1220	672	393	357
MILWAUKEE	33	498,521	96	95	110	187	230	310	246	120	115
MINNEAPOLIS-ST. PAUL	14	968,813	263	204	247	355	443	561	460	283	265
MINOT-BISMARCK-DICKINSON	159	67,766	24	20	23	32	31	38	35	37	30
MISSOULA	169	54,293	26	26	27	37	38	39	40	27	27
MOBILE-PENSACOLA (FT WALT	62	284,843	44	35	61	97	103	143	113	69	65
MONROE-EL DORADO	135	100,169	13	13	20	29	32	57	44	26	23

City	Rank	Population										
MONTEREY-SALINAS	121	158,550	46	58	83	86	90	150	115	77	80
MONTGOMERY (SELMA)	115	139,623	28	20	29	44	47	56	51	28	29
MYRTLE BEACH-FLORENCE	109	148,825	37	30	47	65	59	105	79	56	52
NASHVILLE	30	533,357	76	81	119	163	221	241	180	123	121
NEW ORLEANS	42	412,041	59	57	62	93	93	157	117	54	58
NEW YORK	1	4,746,411	1143	798	1341	1467	2462	3822	2004	1744	1543
NORFOLK-PORTSMTH-NEWPT NW	41	423,723	79	57	99	142	144	230	146	83	91
NORTH PLATTE	209	7,821	11	31	25	10	14	18	8	11	18
ODESSA-MIDLAND	157	80,163	16	16	21	31	32	51	36	24	23
OKLAHOMA CITY	45	365,679	66	56	70	79	103	132	131	73	72
OMAHA	77	222,058	63	50	59	86	94	118	97	89	74
ORLANDO-DAYTONA BCH-MELBR	20	684,642	268	148	260	341	308	473	429	231	246
OTTUMWA-KIRKSVILLE	197	26,146	12	10	10	15	11	25	18	17	14
PADUCAH-CAPE GIRARD-HARSB	76	201,767	30	27	36	54	74	86	73	41	39
PALM SPRINGS	160	65,897	46	38	62	92	84	149	103	72	67
PANAMA CITY	158	68,661	12	13	16	22	29	48	34	19	18
PARKERSBURG	187	33,446	21	19	51	53	48	102	52	31	41
PEORIA-BLOOMINGTON	117	133,895	29	26	37	70	64	72	66	44	41
PHILADELPHIA	4	1,706,206	374	350	447	680	781	1361	925	476	462
PHOENIX (PRESCOTT)	15	920,284	241	232	259	336	441	591	388	325	292
PITTSBURGH	22	608,776	130	125	192	215	258	483	300	222	207
PORTLAND, OR	24	627,700	173	120	174	215	224	379	244	188	181
PORTLAND-AUBURN	74	211,977	58	60	86	110	111	138	126	110	98
PRESQUE ISLE	205	14,491	13	29	52	20	28	32	22	21	37
PROVIDENCE-NEW BEDFORD	48	366,214	117	95	133	179	179	251	162	170	152
QUINCY-HANNIBAL-KEOKUK	166	53,949	19	12	18	22	21	35	29	17	18
RALEIGH-DURHAM (FAYETVLLE	29	583,543	92	83	136	192	164	400	281	119	128
RAPID CITY	174	51,488	20	18	26	42	33	50	51	37	32
RENO	116	136,424	35	35	50	62	59	89	70	53	52
RICHMOND-PETERSBURG	58	296,164	60	58	81	86	110	146	114	80	81
ROANOKE-LYNCHBURG	66	232,801	50	38	78	104	85	144	122	86	82
ROCHESTER, NY	75	224,936	79	51	80	100	109	167	132	118	99
ROCHESTR-MASON CITY-AUSTI	152	74,703	19	19	29	52	37	66	45	33	31
ROCKFORD	133	101,005	26	26	44	42	61	60	58	49	47
SACRAMNTO-STKTON-MODESTO	19	805,113	255	143	244	326	262	449	295	188	216
SALISBURY	149	74,094	23	39	40	67	58	70	66	31	36
SALT LAKE CITY	36	573,181	149	116	152	211	210	323	253	138	145
SAN ANGELO	195	29,843	20	16	17	29	22	33	30	23	20
SAN ANTONIO	37	472,804	105	91	133	167	167	304	213	110	122
SAN DIEGO	26	669,351	268	185	246	317	365	520	432	366	306
SAN FRANCISCO-OAK-SAN JOS	5	1,568,746	717	485	1032	980	1114	2031	1143	1026	1029
SANTABARBRA-SANMAR-SANLUO	119	141,172	35	49	75	87	90	105	99	59	67
SAVANNAH	98	174,222	34	33	49	65	68	98	81	67	58
SEATTLE-TACOMA	12	986,374	259	210	282	331	385	693	450	287	285
SHERMAN-ADA	161	64,464	18	22	27	43	49	58	36	43	35

(continued)

Target: Women 18-49

MARKET	RANK	POP	EM	DAY	EF	EN	PA	PR	LN	LF	CF
SHREVEPORT	81	213,215	36	37	58	71	77	107	84	62	60
SIOUX CITY	144	83,045	27	25	24	38	40	56	52	34	29
SIOUX FALLS(MITCHELL)	113	130,462	25	32	35	53	52	71	54	34	35
SOUTH BEND-ELKHART	87	188,289	49	44	70	71	76	110	88	73	72
SPOKANE	80	211,155	33	36	68	73	72	100	75	68	68
SPRINGFIELD, MO	78	201,961	46	38	44	69	63	87	97	58	51
SPRINGFIELD-HOLYOKE	106	148,557	40	37	68	78	119	167	101	89	79
ST. JOSEPH	201	27,019	38	49	26	40	65	86	38	22	24
ST. LOUIS	21	690,904	120	119	161	198	241	391	299	173	167
SYRACUSE	79	215,716	43	47	84	66	72	133	101	85	85
TALLAHASSEE-THOMASVILLE	111	154,620	43	37	56	64	63	104	102	58	57
TAMPA-ST. PETE (SARASOTA)	13	774,348	163	148	217	250	335	614	358	241	229
TERRE HAUTE	148	76,335	17	22	39	44	37	60	51	52	46
TOLEDO	69	238,033	42	44	72	73	71	115	118	80	76
TOPEKA	137	95,199	15	17	23	33	34	50	28	33	28
TRAVERSE CITY-CADILLAC	112	123,807	46	44	54	65	61	81	86	64	59
TRI-CITIES, TN-VA	91	165,515	32	29	56	76	71	91	113	66	61
TUCSON (SIERRA VISTA)	71	227,921	61	60	64	80	98	126	122	74	69
TULSA	60	277,731	52	43	65	85	102	124	124	72	69
TWIN FALLS	192	33,431	18	17	21	26	26	32	31	20	21
TYLER-LONGVIEW(LFKN&NCGD)	107	145,355	44	39	46	73	75	134	84	76	61
UTICA	167	55,269	24	21	43	48	34	67	53	40	42
VICTORIA	204	18,879	21	20	37	31	32	62	33	32	35
WACO-TEMPLE-BRYAN	92	198,573	33	39	53	63	77	108	84	78	66
WASHINGTON, DC (HAGRSTWN)	8	1,404,880	449	380	580	659	1079	1513	1018	708	644
WATERTOWN	177	51,533	18	20	43	52	42	75	39	27	35
WAUSAU-RHINELANDER	134	93,129	17	20	26	39	36	54	33	37	32
WEST PALM BEACH-FT. PIERC	39	320,837	96	80	113	176	144	262	173	141	127
WHEELING-STEUBENVILLE	151	69,254	15	19	24	32	39	69	39	31	28
WICHITA FALLS & LAWTON	143	86,726	20	21	25	37	47	49	44	23	24
WICHITA-HUTCHINSON PLUS	67	245,586	34	34	48	61	80	113	102	62	55
WILKES BARRE-SCRANTON	53	304,703	48	45	81	86	86	144	118	95	88
WILMINGTON	142	83,212	19	21	27	32	32	70	38	34	31
YAKIMA-PASCO-RCHLND-KNNWC	127	122,829	24	22	39	42	41	53	43	26	33
YOUNGSTOWN	101	144,499	36	36	47	67	72	79	76	53	50
YUMA-EL CENTRO	172	65,072	25	29	31	54	50	86	62	28	30
ZANESVILLE	202	18,079	26	12	13	31	42	29	29	22	18
TOTALS		64,820,339	16,222	13,932	20,653	25,865	29,946	47,807	32,912	22,522	21,637
FACTORS			1.000	1.000	1.000	1.000	1.000	1.000	1.000	1.000	1.000

Source: NSI TV. Copyright © SQAD Inc. All rights reserved. Reprinted with permission.

Notes: PA = Prime Access; PR = Prime Regular.

Level: Average; Pop Base: DMA (CPP).

Table 25.5 *(continued)*

SQAD QuickView Report, TV

Target: Men 18–49

MARKET	RANK	POP	EM	DAY	EF	EN	PA	PR	LN	LF	CF
ABILENE-SWEETWATER	163	61,106	12	18	26	24	31	51	34	24	25
ALBANY, GA	145	94,337	21	23	29	42	43	114	63	66	48
ALBANY-SCHENECTADY-TROY	55	285,531	93	117	161	156	200	275	160	184	173
ALBUQUERQUE-SANTA FE	49	368,933	61	57	79	108	123	190	153	117	98
ALEXANDRIA, LA	176	53,976	18	13	18	37	33	45	41	25	22
ALPENA	208	8,282	13	9	26	18	18	31	26	19	23
AMARILLO	129	108,796	20	17	24	27	38	47	36	30	27
ANCHORAGE	155	88,130	25	22	35	50	32	52	49	29	32
ATLANTA	9	1,355,668	246	277	363	417	536	986	680	431	397
AUGUSTA	114	147,312	29	25	39	56	42	87	66	44	42
AUSTIN	54	376,280	133	98	134	181	166	244	243	138	136
BAKERSFIELD	130	132,799	52	35	53	61	76	120	77	56	55
BALTIMORE	23	645,315	185	163	250	269	347	568	329	274	262
BANGOR	153	73,794	21	26	26	36	31	41	44	34	30
BATON ROUGE	95	191,743	46	53	63	73	77	107	104	64	64
BEAUMONT-PORT ARTHUR	138	98,397	18	23	24	39	37	72	46	27	26
BEND, OR	199	27,684	17	23	29	36	17	30	24	25	27
BILLINGS	170	52,342	15	19	18	26	24	34	34	22	20
BILOXI-GULFPORT	156	80,820	35	35	58	58	65	133	50	65	62
BINGHAMTON	154	71,189	19	27	32	34	35	47	45	34	33
BIRMINGHAM (ANN AND TUSC)	40	395,422	48	52	87	111	122	199	135	59	73
BLUEFIELD-BECKLEY-OAK HIL	150	72,518	26	27	39	45	39	93	47	28	34
BOISE	123	135,147	43	33	46	52	48	74	66	49	48
BOSTON (MANCHESTER)	6	1,420,880	461	407	615	606	966	1727	1004	644	630
BOWLING GREEN	181	45,579	17	13	23	39	35	65	43	37	30
BUFFALO	44	348,241	74	65	119	118	135	201	175	128	124
BURLINGTON-PLATTSBURGH	89	178,595	41	42	63	81	90	122	98	68	66
BUTTE-BOZEMAN	194	31,177	21	18	22	29	27	32	31	20	21
CASPER-RIVERTON	200	26,851	11	20	19	29	19	22	27	13	16
CEDAR RAPIDS-WTRLO-IWC&DU	88	181,481	31	34	44	61	68	83	73	54	49
CHAMPAIGN&SPRNGFLD-DECATU	82	205,338	34	32	43	63	64	89	82	61	52
CHARLESTON, SC	104	161,408	27	30	40	44	41	82	44	43	42
CHARLESTON-HUNTINGTON	63	267,821	46	34	57	90	84	114	118	84	71
CHARLOTTE	28	585,022	108	91	109	154	145	287	197	113	111
CHARLOTTESVILLE	186	42,480	20	20	35	49	42	72	49	33	34
CHATTANOOGA	86	195,955	49	38	61	68	73	121	96	66	64
CHEYENNE-SCOTTSBLUF	196	27,851	19	21	20	45	29	48	38	25	23
CHICAGO	3	2,195,850	441	455	662	990	1018	2196	1256	551	607
CHICO-REDDING	132	99,438	19	17	19	33	34	40	33	26	23

(continued)

179

Target: Men 18-49

MARKET	RANK	POP	EM	DAY	EF	EN	PA	PR	LN	LF	CF
CHICO-REDDING	132	52,545	32	30	14	21	23	48	23	17	
CINCINNATI	32	248,574	221	226	159	111	161	343	140	130	
CLARKSBURG-WESTON	165	27,389	59	32	35	32	19	39	65	39	
CLEVELAND-AKRON (CANTON)	16	398,755	479	363	327	352	472	658	585	279	
COLORADO SPRINGS-PUEBLO	93	90,568	176	156	68	57	79	102	163	78	
COLUMBIA, SC	84	102,764	96	87	67	100	98	127	117	58	
COLUMBIA-JEFFERSON CITY	139	50,479	31	35	28	32	39	45	44	31	
COLUMBUS, GA	125	67,661	46	23	32	48	35	71	75	29	
COLUMBUS, OH	34	255,418	276	235	239	225	279	444	321	287	
COLUMBUS-TUPELO-WEST POIN	131	57,249	41	25	30	29	39	66	40	26	
CORPUS CHRISTI	128	63,483	58	45	55	62	59	69	57	59	
DALLAS-FT. WORTH	7	782,952	743	675	730	796	925	1329	1207	402	
DAVENPORT-R.ISLAND-MOLINE	94	81,362	138	77	69	61	85	113	169	88	
DAYTON	59	136,925	144	208	89	92	109	180	204	132	
DENVER	18	448,389	678	360	266	392	429	560	494	285	
DES MOINES-AMES	73	113,905	81	73	93	65	88	129	109	90	
DETROIT	10	556,988	488	409	362	319	489	741	696	303	
DOTHAN	171	26,317	53	40	37	37	24	58	71	47	
DULUTH-SUPERIOR	136	42,499	63	63	31	38	46	73	107	50	
EL PASO (LAS CRUCES)	100	107,189	86	65	79	73	107	114	85	62	
ELMIRA (CORNING)	173	24,629	65	35	46	44	31	71	53	36	
ERIE	141	43,470	56	42	35	51	39	71	52	31	
EUGENE	120	64,934	71	61	40	37	38	81	56	28	
EUREKA	193	16,568	34	15	19	26	13	33	15	14	
EVANSVILLE	99	75,957	62	71	69	86	171	141	189	70	
FAIRBANKS	203	10,762	11	14	15	16	13	13	19	17	
FARGO-VALLEY CITY	118	67,272	37	41	42	50	63	64	82	26	
FLINT-SAGINAW-BAY CITY	64	130,821	182	134	82	105	63	133	137	68	
FRESNO-VISALIA	57	210,694	148	126	115	148	186	246	189	131	
FT. MYERS-NAPLES	70	88,351	233	219	58	75	79	126	117	91	
FT. SMITH-FAY-SPRNGDL-RGR	108	82,265	66	59	45	71	62	109	113	34	
FT. WAYNE	105	80,513	61	62	58	38	52	96	79	56	
GAINESVILLE	162	44,485	75	48	42	49	34	106	84	41	
GLENDIVE	210	1,138	36	33	31	16	13	14	21	27	
GRAND JUNCTION-MONTROSE	190	15,872	53	72	40	33	35	44	61	31	
GRAND RAPIDS-KALMZOO-B.CR	38	226,576	364	210	163	214	241	334	316	195	
GREAT FALLS	188	16,311	24	16	19	21	17	23	32	20	
GREEN BAY-APPLETON	68	117,920	106	90	94	74	117	106	144	61	
GREENSBORO-H.POINT-W.SALE	46	178,866	83	89	83	100	91	216	98	96	
GREENVILLE-N.BERN-WASHNGT	103	83,365	55	49	45	75	72	100	55	31	
GREENVLL-SPART-ASHEVLL-AN	35	215,734	191	127	92	107	123	228	192	121	
GREENWOOD-GREENVILLE	182	25,603	27	16	16	21	25	32	28	23	
HARLINGEN-WSLCO-BRNSVL-MC	97	131,071	116	97	140	99	142	201	113	84	
HARRISBURG-LNCSTR-LEB-YOR	47	169,104	370	175	135	130	158	314	222	159	

180	HARRISONBURG	26,251	64	59	55	60	79	145	88	48
27	HARTFORD & NEW HAVEN	250,043	273	366	225	244	350	470	448	253
168	HATTIESBURG-LAUREL	32,995	49	23	41	41	31	51	42	26
207	HELENA	5,815	27	21	15	15	16	18	21	17
72	HONOLULU	131,431	89	78	69	107	105	138	190	81
11	HOUSTON	652,349	528	462	406	535	492	802	1005	352
83	HUNTSVILLE-DECATUR (FLOR)	98,571	72	68	90	70	128	145	151	77
164	IDAHO FALLS-POCATELLO	40,977	27	32	45	29	46	50	50	18
25	INDIANAPOLIS	298,965	325	330	212	251	240	477	379	208
90	JACKSON, MS	99,188	46	44	55	52	82	140	94	52
183	JACKSON, TN	20,855	63	27	42	40	29	132	58	48
52	JACKSONVILLE	169,497	164	142	119	143	128	283	159	122
96	JOHNSTOWN-ALTOONA	85,563	83	59	59	57	53	109	73	49
179	JONESBORO	24,733	72	24	51	29	33	49	44	46
146	JOPLIN-PITTSBURG	44,524	63	37	34	36	49	49	45	30
206	JUNEAU	6,685	67	72	46	43	40	42	49	17
31	KANSAS CITY	258,087	202	338	260	197	264	327	405	178
61	KNOXVILLE	133,493	154	94	91	103	94	156	172	102
126	LA CROSSE-EAU CLAIRE	61,312	51	45	64	49	80	71	110	62
189	LAFAYETTE, IN	26,899	38	24	21	38	40	57	48	33
124	LAFAYETTE, LA	66,732	88	89	86	65	80	90	110	44
175	LAKE CHARLES	27,838	39	39	60	43	61	93	52	40
110	LANSING	76,997	72	72	74	81	59	115	100	43
191	LAREDO	28,817	94	74	79	65	66	110	59	44
51	LAS VEGAS	191,433	335	240	178	217	201	330	411	209
65	LEXINGTON	139,466	210	83	105	91	83	162	95	104
185	LIMA	20,197	41	44	12	47	52	60	35	26
102	LINCOLN & HASTINGS-KRNY	80,448	41	41	84	60	74	112	139	62
56	LITTLE ROCK-PINE BLUFF	144,528	124	120	117	120	143	167	150	72
2	LOS ANGELES	2,031,131	1166	1173	1383	900	1596	3278	1428	1034
50	LOUISVILLE	171,923	108	119	120	93	88	210	133	94
147	LUBBOCK	51,861	65	56	67	65	61	55	64	38
122	MACON	65,123	63	56	42	85	51	97	130	96
85	MADISON	107,514	116	96	81	77	113	114	168	96
198	MANKATO	16,659	106	110	134	87	64	69	72	57
178	MARQUETTE	23,218	33	13	23	33	29	41	44	17
140	MEDFORD-KLAMATH FALLS	37,184	94	43	34	31	29	52	54	24
43	MEMPHIS	200,565	122	116	149	132	177	194	198	101
184	MERIDIAN	20,082	53	30	30	27	28	40	52	40
17	MIAMI-FT. LAUDERDALE	445,268	519	524	377	584	682	933	884	512
33	MILWAUKEE	245,102	236	206	201	210	326	329	279	128
14	MINNEAPOLIS-ST. PAUL	488,348	439	344	266	310	421	625	710	389
159	MINOT-BISMARCK-DICKINSON	34,555	41	37	26	32	41	45	34	37
169	MISSOULA	27,125	63	37	40	33	50	39	49	27
62	MOBILE-PENSACOLA (FT WALT)	137,889	118	89	112	88	112	163	185	86
135	MONROE-EL DORADO	51,147	36	30	58	46	43	71	88	33

(continued)

Target: Men 18–49

MARKET	RANK	POP	EM	DAY	EF	EN	PA	PR	LN	LF	CF
MONTEREY-SALINAS	121	86,623	90	90	66	62	81	164	64	62	
MONTGOMERY (SELMA)	115	66,144	73	37	47	64	52	66	85	39	
MYRTLE BEACH-FLORENCE	109	74,712	119	62	58	76	77	121	91	60	
NASHVILLE	30	274,402	176	225	196	178	252	293	327	133	
NEW ORLEANS	42	197,051	164	126	91	112	107	186	124	67	
NEW YORK	1	2,249,838	2807	2031	2023	2200	2096	5470	2092	1632	
NORFOLK-PORTSMTH-NEWPT NW	41	203,114	168	143	132	160	146	242	214	103	
NORTH PLATTE	209	4,082	38	86	39	16	20	21	12	14	
ODESSA-MIDLAND	157	40,093	37	37	61	35	35	63	48	22	
OKLAHOMA CITY	45	194,718	138	136	122	104	140	196	184	94	
OMAHA	77	114,200	153	88	70	76	103	156	129	99	
ORLANDO-DAYTONA BCH-MELBR	20	332,920	564	273	256	358	284	524	516	288	
OTTUMWA-KIRKSVILLE	197	14,001	34	21	21	13	14	27	25	19	
PADUCAH-CAPE GIRARD-HARSB	76	105,267	53	53	68	55	87	116	111	40	
PALM SPRINGS	160	36,748	84	93	73	91	79	162	80	41	
PANAMA CITY	158	34,367	37	32	38	27	37	49	52	32	
PARKERSBURG	187	15,869	53	53	56	46	45	110	76	47	
PEORIA-BLOOMINGTON	117	68,969	82	47	52	52	74	84	126	62	
PHILADELPHIA	4	789,494	833	666	637	866	756	1511	1300	661	
PHOENIX (PRESCOTT)	15	506,029	600	544	467	568	569	608	690	238	
PITTSBURGH	22	288,657	357	357	307	252	258	701	474	239	
PORTLAND, OR	24	320,889	427	269	245	206	218	313	272	225	
PORTLAND-AUBURN	74	94,848	114	92	105	140	99	155	127	79	
PRESQUE ISLE	205	6,731	39	62	88	24	33	37	37	30	
PROVIDENCE-NEW BEDFORD	48	170,713	360	235	184	224	174	333	271	212	
QUINCY-HANNIBAL-KEOKUK	166	27,814	43	25	35	29	30	38	49	27	
RALEIGH-DURHAM (FAYETVLLE)	29	300,670	177	195	182	202	164	444	275	125	
RAPID CITY	174	26,041	56	58	44	37	34	45	71	65	
RENO	116	68,595	71	73	34	39	52	95	56	62	
RICHMOND-PETERSBURG	58	132,091	125	107	75	91	107	171	131	79	
ROANOKE-LYNCHBURG	66	116,346	115	63	89	139	106	184	92	83	
ROCHESTER, NY	75	104,503	185	149	161	94	126	203	131	112	
ROCHESTR-MASON CITY-AUSTI	152	37,591	64	43	36	52	50	69	55	33	
ROCKFORD	133	49,964	87	45	62	40	66	59	80	49	
SACRAMNTO-STKTON-MODESTO	19	400,527	417	314	249	358	350	518	453	243	
SALISBURY	149	34,365	75	64	44	88	66	89	107	39	
SALT LAKE CITY	36	347,644	383	302	250	240	270	351	330	185	
SAN ANGELO	195	14,991	57	31	24	29	25	47	48	37	
SAN ANTONIO	37	238,371	203	198	145	234	187	374	247	126	
SAN DIEGO	26	352,951	733	488	357	311	379	639	485	291	
SAN FRANCISCO-OAK-SAN JOS	5	786,866	1106	1119	872	841	1058	1849	1166	706	
SANTABARBRA-SANMAR-SANLUO	119	78,886	75	124	94	65	67	156	97	60	

Market										
SAVANNAH	98	93,131	85	79	80	87	69	123	86	73
SEATTLE-TACOMA	12	480,962	834	911	436	576	566	690	731	353
SHERMAN-ADA	161	33,282	52	33	43	61	67	65	58	50
SHREVEPORT	81	107,718	66	82	80	59	100	115	105	61
SIOUX CITY	144	45,405	44	39	24	33	45	51	69	32
SIOUX FALLS(MITCHELL)	113	69,985	44	44	58	57	60	90	105	58
SOUTH BEND-ELKHART	87	97,838	97	69	70	57	71	115	127	65
SPOKANE	80	109,073	80	68	90	65	68	126	94	47
SPRINGFIELD, MO	78	102,367	134	80	48	56	70	101	138	64
SPRINGFIELD-HOLYOKE	106	69,742	79	44	72	81	94	184	105	85
ST. JOSEPH	201	13,921	126	150	56	60	98	97	65	41
ST. LOUIS	21	330,294	213	214	267	143	259	373	288	169
SYRACUSE	79	105,060	86	124	114	48	91	148	107	58
TALLAHASSEE-THOMASVILLE	111	83,575	69	93	72	80	61	115	117	71
TAMPA-ST. PETE (SARASOTA)	13	366,094	362	344	252	342	352	556	462	266
TERRE HAUTE	148	40,658	70	35	46	72	46	81	66	58
TOLEDO	69	121,581	92	94	66	68	76	137	124	75
TOPEKA	137	52,662	36	30	29	25	42	59	48	36
TRAVERSE CITY-CADILLAC	112	60,846	79	116	87	81	55	81	132	76
TRI-CITIES, TN-VA	91	81,139	106	66	61	86	71	111	136	58
TUCSON (SIERRA VISTA)	71	116,531	134	110	88	83	133	161	198	65
TULSA	60	141,321	182	129	92	100	136	156	165	78
TWIN FALLS	192	18,696	43	29	31	28	34	34	45	39
TYLER-LONGVIEW (LFKN&NCGD)	107	75,456	98	72	67	93	99	149	128	63
UTICA	167	27,443	51	49	46	62	41	77	77	50
VICTORIA	204	9,474	45	34	74	61	62	76	61	34
WACO-TEMPLE-BRYAN	92	118,179	53	90	74	62	92	129	98	81
WASHINGTON, DC (HAGRSTWN)	8	647,383	852	957	860	680	988	1715	1265	688
WATERTOWN	177	26,730	43	41	55	70	38	88	43	32
WAUSAU-RHINELANDER	134	46,832	41	56	51	51	57	65	79	46
WEST PALM BEACH-FT. PIERC	39	148,373	182	163	99	146	143	239	122	121
WHEELING-STEUBENVILLE	151	32,762	57	35	33	45	51	81	52	31
WICHITA FALLS & LAWTON	143	43,692	55	35	32	32	46	47	84	29
WICHITA-HUTCHINSON PLUS	67	129,459	85	73	64	71	106	147	109	77
WILKES BARRE-SCRANTON	53	147,567	137	81	98	146	75	154	134	86
WILMINGTON	142	42,456	46	52	27	41	22	79	39	30
YAKIMA-PASCO-RCHLND-KNNWC	127	67,488	47	41	41	38	35	58	50	28
YOUNGSTOWN	101	69,230	122	76	55	73	76	97	109	57
YUMA-EL CENTRO	172	32,787	67	72	48	73	60	101	95	40
ZANESVILLE	202	8,762	61	44	20	42	59	33	39	37
TOTALS		32,460,489	35,784	30,347	26,992	28,159	31,310	53,260	41,523	23,438
FACTORS			1.000	1.000	1.000	1.000	1.000	1.000	1.000	1.000

Notes: PA = Prime Access; PR = Prime Regular.

Level: Average; Pop Base: DMA (CPP).

There is a specific CPP for each daypart, beginning with early morning and ending with late fringe. All of the costs are based on :30 creative units.

The population figures for each market are based on Nielsen estimates for the demographic targets of women ages 18–49 and men ages 18–49. These population figures can come in handy if you are converting CPPs into CPMs.

Table 25.6 is a radio CPP chart from SQAD for first quarter 2004. The costs are for the top 100 radio markets in the United States for both men and women ages 18 and up. There is a specific CPP for each daypart, beginning with morning drive and ending with evening. All of the costs are based on a :60 creative unit.

As you review the markets for television and radio, you should notice some differences in market rank. This has to do with the different geography for each medium. Television is based on DMA, a Nielsen term that stands for *designated market area*. Counties are assigned to a DMA based on the majority of their television viewing. Radio, on the other hand, is based on a metro area, which is smaller in size than a DMA. There are some DMAs that contain multiple radio metro areas. This becomes important when you are considering local market plans across multiple markets. It can have a significant impact on evaluating the appropriate broadcast strategy for a given market.

Table 25.6

SQAD QuickView Report, Radio

Target: Women 18+

MARKET	RANK	POP	AMDRV	DAY	PMDRV	EVE
Abilene, TX	233	61,200	15	14	16	22
Akron	73	277,900	71	69	74	60
Albany, GA	263	47,300	18	19	17	27
Albany-Schenectady-Troy	64	348,400	55	58	66	40
Albuquerque	71	277,100	40	43	47	31
Alexandria, LA	217	71,500	13	14	16	12
Allentown-Bethlehem	70	299,700	40	39	42	15
Altoona	256	52,800	21	12	14	11
Amarillo	193	84,300	17	14	16	15
Anchorage	175	94,200	17	15	16	20
Ann Arbor	146	131,700	74	54	76	53
Appleton-Oshkosh	137	137,900	36	33	50	34
Asheville	160	119,400	35	26	41	27
Atlanta	11	1,663,400	390	311	396	162
Atlantic City	138	144,600	42	35	40	14
Augusta, GA	109	188,100	27	26	27	19
Augusta-Waterville, ME	261	47,500	12	13	17	9
Austin	42	504,800	94	84	101	33
Bakersfield	87	204,600	72	68	76	36
Baltimore	19	1,036,600	164	136	175	63
Bangor, ME	214	73,300	14	19	18	10
Baton Rouge	83	236,200	41	50	51	20
Battle Creek, MI	254	53,800	17	18	24	16
Beaumont-Port Arthur	131	146,500	26	25	26	25
Beckley, WV	283	31,900	10	8	11	11
Billings	257	50,900	8	9	11	5
Biloxi-Gulfport, MS	136	139,400	26	23	27	10
Binghamton	179	99,000	14	15	19	5
Birmingham	57	400,000	67	67	74	34
Bismarck, ND	278	37,100	8	10	9	5
Blacksburg-Christn-Rad-Pu	220	69,300	34	20	15	10
Bloomington	237	62,200	30	33	42	21
Bluefield, WV	270	44,900	16	12	19	12
Boise	121	168,400	25	26	30	9

Target: Women 18+

MARKET	RANK	POP	AMDRV	DAY	PMDRV	EVE
Boston	9	1,837,200	376	317	348	124
Bowling Green	208	76,300	24	25	28	19
Bridgeport	117	184,700	75	74	98	19
Brunswick, GA	286	27,400	11	9	11	7
Bryan-College Station, TX	230	63,300	17	14	15	18
Buffalo-Niagara Falls	51	465,100	66	61	73	45
Burlington, VT	139	137,900	24	23	26	23
Canton	129	162,200	38	29	47	15
Cape Cod, MA	183	98,900	30	30	32	11
Casper	287	25,500	12	10	13	12
Cedar Rapids	209	75,600	19	22	26	13
Champaign, IL	216	71,900	21	22	23	12
Charleston, SC	89	215,200	39	34	42	25
Charleston, WV	177	103,200	44	35	47	26
Charlotte-Gastonia-Rock H	37	611,100	117	97	123	62
Charlottesville, VA	224	69,700	14	13	17	7
Chattanooga	105	195,200	35	33	39	21
Cheyenne, WY	281	30,900	8	6	10	6
Chicago	3	3,469,500	426	393	460	174
Chico, CA	195	84,100	12	14	17	8
Cincinnati	26	773,600	116	110	119	48
Clarksville-Hopkin, TN-KY	204	75,700	50	40	45	38
Cleveland	25	854,400	105	95	114	56
Colorado Springs	96	198,800	41	37	46	17
Columbia, MO	253	56,600	14	17	19	16
Columbia, SC	90	218,400	45	37	47	30
Columbus, GA	181	94,500	19	19	22	20
Columbus, OH	35	626,600	112	105	138	64
Columbus-Strk-W Point	258	49,900	21	16	16	12
Cookeville, TN	276	38,100	13	10	19	14
Corpus Christi	134	143,000	26	25	27	19
Dallas-Ft. Worth	5	1,992,000	347	269	326	145
Danbury, CT	197	85,800	47	50	54	24
Dayton	58	391,800	48	54	62	52
Daytona Beach	94	216,800	55	59	64	42
Decatur, IL	267	45,600	14	14	16	16
Denver-Boulder	22	954,700	172	179	199	84
Des Moines	92	212,900	32	35	40	27
Detroit	10	1,781,000	237	180	229	95
Dothan, AL	191	88,600	15	19	19	10
Dubuque, IA	234	62,200	11	11	11	5
Duluth-Superior	202	78,800	14	13	17	13
Eau Claire, WI	244	59,200	13	12	14	13
El Paso	78	252,900	29	32	36	21
Elizabeth City-Nags Head	248	56,600	18	14	19	14
Elmira-Corning, NY	213	72,500	14	17	17	14
Erie	164	109,500	19	16	21	13
Eugene-Springfield	145	132,000	19	22	27	6
Evansville	157	119,100	20	21	29	21
Fargo-Moorhead	221	69,000	24	26	27	14
Fayetteville, NC	127	156,400	39	38	45	15
Fayetteville-Springdale,	151	124,600	25	25	30	15
Flagstaff-Prescott, AZ	156	119,400	20	15	15	23
Flint	125	168,700	34	32	39	23
Florence, SC	210	78,600	23	20	24	17
Florence-Muscle Shoal, AL	246	59,000	25	14	20	24
Frederick, Md	203	78,200	37	42	37	44
Fredericksburg, VA	166	104,700	36	37	42	66
Fresno	67	290,700	49	53	65	22
Ft. Collins-Greeley, Co	126	158,200	36	27	38	27
Ft. Myers, FL	68	315,000	45	44	53	25
Ft. Pierce, FL	111	192,100	38	38	39	36
Ft. Smith, AR	174	99,400	21	24	25	23
Ft. Walton Beach, FL	219	68,100	15	17	19	8

(continued)

Target: Women 18+

MARKET	RANK	POP	AMDRV	DAY	PMDRV	EVE
Ft. Wayne	103	190,900	33	34	32	19
Gainesville-Ocala, FL	86	233,000	40	39	44	29
Grand Forks, ND-Mn	277	36,500	13	12	15	10
Grand Junction, Co	259	47,400	12	12	12	13
Grand Rapids	66	310,800	50	57	60	31
Great Falls, MT	284	30,100	15	12	21	14
Green Bay	187	87,800	35	31	48	46
Greensboro-Ws-High Point	43	517,200	59	55	79	27
Greenville-Spartanburg	59	369,700	66	59	64	29
Greenville/New Bern, NC	84	224,000	40	37	39	26
Hagerstn-Chambrsg-Wayn	169	102,900	31	31	39	35
Harrisburg-Lebanon-Carlis	79	254,600	53	49	53	19
Harrisonburg, VA	264	47,600	17	11	26	4
Hartford-New Britain-Midd	49	473,200	99	100	113	45
Honolulu	61	339,200	56	50	75	16
Houston-Galveston	7	1,813,200	329	262	328	130
Huntington-Ashland	152	128,400	30	32	32	20
Huntsville	118	177,900	30	39	47	17
INDianapolis	41	580,100	88	87	100	28
Ithaca, NY	274	40,300	23	14	17	21
Jackson, MS	123	174,200	30	36	36	21
Jackson, TN	279	37,500	12	11	11	9
Jacksonville	50	457,000	72	64	75	28
Johnson City-Kingsport-Br	101	201,000	29	27	34	19
Johnstown	184	93,200	15	14	18	10
Jonesboro, AR	280	33,700	32	29	31	15
Joplin, MO	235	63,300	18	17	18	15
Kalamazoo	182	96,600	24	23	28	31
Kansas City	29	684,900	100	93	121	60
Killeen-Temple, TX	155	116,200	20	21	19	11
Knoxville	72	285,700	47	40	47	30
Lafayette, IN	236	59,200	17	13	15	11
Lafayette, LA	100	194,900	26	26	28	14
Lake Charles, LA	218	70,800	17	14	18	16
Lakeland-Winter Haven	98	201,600	28	26	32	32
Lancaster, PA	115	183,600	39	45	50	13
Lansing-East Lansing	120	177,600	34	34	39	22
Laredo, TX	215	70,900	13	12	15	9
Las Vegas	39	577,100	102	96	111	32
Laurel-Hattiesburg, MS	223	70,700	15	15	14	9
Lawton, Ok	269	40,100	9	9	10	2
Lewiston-Auburn, ME	272	41,600	13	13	15	14
Lexington-Fayette, KY	102	198,500	36	39	39	20
Lima, OH	241	58,200	15	11	17	21
Lincoln	176	98,500	25	22	25	10
Little Rock	85	232,800	48	52	51	28
Los Angeles	2	4,759,300	895	810	984	476
Louisville	55	424,700	64	58	66	37
Lubbock	180	96,300	22	20	23	13
Macon	154	124,800	26	26	31	20
Madison	97	202,200	38	43	43	13
Manchester	186	89,400	44	39	62	17
Mankato-New Ulm-St. P, Mn	265	44,500	13	17	22	15
Mason City, IA	282	32,500	8	9	11	15
Mcallen-Brownsville	63	337,200	31	30	31	18
Meadville-Franklin, PA	245	58,600	16	14	15	10
Medford-Ashland, OR	212	74,800	16	16	19	15
Melbourne-Titusville-Coco	99	201,600	47	34	39	43
Memphis	48	473,700	73	67	78	35
Merced, CA	189	81,600	23	16	24	26
Meridian, MS	285	30,700	13	14	15	6
Miami-Ft. Lauderdale-Holl	12	1,604,900	226	192	255	118
Middlesex-Somerset-Union	36	635,100	146	126	143	92
Milwaukee-Racine	33	655,500	88	84	99	56
Minneapolis-St. Paul	16	1,144,700	159	166	197	67

Target: Women 18+ MARKET	RANK	POP	AMDRV	DAY	PMDRV	EVE
Mobile	93	214,300	36	39	42	26
Modesto	122	167,000	57	55	69	25
Monmouth-Ocean, NJ	52	462,800	155	118	154	281
Monroe, LA	251	57,200	13	16	16	4
Monterey-Salinas-Santa Cr	75	249,800	39	41	48	20
Montgomery, AL	150	131,000	31	30	34	24
Morgantown-Clarksbrg-Fair	196	85,600	23	22	24	11
Morristown, NJ	113	188,900	140	108	151	128
Muncie-Marion, IN	201	83,500	22	26	28	18
Muskegon, MI	226	64,400	36	31	37	30
Myrtle Beach, SC	167	108,700	23	15	26	17
Nashville	45	496,800	77	77	92	54
Nassau-Suffolk (Li)	18	1,087,600	224	179	213	141
New Bedford-Fall Riv, MA	172	104,800	45	38	41	34
New Haven	108	194,400	88	97	114	44
New London, CT	173	100,600	39	34	48	11
New ORleans	44	503,700	77	76	87	43
New York	1	7,257,700	791	708	725	378
Newburgh-Middletown, NY	149	125,400	78	87	102	94
Norfolk-Virginia Beach	40	579,700	65	68	74	31
Odessa-Midland, TX	188	87,700	16	13	17	15
Oklahoma City	53	424,500	60	62	61	51
Olean, NY	207	75,300	30	26	31	20
Omaha-Council Bluffs	74	264,500	45	39	48	26
ORlando	38	594,100	131	117	134	65
Oxnard-Ventura	119	169,100	72	62	82	86
Palm Springs, CA	162	107,900	26	28	31	28
Panama City, FL	238	60,100	15	14	15	9
Parkersb-Marietta, WV-OH	242	60,900	12	12	14	7
Pensacola	124	166,000	37	36	41	14
Peoria	143	136,000	22	21	20	12
Philadelphia	6	2,009,800	273	227	268	88
Phoenix	15	1,231,400	182	153	212	112
Pittsburg, KS (SE Kansas)	232	63,900	14	13	14	14
Pittsburgh	23	969,900	102	97	117	45
Portland, ME	165	110,400	54	46	56	17
Portland, OR	24	855,500	136	131	174	53
Portsmouth-Dover-Rochstr	116	178,900	51	69	80	48
Poughkeepsie, NY	163	108,700	50	50	63	74
Providence-Warw-Pawtucket	34	652,100	91	76	100	45
Pueblo	249	56,300	20	14	23	15
Puerto Rico	13	1,543,200	197	182	250	132
Quad Cities (Davnprt-Ri)	141	139,900	22	22	29	13
Raleigh-Durham	46	494,800	109	110	132	43
Rapid City, SD	268	42,400	11	15	17	22
Reading, PA	133	148,900	64	71	72	50
Redding, CA	227	65,400	11	11	14	6
Reno	128	156,000	25	26	28	13
Richmond, VA	56	409,900	65	58	69	22
Riverside-San Bernardino	28	659,800	132	123	169	80
Roanoke-Lynchburg	110	195,600	36	49	52	25
Rochester, Mn	229	63,200	22	24	26	35
Rochester, NY	54	427,800	57	67	71	28
Rockford, IL	153	123,700	18	21	19	10
Sacramento	27	720,500	141	130	165	102
Saginaw-Bay City-Midland	130	157,200	26	30	33	17
Salisbury-Ocean City	148	133,300	16	20	20	14
Salt Lake City-Og-Provo	32	622,000	94	98	120	40
San Angelo, TX	273	41,400	13	12	13	13
San Antonio	31	670,100	90	89	104	53
San Diego	17	1,090,300	216	202	244	97
San Francisco	4	2,739,900	660	545	634	295
San Jose	30	658,200	262	244	304	120
San Luis Obispo, CA	170	99,400	20	20	24	27
Santa Barbara, CA	199	81,400	24	25	35	17

(continued)

Target: Women 18+

MARKET	RANK	POP	AMDRV	DAY	PMDRV	EVE
Santa Fe, Nm	240	59,300	24	21	24	34
Santa Maria-Lompoc, CA	205	76,600	23	31	26	16
Santa Rosa, CA	107	187,800	41	39	41	14
Sarasota-Bradenton	77	273,100	60	65	77	88
Savannah	158	117,000	24	26	29	17
Seattle-Tacoma	14	1,406,400	211	198	250	107
Sebring, FL	275	39,900	19	18	24	18
Sheboygan, WI	266	42,600	27	27	33	15
Shreveport	132	153,700	25	30	29	18
Sioux City, IA	262	46,500	10	9	10	10
South Bend	171	104,700	31	31	34	18
Southern IL, (Mar-Carb)	231	64,200	14	11	17	14
Spokane	91	209,200	26	26	27	10
Springfield, IL	206	80,700	35	22	43	14
Springfield, MA	81	246,800	36	42	46	19
Springfield, MO	144	134,600	26	22	29	16
St. Cloud, Mn	222	66,300	16	13	17	17
St. Louis	20	1,022,800	112	115	150	57
Stamford-Norwalk, CT	142	142,100	96	73	100	114
State College, PA	247	55,600	14	12	14	10
Stockton	88	206,400	53	44	55	13
Sussex, NJ	250	54,300	30	30	35	29
Syracuse	80	252,000	52	49	55	25
Tallahassee	161	117,900	28	24	26	13
Tampa-St. Pete-Clearwater	21	1,034,400	134	126	151	60
Terre Haute	200	81,100	17	16	15	12
Texarkana, TX	255	50,600	18	18	23	13
Toledo	82	241,500	46	38	48	29
Topeka	190	87,500	19	19	24	14
Traverse City-Petoskey	192	85,800	31	22	28	34
Trenton, NJ	140	142,700	127	114	141	149
Tri-Cities, WA (Rich-Ken)	211	69,600	13	12	16	8
Tucson	62	348,500	46	50	58	20
Tulsa	65	327,100	53	55	63	37
Tupelo, MS	185	92,800	24	21	28	16
Tuscaloosa, AL	228	67,500	27	26	26	14
Tyler, TX	147	132,300	33	34	35	27
Utica-Rome	159	114,400	26	25	25	9
Victor Valley	135	137,800	40	36	47	29
Visalia-Tulare-Hanford	104	170,300	36	37	54	28
Waco	194	85,100	25	26	24	24
Washington, DC	8	1,849,700	362	301	350	123
Waterloo-Cedar Falls	243	61,200	17	16	17	14
Watertown, NY	271	39,200	9	10	11	5
Wausau-Stevens Point, WI	168	103,000	20	22	26	29
West Palm Bch-Boca Raton	47	496,600	87	93	99	42
Westchester	60	372,600	103	112	175	102
Wheeling	239	61,500	23	22	26	11
Wichita	95	203,500	31	31	36	23
Wichita Falls, TX	252	52,800	13	13	14	11
Wilkes Barre-Scranton	69	315,100	45	47	54	18
Williamsport, PA	260	48,000	14	17	16	12
Wilmington, DE	76	261,200	63	58	81	25
Wilmington, NC	178	102,100	32	28	32	27
Winchester, VA	225	65,700	15	19	22	34
Worcester	114	185,000	54	58	71	23
Yakima, WA	198	77,900	12	16	15	11
York	106	188,500	43	46	55	29
Youngstown-Warren	112	191,300	23	23	27	24
Totals		**94,166,400**	**17,596**	**16,215**	**19,336**	**10,371**
Factors			1	1	1	1

Notes: Level: Average; Pop Base: Metro (CPP); Qtr Weights: 1Q '04 (1.0000).

Table 25.6 *(continued)*

SQAD QuickView Report, Radio

Target: Men 18+

MARKET	RANK	POP	AMDRV	DAY	PMDRV	EVE
Abilene, TX	233	59,600	14	12	13	13
Akron	73	249,400	74	71	72	58
Albany, GA	263	40,400	13	18	17	27
Albany-Schenectady-Troy	64	315,800	53	54	59	29
Albuquerque	71	257,700	36	39	43	27
Alexandria, LA	217	63,700	11	11	12	9
Allentown-Bethlehem	70	271,300	34	34	35	12
Altoona	256	46,600	18	11	13	14
Amarillo	193	79,900	14	13	15	17
Anchorage	175	95,500	16	14	16	15
Ann Arbor	146	127,800	58	43	62	40
Appleton-Oshkosh	137	133,800	36	29	41	24
Asheville	160	106,200	31	25	35	17
Atlanta	11	1,573,100	359	296	365	164
Atlantic City	138	129,000	33	30	36	16
Augusta, GA	109	170,200	25	24	26	18
Augusta-Waterville, ME	261	43,100	10	11	15	5
Austin	42	512,100	91	79	92	36
Bakersfield	87	214,800	62	59	71	41
Baltimore	19	921,600	147	130	154	51
Bangor, ME	214	68,100	12	17	15	7
Baton Rouge	83	211,400	40	50	50	20
Battle Creek, MI	254	48,600	16	18	22	14
Beaumont-Port Arthur	131	141,900	19	20	24	24
Beckley, WV	283	30,300	11	10	10	12
Billings	257	46,400	8	7	8	4
Biloxi-Gulfport, MS	136	135100	24	23	28	10
Binghamton	179	89600	14	15	21	5
Birmingham	57	350000	66	62	70	33
Bismarck, ND	278	34400	7	7	6	3
Blacksburg-Christn-Rad-Pu	220	69800	32	21	17	11
Bloomington	237	56200	27	25	32	15
Bluefield, WV	270	39400	16	10	16	14
Boise	121	164100	22	24	26	8
Boston	9	1647200	314	280	302	103
Bowling Green	208	70500	21	21	25	17
Bridgeport	117	164300	79	79	96	18
Brunswick, GA	286	24000	10	8	10	8
Bryan-College Station, TX	230	63300	15	10	12	18
Buffalo-Niagara Falls	51	408700	65	58	66	36
Burlington, VT	139	133900	21	19	21	19
Canton	129	143900	32	24	41	11
Cape Cod, MA	183	85000	25	23	26	10
Casper	287	24200	10	6	9	10
Cedar Rapids	209	70600	20	21	24	13
Champaign, IL	216	71300	21	22	25	14
Charleston, SC	89	199900	37	32	41	22
Charleston, WV	177	91100	47	42	52	28
Charlotte-Gastonia-Rock H	37	570200	102	91	111	58
Charlottesville, VA	224	60800	12	12	17	8
Chattanooga	105	173300	33	32	36	20
Cheyenne, WY	281	30700	8	5	9	4
Chicago	3	3203400	386	359	398	154
Chico, CA	195	77200	12	13	16	12
Cincinnati	26	701000	98	106	103	44
Clarksville-Hopkin, TN-KY	204	76900	41	27	31	26
Cleveland	25	748900	94	89	100	45
Colorado Springs	96	195900	34	33	39	16
Columbia, MO	253	51300	15	16	18	11
Columbia, SC	90	196900	39	37	43	27
Columbus, GA	181	89500	18	19	22	17

(continued)

Target: Men 18+

MARKET	RANK	POP	AMDRV	DAY	PMDRV	EVE
Columbus, OH	35	583500	102	94	124	60
Columbus-Strk-W Point	258	44300	19	19	15	10
Cookeville, TN	276	36400	14	9	15	9
Corpus Christi	134	133000	26	24	27	18
Dallas-Ft. Worth	5	1928400	307	246	294	123
Danbury, CT	197	77500	42	50	56	23
Dayton	58	350,100	45	52	57	42
Daytona Beach	94	197,700	45	51	57	40
Decatur, IL	267	39,900	15	15	17	20
Denver-Boulder	22	940,100	150	163	179	79
Des Moines	92	197,300	28	29	35	21
Detroit	10	1,623,600	223	181	219	85
Dothan, AL	191	79,200	15	20	17	10
Dubuque, IA	234	59,100	11	10	11	5
Duluth-Superior	202	74,800	12	11	15	10
Eau Claire, WI	244	54,600	11	10	13	14
El Paso	78	223,700	29	30	32	17
Elizabeth City-Nags Head	248	52,800	14	12	15	13
Elmira-Corning, NY	213	68,000	12	16	13	8
Erie	164	99,800	16	15	19	10
Eugene-Springfield	145	124,700	17	17	22	5
Evansville	157	105,900	19	20	24	17
Fargo-Moorhead	221	66,200	21	22	25	15
Fayetteville, NC	127	153,800	34	34	38	14
Fayetteville-Springdale,	151	120,100	22	20	25	13
Flagstaff-Prescott, AZ	156	112,800	20	14	14	23
Flint	125	149,300	30	29	35	18
Florence, SC	210	66,200	16	13	19	16
Florence-Muscle Shoal,AL	246	52,000	24	19	19	23
Frederick, Md	203	73,400	30	33	29	31
Fredericksburg, VA	166	98,500	31	28	26	39
Fresno	67	283,600	45	51	55	18
Ft. Collins-Greeley, Co	126	154,200	30	26	38	30
Ft. Myers, FL	68	299,300	41	44	49	23
Ft. Pierce, FL	111	177,500	33	33	30	29
Ft. Smith, AR	174	92,800	19	21	23	20
Ft. Walton Beach, FL	219	68,200	13	15	17	9
Ft. Wayne	103	177,900	27	27	28	17
Gainesville-Ocala, FL	86	213,300	31	29	37	25
Grand Forks, ND-Mn	277	36,300	11	9	11	11
Grand Junction, Co	259	43,900	10	11	10	8
Grand Rapids	66	291,200	39	44	53	29
Great Falls, MT	284	28,800	10	8	13	8
Green Bay	187	84,900	32	29	44	31
Greensboro-Ws-High Point	43	465,200	58	52	70	23
Greenville-Spartanburg	59	339,600	62	56	64	30
Greenville/New Bern, NC	84	223,400	32	36	37	21
Hagerstn-Chambrsg-Wayn	169	100,600	29	30	36	33
Harrisburg-Lebanon-Carlis	79	230,700	49	45	49	16
Harrisonburg, VA	264	43,200	16	11	23	5
Hartford-New Britain-Midd	49	426,900	92	91	100	40
Honolulu	61	337,700	59	52	73	15
Houston-Galveston	7	1,757,400	304	252	290	120
Huntington-Ashland	152	115,700	25	25	27	22
Huntsville	118	166,800	32	37	44	15
INDianapolis	41	531,900	76	78	86	23
Ithaca, NY	274	38,100	25	13	15	20
Jackson, MS	123	150,000	29	34	34	21
Jackson, TN	279	32,700	11	10	12	9
Jacksonville	50	419,500	61	54	65	26
Johnson City-Kingsport-Br	101	181,900	27	26	31	16
Johnstown	184	86,800	15	13	15	8
Jonesboro, AR	280	30,200	25	23	24	13
Joplin, MO	235	57,000	14	12	14	14
Kalamazoo	182	86,900	20	17	22	26

Target: Men 18+

MARKET	RANK	POP	AMDRV	DAY	PMDRV	EVE
Kansas City	29	628,300	90	82	106	53
Killeen-Temple, TX	155	116,500	17	16	18	10
Knoxville	72	257,800	43	38	43	27
Lafayette, IN	236	61,800	19	15	17	13
Lafayette, LA	100	175,400	20	18	20	14
Lake Charles, LA	218	64,100	16	16	17	17
Lakeland-Winter Haven	98	186,500	27	24	27	24
Lancaster, PA	115	167,600	34	39	43	12
Lansing-East Lansing	120	161,800	32	31	37	21
Laredo, TX	215	62,300	14	13	16	8
Las Vegas	39	587,700	83	82	99	33
Laurel-Hattiesburg, MS	223	62,000	13	13	16	8
Lawton, Ok	269	42,600	7	8	8	2
Lewiston-Auburn, ME	272	38,000	9	9	12	11
Lexington-Fayette, KY	102	183,300	35	38	38	16
Lima, OH	241	55,500	14	10	16	21
Lincoln	176	96,800	22	16	20	7
Little Rock	85	209,300	42	46	45	20
Los Angeles	2	4,523,600	818	783	866	418
Louisville	55	383,200	62	54	64	26
Lubbock	180	88,700	21	17	21	12
Macon	154	107,800	23	24	28	19
Madison	97	193,800	31	34	34	9
Manchester	186	84,500	36	35	50	19
Mankato-New Ulm-St. P, Mn	265	42,700	11	13	17	12
Mason City, IA	282	29,200	9	10	11	18
Mcallen-Brownsville	63	297,400	31	34	31	17
Meadville-Franklin, PA	245	53,500	13	13	15	7
Medford-Ashland, OR	212	68,100	15	17	19	11
Melbourne-Titusville-Coco	99	187,700	37	29	32	36
Memphis	48	417,100	71	58	70	36
Merced, CA	189	79,100	18	14	21	21
Meridian, MS	285	26,300	11	11	13	6
Miami-Ft. Lauderdale-Holl	12	1,438,300	204	176	240	110
Middlesex-Somerset-Union	36	581,000	124	107	126	84
Milwaukee-Racine	33	596,400	78	79	89	50
Minneapolis-St. Paul	16	1,084,300	137	138	161	54
Mobile	93	190,300	34	34	36	26
Modesto	122	155,600	44	40	53	19
Monmouth-Ocean, NJ	52	410,500	116	105	126	227
Monroe, LA	251	48,300	11	11	12	4
Monterey-Salinas-Santa Cr	75	258,100	33	36	42	19
Montgomery, AL	150	117,400	30	28	34	25
Morgantown-Clarksbrg-Fair	196	79,400	19	18	19	10
Morristown, NJ	113	174,800	114	94	129	131
Muncie-Marion, IN	201	74,400	21	22	25	22
Muskegon, MI	226	60,600	32	31	35	27
Myrtle Beach, SC	167	100,700	20	14	22	18
Nashville	45	461,100	81	87	91	51
Nassau-Suffolk (Li)	18	985,800	186	156	185	104
New Bedford-Fall Riv, MA	172	92,500	39	30	39	29
New Haven	108	171,300	77	82	95	34
New London, CT	173	96,800	35	31	38	12
New ORleans	44	439,700	73	74	84	45
New York	1	6,398,400	720	687	663	334
Newburgh-Middletown, NY	149	121,000	67	60	76	76
Norfolk-Virginia Beach	40	547,800	56	62	70	28
Odessa-Midland, TX	188	79,100	15	11	15	16
Oklahoma City	53	394,200	51	48	50	42
Olean, NY	207	71,700	25	21	27	13
Omaha-Council Bluffs	74	246,300	41	34	42	20
Orlando	38	561,200	114	110	123	52
Oxnard-Ventura	119	167,400	61	62	72	80
Palm Springs, CA	162	104,700	25	24	29	29
Panama City, FL	238	57,100	15	14	15	8

(continued)

Target: Men 18+

MARKET	RANK	POP	AMDRV	DAY	PMDRV	EVE
Parkersb-Marietta, WV-OH	242	54,700	10	11	12	8
Pensacola	124	160,900	34	31	35	15
Peoria	143	123,600	22	24	20	11
Philadelphia	6	1,768,700	253	218	256	84
Phoenix	15	1,203,200	149	133	198	104
Pittsburg, KS (Se Kansas)	232	58,100	13	12	13	11
Pittsburgh	23	848,500	89	88	103	39
Portland, ME	165	98,800	52	40	51	15
Portland, OR	24	823,500	128	128	153	50
Portsmouth-Dover-Rochstr	116	167,900	42	53	62	42
Poughkeepsie, NY	163	106,400	47	49	52	50
Providence-Warw-Pawtucket	34	575,500	77	65	81	35
Pueblo	249	52,100	19	14	23	15
Puerto Rico	13	1,353,900	186	183	221	114
Quad Cities (Davnprt-Ri)	141	128,300	22	18	26	12
Raleigh-Durham	46	463,500	99	91	115	42
Rapid City, SD	268	41,000	9	13	16	26
Reading, PA	133	137,400	55	70	71	45
Redding, CA	227	59,400	11	12	15	5
Reno	128	158,800	23	23	26	12
Richmond, VA	56	362,800	60	54	63	19
Riverside-San Bernardino	28	640,300	128	126	157	64
Roanoke-Lynchburg	110	170,800	32	45	45	22
Rochester, Mn	229	59,600	19	20	25	30
Rochester, NY	54	388,600	54	62	62	25
Rockford, IL	153	115,100	16	17	18	8
Sacramento	27	669,100	127	117	143	86
Saginaw-Bay City-Midland	130	141,200	25	29	29	13
Salisbury-Ocean City	148	122,900	13	16	16	11
Salt Lake City-Og-Provo	32	608,500	80	86	104	35
San Angelo, TX	273	36,800	12	12	11	10
San Antonio	31	614,200	84	82	100	49
San Diego	17	1,081,600	205	207	234	86
San Francisco	4	2,662,000	600	548	599	255
San Jose	30	668,800	244	257	278	108
San Luis Obispo, CA	170	102,100	16	16	21	23
Santa Barbara, CA	199	78,700	26	24	31	13
Santa Fe, Nm	240	55,700	25	21	25	31
Santa Maria-Lompoc, CA	205	75,600	17	20	20	12
Santa Rosa, CA	107	176,000	36	31	36	13
Sarasota-Bradenton	77	241,700	52	57	65	94
Savannah	158	106,100	25	27	29	16
Seattle-Tacoma	14	1,363,700	193	180	222	95
Sebring, FL	275	36,600	19	17	21	12
Sheboygan, WI	266	42,300	22	22	27	12
Shreveport	132	133,600	22	24	29	19
Sioux City, IA	262	43,200	8	7	8	10
South Bend	171	93,800	28	27	34	16
Southern IL, (Mar-Carb)	231	60,800	16	13	18	11
Spokane	91	195,600	21	21	24	9
Springfield, IL	206	70,500	34	20	40	12
Springfield, MA	81	213,700	32	38	40	16
Springfield, MO	144	123,200	24	20	26	12
St. Cloud, MN	222	65,600	13	11	14	13
St. Louis	20	904,400	103	100	131	54
Stamford-Norwalk, CT	142	127,000	99	79	102	92
State College, PA	247	57,700	13	10	14	11
Stockton	88	200,000	50	44	52	11
Sussex, NJ	250	52,000	21	20	23	38
Syracuse	80	225,100	49	46	52	19
Tallahassee	161	105,200	27	25	28	15
Tampa-St. Pete-Clearwater	21	927,800	114	106	122	52
Terre Haute	200	77,100	14	13	16	11
Texarkana, TX	255	48,500	19	17	20	11
Toledo	82	215,800	45	40	47	22

Target: Men 18+

MARKET	RANK	POP	AMDRV	DAY	PMDRV	EVE
Topeka	190	79,900	20	18	22	13
Traverse City-Petoskey	192	81,000	23	18	22	32
Trenton, NJ	140	130,700	113	112	126	117
Tri-Cities, WA (Rich-Ken)	211	69,000	13	13	16	7
Tucson	62	322,400	36	36	47	18
Tulsa	65	300,900	49	51	54	31
Tupelo, MS	185	81,600	21	16	21	12
Tuscaloosa, AL	228	60,600	25	20	24	10
Tyler, TX	147	119,100	31	30	32	28
Utica-Rome	159	108,700	25	22	23	11
Victor Valley	135	132,700	33	31	37	20
Visalia-Tulare-Hanford	104	183,100	31	29	47	26
Waco	194	76,500	21	22	25	22
Washington, Dc	8	1,691,800	335	307	311	111
Waterloo-Cedar Falls	243	54,000	12	11	13	12
Watertown, NY	271	41,300	9	9	10	4
Wausau-Stevens Point, WI	168	98,800	19	19	21	19
West Palm Bch-Boca Raton	47	448,100	73	85	87	35
Westchester	60	324,700	94	96	149	90
Wheeling	239	55,400	20	18	22	10
Wichita	95	193,400	29	28	32	23
Wichita Falls, TX	252	53,600	12	13	14	12
Wilkes Barre-Scranton	69	280,800	39	41	46	15
Williamsport, PA	260	44,100	12	14	12	9
Wilmington, DE	76	237,900	65	60	77	22
Wilmington, NC	178	93,400	26	23	26	16
Winchester, VA	225	62,100	14	15	15	27
Worcester	114	170,300	51	52	59	21
Yakima, WA	198	75,400	14	16	13	10
York	106	176,400	38	38	45	24
Youngstown-Warren	112	170,000	23	23	26	21
TOTALS		87,101,100	15,850	14,938	17,272	9,129
FACTORS			1	1	1	1

Source: SQAD RADIO. Copyright © SQAD Inc. All rights reserved. Reprinted with permission.

Notes: Level: Average; Pop Base: Metro (CPP); Qtr Weights: 1Q '04 (1.0000).

Unit 25 Exercises
Working with Broadcast Media Costs

1. You have scheduled commercials in early fringe, prime time, and late fringe. You received your invoice with commercial times airing at 5:05 P.M., 7:10 P.M., and 11:09 P.M. How do these times match up with your buy?

2. What is the comparison in costs between men and women for a national buy for 100 gross rating points (GRPs) that is split 60/40 between network morning and prime-time cable?

3. The previous buy was done in the scatter market but this year you can purchase it in the upfront market. What would be the impact on the latter buy if costs have increased by 6 percent yet you moved from the scatter to the upfront market?

4. You are asked to develop a plan to target women ages 18–49 in the top five spot television markets. Using an equal weighting of daytime, prime time, and late fringe dayparts, what would be the cost for such a plan?

5. The costs you have developed for these top five markets were based on first quarter costs, but the client must delay the plan until the fourth quarter. How will this change in timing affect the costs of the plan?

6. You have a budget of $5 million. Your client has asked to see two plans: one that is a national cable-only plan using an equal weighting of daytime and prime time, and the other is a spot television plan for the top 15 markets using the same daytime and prime-time daypart mix. Based on a women-buying target, which plan delivers more impressions?

7. Compare a spot television news-only buy using 15-second commercials in the top five markets with a spot radio A.M. drive-time buy using 60-second commercials in the same markets with men as the buying demographic. What plan would offer the best media delivery on a $3 million budget?

8. Your client wants to run radio in the top 20 markets. Would he be better off scheduling spot radio or moving to network radio?

9. Your client wants to compare media in Detroit and Dallas. With a schedule of 125 GRPs per week in prime time and 75 GRPs per week on A.M. drive radio, what is a four-week schedule in each of these markets?

Unit 26

Working with Broadcast Negotiations

Broadcast negotiation is both an art and a science. It is the art of negotiating the best deal whereby both the buyer and the seller believe that they can win. And it is a science in terms of delivering the specifications outlined in the media plan. The broadcast negotiation process begins with a briefing by the media planning team. In this briefing, the team reviews the target, the daypart goals, the types of programming that best fit the target, the cost goals, and what items outside the paid media purchase would be of benefit to the brand. Then it is up to the broadcast negotiator to make it happen.

There are differences in negotiating national versus local broadcast, as there are for radio versus television versus cable. Each medium has its own set of measurement, costs, dayparts, and protocol. In large media companies, there are negotiation specialists for each. However, the fundamentals of broadcast buying are largely the same. For the purposes of this unit we focus on purchasing national broadcast. Our example is network cable.

Negotiation Process

The negotiation process begins with the request for packages from selected networks. Not every network is asked to participate in the negotiating process. Only those networks that have the audience that is desirable for the brand are asked to participate.

The networks are provided with a briefing not dissimilar to that of the negotiators. They are provided with the brand's goals, budget, cost-per-thousand target, GRP or impression target, daypart distribution, flight dates, creative unit, and added-value requests. The networks may also be asked to develop packages at specific budget levels.

The networks then develop packages based on their available inventory and sales goals. Networks mix inventory that is highly desirable with inventory that is less desirable to meet the overall brand goals. The objective of the network is to gain the largest share of the brand's budget. If the network had 10 percent of the brand's budget in the past year, they would like to up that to 15 percent in the subsequent year. Networks participate in the negotiation process to gain market share just like the brand is trying to gain market share.

The networks submit their first-round packages to the negotiator for evaluation. The negotiator then evaluates each package. Table 26.1 shows a rudimentary comparison of

Table 26.1

Cable News Comparison

Buy Item	CNN	Fox News
# :30	160	140
Imp (000)	55,000	85,000
Cost	$1,000,000	$1,000,000
CPM	$18.18	$11.76
Avg. unit cost	$6,250	$7,140
Added value		
# Billboards	30	25
Sponsorship	Set signage for 6 P.M. news	—
Cross platform	140 units; Bonus on CNN	—
	Airport news	

two national cable news proposals. At this point, the negotiator will counsel each network on where they stand in the process. And they will ask each network to adjust their packages to better meet the goals. The negotiator will then ask for another round of packages to evaluate.

Some negotiations go three rounds or more. Other negotiators ask for the networks' best effort on the first round. It is simply a matter of the negotiators' style and the time frame in which they have to negotiate. As you can imagine, it takes a week or more for a network to thoroughly develop a package. So, if the negotiator is working in three or more rounds of negotiation, the time frame to make the purchase can drag on for a month or more. However, with millions of dollars at stake for the brand and the networks, there is certainly spirited negotiations and give and take on each side. At the end of the day, both sides must believe that they have gotten a fair deal.

Components of Negotiation

The negotiation of broadcast advertising is a complex process. Of course all negotiations depend on the brand's specific goals, and there are many components to the negotiation process. The following are the key components of any negotiation.

Currency

It does seem funny that a part of the negotiation process is over what is used as currency. But, with continued changes in measurement of broadcast, the buyer and seller must agree on the measurement service and specifics for pegging an audience. For example, in network television and cable, Nielsen is the measurement company. Nielsen has recently moved from just providing program audience information to providing specific commercial rating information. Those are two different numbers and impact the outcome of the purchase. Change is happening on the local broadcast front as well. Nielsen has been moving from a diary-based method to a home meter method to capture television viewing information. Arbitron is moving from a diary method to a portable meter system to measure radio audience listening. Each method produces radically different numbers. These audience numbers are the "currency" for pegging commercial rates. So, agreeing on the currency is important.

Audience Guarantee

This leads to audience guarantees. Nearly all network purchases and many local purchases include audience guarantees. Based on the audience method, the buyer negotiates a specific audience delivery for the dollars invested. If the network does not meet that goal, they agree to add additional commercials at no charge to attain the guarantee.

CPM

The buyer negotiates a package CPM, or cost-per-thousand. By negotiating a package CPM, the agency negotiator allows the network to price individual programming up or down to meet the overall goals. While there can be program unit rate negotiation, the majority of negotiation is based on overall package CPM.

Delivery

The negotiator ensures that the network meets delivery goals for the target, for the daypart distribution, and for the specific timing. This is then tied back to audience guarantees. A sub-part of delivery is where the commercials will air in the program commercial pod. Research shows that the first commercial in the pod is viewed more than ones in the middle. These commercial placements will be negotiated, as well as placements within a special editorial or feature that is relevant to the brand. A big aspect of placement negotiation is exclusivity. This is when the brand is the only brand in the category in a program.

Added Value

A big aspect of broadcast negotiation is in the arena of added value. Added value is a catch-all for additional items above and beyond the paid media portion of the purchase. The following is a sample of added-value elements that are negotiated.

- *Bonus weight.* The network provides additional commercial units at no charge.
- *Brand mentions.* An announcer will mention the brand on the air.
- *Sponsorship.* The brand is the sole or shared sponsor of a program.
- *Promotion.* The network will develop a promotion for the brand.
- *Contests and performance tickets.* The network will provide a contest for the brand or tickets to a performance they are airing.

These are examples of items that are negotiated and packaged to gain favor for the brand's dollars.

Cross Platform

Most networks and even local stations offer more than one way to see or hear their programming. This can be in digital form such as streaming video or audio, podcasts, and website content, or as place-based media such as airport screens and mall televisions. Another avenue for negotiation is to add other outlets to the buy from the network.

Broadcast negotiation is a specialized media activity. Negotiators specialize either in a specific medium or in national or local broadcast. It is a complex process. The negotiator wants to get the most he or she can for the brand within the budget. This means assessing the audience and the costs as well as the extras that help the brand achieve their goals.

Unit 26 Exercises
Working with Broadcast Negotiations

1. What is meant by the term "currency" in broadcast negotiations?

2. What is an example of "added value"?

3. Looking at Table 26.1, which cable news channel is the most cost efficient based on the purchase CPM?

4. Looking at Table 26.1, which cable news network offers the most added value?

5. What would you need to know to better evaluate the impact of the added-value portion of the purchase?

6. If CNN had a 30 percent greater composition of the brand's audience than Fox News, how would that impact your decision on purchasing one versus the other?

7. Which of the two networks would you select and why?

Part V
Print Media

Unit 27
Working with Print Media Estimates

While broadcast takes the lion's share of media dollars, many advertisers focus their attention on print as a primary or secondary medium. Consumer magazines are used either as a primary medium for many consumer goods and services or as a support medium for broadcast. Because magazines have a selective audience, advertisers can direct their message to complement the relevant content of a publication. For example, a food manufacturer may run a recipe advertisement in a women's magazine with a food editorial page, while a car manufacturer may run a performance advertisement in a car-buff publication.

Newspapers are a vital medium, particularly for local and national retailers. In fact, for some retail categories such as furniture and tires, the newspaper becomes a directory for comparative prices and styles. A newspaper's greatest strength is its immediacy, so retailers who want to convey short-term sales events use it frequently.

Both consumer magazines and newspapers use the term *coverage* to denote reach. If a newspaper has 40 percent household coverage in Peoria, Illinois, that means that 40 percent of all households in Peoria receive the daily newspaper. The same would be true for *Good Housekeeping* magazine, which is read by nearly 25 percent of all women in the United States. In this case, *Good Housekeeping* would have 25 percent coverage of women.

In print media, there are two dimensions that impact the reach potential of any publication. The first of these is total circulation. A daily newspaper or a monthly magazine has either home or newsstand subscribers who pay for the respective publications. One basic reach analysis of a publication is the percent of households in a given market or demographic that subscribe to the publication. For example, if the *Houston Chronicle* has a daily circulation of 500,000 and Houston has 2 million households, then the *Chronicle* would have a daily household coverage of 25 percent of the Houston market.

The second dimension that impacts the reach potential of a publication is the number of readers who read a given issue of the publication. This is called *readers per copy* and is a factor that is multiplied by the circulation of the publication to calculate its total audience. For example, if *People* magazine has 2 million in circulation yet has eight readers per copy, it would then have 16 million total readers. Because magazines such as *People* are distributed in public places such as doctors' offices and barbershops, they can gain a large number of readers per copy.

One of the questions media planners must answer when working with print audiences is how many advertisements to place in a given publication. At what point is there little to be

Table 27.1

Newspaper Reach and Frequency

Number of ads	Percentage market coverage (circulation/households)							
	25	35	40	45	50	55	60	65
1								
Reach	25	35	40	45	50	55	60	65
Frequency	1.0	1.0	1.0	1.0	1.0	1.0	1.0	1.0
2								
Reach	32	45	51	58	64	70	77	83
Frequency	1.6	1.6	1.6	1.6	1.6	1.6	1.6	1.6
3								
Reach	36	50	58	64	71	78	84	90
Frequency	2.1	2.1	2.1	2.1	2.1	2.1	2.1	2.2
4								
Reach	38	54	62	68	75	82	89	94
Frequency	2.6	2.6	2.6	2.6	2.7	2.7	2.7	2.8
5								
Reach	40	57	64	71	78	85	91	95
Frequency	3.1	3.1	3.1	3.2	3.2	3.2	3.3	3.4
6								
Reach	42	60	66	74	81	87	93	95
Frequency	3.6	3.5	3.6	3.6	3.7	3.8	3.9	4.1
8								
Reach	44	62	68	77	84	91	94	95
Frequency	4.5	4.5	4.7	4.7	4.8	4.8	5.1	5.5
10								
Reach	46	64	70	79	86	92	95	96
Frequency	5.4	5.5	5.7	5.7	5.8	6.0	6.3	6.8
12								
Reach	48	65	72	81	87	93	95	96
Frequency	6.3	6.5	6.7	6.7	6.9	7.1	7.6	8.1
14								
Reach	49	66	74	82	88	94	96	96
Frequency	7.1	7.4	7.6	7.7	8.0	8.2	8.8	9.5
16								
Reach	50	67	76	83	89	94	96	96
Frequency	8.0	8.4	8.4	8.7	9.0	9.4	10.0	10.8
18								
Reach	51	68	77	84	90	95	96	96
Frequency	8.8	9.3	9.4	9.6	10.0	10.4	11.3	12.2
20								
Reach	52	69	78	85	91	95	96	96
Frequency	9.6	10.1	10.3	10.6	11.0	11.6	12.5	13.5

gained in reach potential by adding incremental insertions to the media plan? Table 27.1 is designed to help address this question. The column on the left is the number of ads you might place in a newspaper campaign—but not on the same day. It could be on sequential days or every week. Or it might be based on a flight, that is, a short period of intense advertising (not part of the table).

The horizontal axis is the percentage of households in a given market that receive the newspaper. This is the percentage of household coverage we described earlier by dividing circulation into the number of households in a market.

If a newspaper had 40 percent household penetration (or coverage), you would start your analysis at the 40 percent number on the horizontal axis. If you put one insertion in that publication you would reach 40 percent of all households at one time. In this table, we do not account for readers per copy. It is strictly a household number.

If you wanted to know the reach and frequency impact of placing six insertions in this same newspaper, you would move down to the reach number that is across from six insertions. For the 40 percent coverage, the household reach at six insertions is 66 percent. So, by scheduling five more insertions, you have added 26 percentage points to your total household coverage of the market while also adding frequency.

If you decided to double the frequency to 12, you would see that the reach only moves up to 72 percent. Those six incremental insertions only gained you six reach points. You can see that reach quickly tops out in newspaper schedules. As you add incremental insertions to a schedule, you are adding more frequency than reach to any given campaign.

In today's marketplace, the majority of markets have only a single daily newspaper, so determining the number of insertions is one of the most important facets in newspaper planning. Magazines, on the other hand, require an analysis of the number of insertions you place in a given publication as well as how many publications you might have for your campaign.

Media planners typically use software programs that calculate reach and frequency for a variety of magazine schedules. Magazine optimizers can be run via this software to determine the best schedule combination for a given budget parameter and a given set of publications that fit the brand's specifications.

Table 27.2 is an example of magazine reach and frequency based on two target audience coverage percentages. The first set of reach and frequency numbers is based on all publications having 7 percent coverage. The second set of reach and frequency numbers is based on all publications having 12 percent coverage.

The far left column lists the number of publications (1 through 8) you may consider for a campaign. Along the first row across the top are the number of insertions (1 through 12) you may select per publication. For example, if you selected one publication for the first set of reach and frequency numbers with one insertion, the corresponding set of delivery would be 7 percent reach, 7 gross rating points (GRPs), and a 1.0 frequency. If you selected four insertions for this same publication, then your delivery numbers would be 11 percent reach, 28 GRPs, and a 2.5 average frequency.

Say that you elected to schedule four publications with four insertions per publication. Find the intersection where the number of publications and the number of insertions meet. The corresponding delivery numbers for this are 26 percent reach, 112 GRPs, and a 4.3 average frequency. Remember that in this example all the publications will have a 7 percent coverage of the market. So, the 16 insertions multiplied by a 7 percent coverage equals 112 GRPs.

You read the 12 percent magazine coverage set just like the 7 percent coverage set. In this case, using our same schedule of four publications with four insertions per publication, the corresponding delivery information would be 36 percent reach, 192 GRPs, and a 5.3 average frequency.

A key item we learn from Table 27.2 is the difference between adding a new publication to a schedule and adding another insertion to the same publication. Take a look again at the 7 percent publication: two insertions in this one magazine produce a reach of 9 percent; yet one insertion in two magazines with 7 percent coverage produces a reach of 10 percent. This gap is more magnified with eight insertions in one publication versus a single insertion in eight different publications. The difference in this example, still using the 7 percent coverage publication, is 14 percent compared with 25 percent. In both of these examples the GRPs would be the same.

This table is similar to the multimedia duplication chart we discussed earlier. Just review the two dimensions on the earlier chart: the number of publications and the number of insertions per publication. These two factors will lead you to understand the meaning behind the numbers.

Table 27.2

Magazine Reach and Frequency

Number of publications		Number of issues per magazine[a]							Number of issues per magazine[b]						
		1	2	3	4	6	8	12	1	2	3	4	6	8	12
1	Reach, %	7	9	10	11	13	14	16	12	15	18	20	22	24	26
	GRPs, %	7	14	21	28	42	56	84	12	24	36	48	72	96	144
	Frequency	1.0	1.6	2.1	2.5	3.2	4.0	5.3	1.0	1.6	2.0	2.4	3.3	4.0	5.5
2	Reach, %	10	14	16	18	20	22	24	17	20	24	27	30	32	34
	GRPs, %	14	28	42	56	84	112	168	24	48	72	96	144	192	288
	Frequency	1.4	2.0	2.6	3.1	4.2	5.1	7.0	1.4	2.4	3.0	3.6	4.8	6.0	8.5
3	Reach, %	13	17	19	21	23	25	27	22	26	30	34	38	41	43
	GRPs, %	21	42	63	84	126	168	252	36	72	108	144	216	288	432
	Frequency	1.6	2.5	3.3	4.0	5.5	6.7	9.3	1.6	2.8	3.6	4.2	5.7	7.0	10.0
4	Reach, %	16	20	23	26	28	30	32	27	30	33	36	40	43	46
	GRPs, %	28	56	84	112	168	224	336	48	96	144	192	288	384	576
	Frequency	1.8	2.8	3.7	4.3	6.0	7.5	10.5	1.8	3.2	4.4	5.3	7.2	8.9	12.5
5	Reach, %	18	23	26	30	32	34	36	31	34	37	40	43	46	49
	GRPs, %	35	70	105	140	210	280	420	60	120	180	240	360	480	720
	Frequency	1.9	3.0	4.0	4.7	6.6	8.2	11.7	1.9	3.5	4.9	6.0	8.4	10.4	14.7
6	Reach, %	21	25	29	33	36	39	41	35	38	41	44	47	50	53
	GRPs, %	42	84	126	168	252	336	504	72	144	216	288	432	576	864
	Frequency	2.0	3.4	4.3	5.1	7.0	8.6	12.3	2.1	3.8	5.3	6.5	9.2	11.5	16.3
8	Reach, %	25	29	33	37	41	44	47	40	43	46	49	52	55	58
	GRPs, %	56	112	168	224	336	448	672	96	192	288	384	576	768	1,152
	Frequency	2.2	3.9	5.1	6.1	8.2	10.2	14.3	2.4	4.5	6.3	7.8	11.1	14.0	19.9

Notes: Average target coverage: [a]7 percent per publication; [b]12 percent per publication.

Unit 27 Exercises
Working with Print Media Estimates

Use the tables in this unit to answer the following questions:

1. You are advertising in a newspaper that achieves 35 percent coverage of its market.

   a. What percentage of the households would you reach with five advertising insertions?

   b. What frequency level would you achieve with those same five advertising insertions?

2. You are running 10 advertisements in a newspaper that has 40 percent coverage of its market.

   a. What reach will you achieve?

b. Is it percentage reach or numerical reach?

c. What frequency level will you achieve?

d. Your market has 925,000 people in it. How many can you expect to reach with your newspaper advertising?

3. You are advertising in a newspaper that achieves 45 percent coverage of its market.

a. How many advertising insertions would be required to reach 80 percent of the market's households?

b. How many insertions would be required to reach your audience an average of seven times?

4. You are advertising in (a) magazine(s) having 7 percent circulation of U.S. households.

    a. What percentage of the audience will you reach with advertising insertions in four issues of one magazine?

    b. What percentage of the audience will you reach with advertising insertions in eight issues of each of three magazines?

    c. What will be the average frequency achieved by six insertions per magazine in six different publications?

    d. How many GRPs will you achieve with two insertions in each of five magazines?

5. You are advertising in (a) magazine(s) having 12 percent circulation of U.S. households.

    a. How many magazines and how many advertisements per magazine would be required to achieve a 1,000 GRP level?

b. What is one combination of magazines and advertisements per magazine that would achieve a reach of 50 percent?

c. What is another combination of magazines and advertisements per magazine that would also achieve a reach of 50 percent?

d. If there are 90,000,000 households in the United States, how many will you reach with your advertising?

6. Use the 7 percent publication chart for this problem.

a. What is the reach for advertising eight times in a single magazine?

b. What is the reach for advertising only once in each of eight different magazines?

c. Why is there a difference in these two reach figures?

7. Use the 12 percent publication chart for this exercise.

   a. What is the GRP level for advertising eight times in a single magazine?

   b. What is the GRP level for advertising only once in each of eight different magazines?

   c. Please explain your results.

Unit 28
Working with Print Media Costs

Some advertising media make use of *contracts*. Contracts are most common in print media, especially for advertising in newspapers.

An advertising contract is not a legally binding document. Instead, it is a statement of intent, agreed to by both the advertiser and the media vehicle, indicating how much advertising that advertiser is expected to use in that particular media outlet.

A contract is a "good faith" estimate by both parties, and it helps both parties. For the advertiser, a contract encourages planned advertising and permits the advertiser to begin buying advertising at a discounted rate. For the advertising medium, such as a newspaper, the contract permits planning, such as ordering newsprint paper, and also makes the selling job easier, because the newspaper knows in advance which advertisers will want to place advertisements on which days.

Advertising Rates

The cost of advertising is called the *advertising rate*. In print media, a *flat rate* indicates that no discounts are available; no matter how much advertising you use or how often you advertise, you will pay the same flat rate.

An *open rate* indicates that discounts are available. The open rate is not yet a discounted rate; it is the highest advertising rate you will pay before you begin earning a discount. The term "open rate" means that you may be able to qualify for a discounted advertising rate.

Discounts

To understand contracts, it is necessary to understand *discounts*. Generally, there are two kinds of discounts, which are reductions in the cost of advertising. A *quantity discount* is a reduced advertising rate for buying more advertising. A *frequency discount* is a reduced advertising rate for advertising more often, usually on a regular basis. Each media vehicle sets its own rules, but in general, the advertiser may earn either a quantity or a frequency discount, but not both; that is, an advertiser who qualifies for both kinds of discounts is entitled to the better (i.e., the larger) of the two discounts but cannot apply both discounts to reduce the cost of advertising. Of course, there are some advertising vehicles that may permit an advertiser to combine discounts, but the general rule is that the advertiser gets the better of the two kinds of discounts, not both.

Rebates and Short Rates

If an advertiser fails to use as much advertising as was contracted, the advertiser might not qualify for the discounted rate; in that case, the advertiser would pay the difference between the discounted rate and the higher rate, which is called a *short rate*. Similarly, if an advertiser uses more advertising than was contracted and thus earns a better (lower) advertising rate, the advertiser may earn a credit for the difference between the rate paid so far and the rate earned, which is called a *rebate*.

One example of advertising rates can be found in the newspaper medium. The *column-inch rate* is the price (or advertising rate) for each column-inch of advertising space that is purchased.

No. of column-inches used per year	Advertising rate per column-inch
0–49,999	$10.00
50,000–99,999	9.50
100,000–149,999	9.00
150,000–199,999	8.50
200,000–249,999	8.00
250,0000 and more	7.50

Say that a local store chain plans to use 140,000 column-inches of advertising during the coming year, so it signs a contract to pay at the corresponding advertising rate, which would be $9.00 per column-inch of space. By the end of the year, the advertiser actually used 160,000 column-inches of advertising space, so it should have been paying $8.50 per column-inch. So you take the space actually used (160,000) and multiply the rate differential of $0.50 per column-inch ($9.00 contract rate less the $8.50 earned rate).

$$\begin{array}{ll} 160,000 & \text{column-inches used} \\ \underline{\times\ \$0.50} & \text{rate differential} \\ \$80,000 & \end{array}$$

And because the advertiser has been paying a higher rate than actually earned, the advertiser would receive a rebate—money paid by the advertising medium back to the advertiser because the advertiser earned a lower advertising rate than the one contracted.

Similarly, if the advertiser had that same contract of 140,000 column-inches at $9.00 per column-inch, and the advertiser actually used only 95,000 column-inches, there would be a short rate of $47,500.

$$\begin{array}{ll} 95,000 & \text{column-inches used} \\ \underline{\times\ \$0.50} & \text{rate differential} \\ \$47,500 & \end{array}$$

Note that the rebate or short rate is based on the amount of advertising actually used, not on the amount contracted. Once the contract is set, it determines the advertising rate being charged, but the advertiser actually owes for the space used, not for the space contracted.

Sometimes print media appear to be a stepchild to broadcast media. Yet, throughout the introduction of radio, television, cable, and now the Internet, print media have continued to thrive. In fact, as content-rich media, print media have many times actually expanded their own franchises into other media forms.

Over time, there have been changes in the way that print media are bought and sold. Print media, historically, produced an annual rate card that offered the various methods and rates for purchasing each vehicle. Today, most media planners and buyers request formal proposals from the print media that require the print media to develop very tailored media packages to large print buyers. The rate card is still around, but it serves more as a benchmark for rates as opposed to the firm source of costs.

Standard Rates and Data Services (SRDS) is the research tool used by many media planners and buyers as a quick compendium for print rate cards and audit statements. SRDS provides monthly updates of print media costs and, being an online tool, it is quite easy to compile newspaper or magazine lists. It is certainly a timesaver compared with gathering information from each publication's website.

Like broadcast, there are factors that impact the media cost of print. The first factor is the creative unit itself. The larger the unit, the more it costs. Color ads cost more than black-and-white ads. Basically, the more space and the more complicated the production of the ad, the more it will cost. So, adding a response card to a magazine ad or developing an insert will cost more than a standard page unit.

With the increased sophistication of printing, there are now a myriad of ways to deliver one's message. Newspapers routinely produce zoned editions that allow advertisers to purchase only the circulation in a certain area of town. Magazines can segment their message by a number of factors based on subscriber information. Many publications can separate homeowners from renters or Democrats from Republicans. Some publications literally send out hundreds of segmented versions of the same publication based on various subscriber profiles. One of the forerunners of this type of customization was *Progressive Farmer* magazine. They published different versions of the publication depending upon the crop that the farmer was growing.

One other factor in finalizing print rates is the amount of advertising you do with a given publication. The basis for most print rate discounts is the frequency of the number of ads placed within the publication. Higher levels of frequency lead to higher dollar amounts spent with the publication and impact the unit rates charged. For example, many magazine rate cards offer three times (3x), six times (6x), and twelve times (12x) rate breaks for advertisers who run that many pages in their publication. Newspapers often offer similar rate breaks, or they may just offer specific dollar thresholds that constitute specific rate levels.

The last factor—timing—is more related to newspapers than magazines. A Sunday ad in the newspaper typically costs more than a weekday ad because there are more subscribers to the Sunday newspaper than to a weekday newspaper. Some magazines that rely heavily on newsstand sales vary their costs based on historical circulation swings. Many women's magazines have stronger newsstand circulation sales near the Thanksgiving and Christmas season. Subsequently, they charge more for these issues than for issues during a slower period in the summer.

Table 28.1

Newspaper Advertising

Newspaper	Total circulation		Full-page measure-ments	Cost per column-inch gross		Total full-page BW gross cost	
	Daily	Sunday		Daily	Sunday	Daily	Sunday
New York Times	2,179,869	1,672,965	6cX21"	$965	$1,051	$121,590	$132,426
Chicago Tribune	1,764,152	1,002,166	6cX21"	$547	$801	$68,922	$100,926
Atlanta Journal-Constitution	228,146	92,359	6cX21"	$422	$545	$53,172	$68,670
Columbus Dispatch	252,564	368,334	6cX21"	$135	$211	$17,010	$26,586
Cincinnati Enquirer Post	465,852	306,093	6cX21"	$263	$275	$33,138	$34,650
Plain Dealer (Cleveland)	365,288	485,543	6cX21"	$263	$351	$33,138	$44,226
Philadelphia Daily News	926,122	768,237	6cX21"	$511	$695	$64,386	$87,570
Charlotte Observer	226,849	283,339	6cX21"	$188	$195	$23,688	$24,570
St. Louis Post-Dispatch	285,869	459,220	6cX21"	$299	$394	$37,674	$49,644
San Francisco Chronicle	1,019,909	561,118	6cX21"	$459	$479	$57,834	$60,354
Rocky Mtn. New/Denver Post	899,919	785,671	6cX21"	$477	$632	$60,102	$79,632
Kansas City Star	267,273	377,094	6cX21"	$379	$414	$47,754	$52,164
Miami Herald	304,795	419,667	6cX21"	$372	$452	$46,872	$56,952
Orlando Sentinel	266,770	319,145	6cX21"	$249	$365	$31,374	$45,990

Take a look at an example of newspaper costs (see Table 28.1). Newspapers charge a column-inch rate that is based on the dimensions of the newspaper. The majority of newspapers have standardized their dimensions to make advertising across multiple markets more economical for large advertisers. In Table 28.1, all the newspapers are 6 columns wide by 21 inches deep. This gives them a total page size of 126 column-inches.

In this example, the rates are quoted as gross, so they include a 15 percent agency commission. Most newspaper rates are quoted as net, so if you are a media planner at an advertising agency, it is important to note if the rates are net or gross. Also, in this case, the advertiser is working on a 6x rate discount, which is factored into the individual column-inch rates.

As you can see from the example, certain markets are much more expensive on Sunday relative to their weekday costs than others. This reflects both circulation strength and the premium price that a Sunday newspaper commands.

Unlike newspapers, magazines quote their rates by advertising sizes and not by column-inches. Magazines establish standard rates for full-page ads, two-thirds-page ads, half-page ads, and so on. There are different rates for color ads versus black-and-white, as well.

In Table 28.2, we have consumer magazines by selective editorial categories. There are times when a media planner will select magazines that complement each other from an editorial perspective. For example, you may want to mix in an epicurean publication with a women's service publication if you are marketing a food product.

The other aspects of the example are the frequency of the publication, which can range from six times per year to every week, as well as the issue circulation and the advertising rates. In this example, we have costs for full-page and half-page ad units. All units are quoted using four-color process, and the rates are gross. This example also reflects different frequency levels showing a single-time rate and a three-times rate.

You can begin to see the magnitude in differences in publication circulation and costs from this example. You have a niche publication such as *Food and Wine* that has a circulation of 900,000 and then huge publications such as *Parade* that has a circulation of 34 million. As a media planner, it is your role to evaluate each publication's strength and how it might fit into a schedule.

Table 28.2

Magazine Advertising

Category/publication	Yearly freq.	Circulation	1X 4C gross rate		3X 4C gross rate	
			Full page	1/2 page	Full page	1/2 page
Epicurean						
Bon Appétit	12X	1,302,311	$79,645	$47,780	$77,256	$46,347
Cooking Light	11X	1,617,193	76,400	43,340	73,344	41,606*
Cooking Pleasures	24X	571,967	30,530	19,845	29,614	19,250
Food & Wine	12X	900,000	60,105	33,090	57,705	31,765
Gourmet	12X	985,165	72,185	46,885	69,298	45,010*
Health						
Fitness	12X	1,384,067	109,500	66,800	105,120	64,128*
Health	10X	1,389,350	77,000	48,510	73,750	46,085
Prevention	12X	3,277,746	105,900	60,900	101,664	58,464*
Self	12X	1,347,650	87,785	59,225	85,151	57,477
Shape	12X	1,635,266	95,215	60,765	92,840	59,240
Women's service						
Better Homes & Gardens	12X	7,611,005	320,400	208,700	307,584	200,352*
Family Circle	15X	4,585,685	230,110	139,565	220,906	133,982*
Good Housekeeping	12X	4,603,989	255,025	155,570	244,824	149,347*
Ladies' Home Journal	12X	4,100,068	189,500	113,700	181,920	109,152*
O Oprah	12X	2,532,621	129,000	83,870	125,130	81,354
Real Simple	10X	1,375,355	105,700	68,700	101,472	65,952*
Redbook	12X	2,371,371	110,200	66,100	105,792	63,456*
Southern Living	13X	2,600,732	124,000	70,300	119,040	67,488*
Sunset	12X	1,429,656	74,300	44,910	71,328	43,114*
Woman's Day	17X	4,065,406	200,120	123,010	192,115	118,090*
Ethnic						
Ebony	12X	1,884,533	57,934	38,802	56,775	38,026
Essence	12X	1,068,214	57,930	34,745	55,613	33,355*
Jet	6X	912,061	23,588	17,688	22,644	16,980*
Latina	12X	263,165	19,500	12,670	18,720	12,163*
People en Espanol	11X	400,000	40,500	17,701	38,880	16,993*
Ser Padres	6X	510,000	39,500	23,800	37,920	22,848*
Parenting						
Child	10X	1,035,505	71,895	46,810	69,019	44,938*
Family Fun	10X	1,769,003	104,825	62,900	102,730	61,640
Parenting	11X	2,207,543	122,100	81,805	117,216	78,533*
Parents	12X	2,232,793	117,100	70,200	112,416	67,392*
General interest						
Parade	52X	34,286,728	794,000	452,700	762,240	434,592*
Reader's Digest	12X	11,090,349	221,600	133,000	212,736	127,680*
Entertainment Weekly	52X	1,725,053	103,060	66,990	98,938	64,310*
People	52X	3,628,982	171,000	116,000	164,160	111,360*

Source: SRDS.

Note: *Rate card discounts of 3–5 percent, average 4 percent, for nonpublished 3x levels (actual negotiations typically 20 percent off published rates).

Unit 28 Exercises
Working with Print Media Costs

1. A local newspaper distributes this list of advertising rates on its rate card:

No. of column-inches	Advertising rate per column-inch
0–35,000	$2.00
35,001–70,000	1.90
70,001–100,000	1.75
100,001–150,000	1.65
More than 150,000	1.50

   A retail advertiser contracted for 100,000 column-inches of advertising space during the past year. At the end of the year, the retailer had purchased 110,000 column-inches of space in that newspaper. Did the retailer earn the contract—or a rebate, or a short rate—and if so, how much? Please show any calculations you make. Clearly indicate your answer.

2. Using the figures from question 1, what if the advertiser actually had used 68,000 column-inches of advertising during the year? Did the retailer earn the contract (or a rebate or a short rate) and if so, how much? Again, please show your calculations and clearly indicate your answer.

3. Using the same figures once more, what if the advertiser actually had used 90,000 column-inches of advertising during the year? Did the retailer earn the contract, rebate, or short rate, and if so, how much? Again, please show any calculations you make and clearly indicate your answer.

4. A local newspaper distributes this list of advertising rates on its rate card:

No. of column-inches	Advertising rate per column-inch
0–35,000	$2.00
35,001–75,000	1.90
75,001–115,000	1.75
115,001–175,000	1.65
More than 175,000	1.50

A retailer contracted for 100,000 column-inches of advertising space in one year. At the end of the year, the retailer had purchased 90,000 column-inches of advertising. Did the retailer earn the contract—or a rebate, or a short rate, and if so, how much?

5. At the end of the year, the retailer from question 4 had purchased 71,000 column-inches of advertising. Did the retailer earn the contract—or a rebate, or a short rate, and if so, how much?

6. At the end of the year, the same retailer had purchased 120,000 column-inches of advertising. Did the retailer earn the contract—or a rebate, or a short rate, and if so, how much?

7. At the end of the year, the same retailer had purchased 80,000 column-inches of advertising. Did the retailer earn the contract—or a rebate, or a short rate, and if so, how much?

8. Estimate the cost of a 3-column by 8-inch newspaper advertisement in the *Chicago Tribune*. Show your calculations.

9. Estimate the cost of ten insertions in the *Columbus Dispatch* if each advertisement is 13 inches high by 4 columns wide. Show your calculations.

10. Estimate the cost for a year of a weekly full-page insertion in the Sunday editions of the *Orlando Sentinel*. Show your calculations.

11. How many 26 column-inch insertions in the *St. Louis Post-Dispatch* could you afford on a budget of $100,000? Show your calculations.

12. You have an advertising budget of $850,000 and you want to buy equal amounts of advertising space in each of three newspapers: the *Miami Herald,* the *Kansas City Star,* and the *Charlotte Observer.* How much money would you spend in each of the three newspapers? Show your calculations.

13. You are buying six full-page, four-color (4/c) advertisements this year in *Family Circle.* Estimate the total costs. Show your calculations.

14. Estimate the total cost of a 1/2-page, 4/c advertisement to run in each of the five magazines listed in the Epicurean category. Show your calculations.

15. If you have a budget of $500,000 that you can spend on advertising in *Real Simple* this year, how many 1/2-page, 4/c advertisements could you afford to purchase? Show your calculations.

16. If the black-and-white (b&w) advertising rates for *Fitness* magazine are 65 percent of the cost of 4/c advertisements, how many b&w full-page advertisements could you afford in *Fitness* on a budget of $450,000? Show your calculations.

Unit 29

Working with Print Negotiations

Print negotiation is in an evolution. Twenty years ago, media negotiation was largely reserved for broadcast. Print was purchased based on a published rate card. While there were off-rate card deals, print had an aura of limited negotiation. All of that has changed. Print is now highly negotiable. Just like broadcast, large media agencies and advertisers employ print negotiation specialists to deal with this aspect of the media world.

Print negotiation is very different between consumer magazines, trade magazines, and newspapers. In magazine negotiation, each publication is fighting to be on the advertiser's schedule. There are big winners and equally as big losers. In newspaper negotiation, the fight is more how much you can get from the newspaper since most cities now have one dominant daily newspaper. The fundamentals of print buying are basically the same. For the purpose of this unit, we will focus on purchasing consumer magazines.

Negotiation Process

The negotiation process begins with a request for proposal (RFP) from the print negotiator to the publications that the media planning team has selected to be a part of the consideration set. The RFP is a memo to the respective media publications that details the parameters of the campaign.

This includes requests for packages of specific numbers of insertions, the creative unit, the brand goals, and guidelines for value-added support. Based on the input received, the publications will develop packages.

In some cases, the negotiation team will also incorporate or consolidate packages. For example, if the media purchase is weighted toward news and sports publications, then Time, Inc., which owns *Time* magazine and *Sports Illustrated* among others, may be asked to develop a joint package between the two or more publications that fit the buying parameters within their overall publishing empire.

Similar to broadcast negotiation, the publications submit a first round of packages to the print negotiator for review. Table 29.1 shows a basic comparison of two publications being evaluated for a premium-priced package food brand. At this point in the negotiation process,

227

Table 29.1

Working with Print Negotiations

Item	Epicurean	Good Housekeeping
# issues per year	10	12
Full-page 4/c unit lost rate card	$77,000	$315,430
Negotiated rate	$73,920	$147,060
% discount from rate card	4%	53%
Circulation rate base	1,000,000	4,600,000
Circulation CPM	$73.92	$31.97
Brand usage index	220	120
Brand audience	900,000	2,020,000
Brand CPM	$82.13	$72.80
Added value	Placement in 200,000 books	Placement adjacent food editorial
	Advertorial 2x year inside front cover placement	Eligible for Good Housekeeping Seal
Cross platform	Website and iPad app sponsorship	
	Sponsor of cable show to be developed	

the negotiator will counsel each publication on where they stand in the process. Then the negotiator will request a final round of packages.

The majority of print negotiations are done on an annual basis. Rates are then locked in for the year. Because negotiations impact a full year and can be a significant amount of dollars, print negotiations can take months to complete. The outcome of print negotiations is a signed contract between the print publication and the advertiser which details the agreed-upon purchase parameters.

Components of Negotiation

The negotiation process for print is highly detailed. Since it ends in a legally binding document, it is crucial for the print negotiator to be very specific in each area of the negotiation. While all negotiations are unique, the following are the key components of a typical consumer magazine negotiation.

Unit Cost

The fundamental part of negotiation in print is the actual unit cost. An example of this would be the cost of a full-page four-color ad unit. Negotiators will review unit costs in comparison with the published rate card or will compare the cost to the prior year. Both of these items will be used as benchmarks for where costs are and where they can be negotiated.

Circulation Guarantee

Publications have independent auditing companies review and verify their circulation. The Audit Bureau of Circulation, or ABC, is the largest independent auditor of magazines and newspapers. Print negotiators will review the ABC statement of a publication and negotiate a specific circulation level to be achieved. If that circulation level isn't met by the publication, the negotiator will request additional insertions to make up for the deficit.

Brand Audience

The media planning team and the print negotiator will review syndicated research to understand how the magazine's audience matches with the brand's audience. MRI is the most used syndicated research service for magazines. A negotiator will use MRI data to determine if one publication is more targeted than another and to establish an overall audience base for negotiation.

CPM

Print negotiators use a combination of CPM analysis for reviewing the respective cost efficiencies of the publications. The first base for CPM is circulation. One CPM analysis, then, is taking the unit cost of each publication and comparing it with the circulation to derive a CPM. A second analysis uses syndicated research as the base. In this case, the unit cost is compared with brand audience or other criteria such as responsiveness to advertising, category usage, or other qualitative dimensions. Print negotiators then may develop a system to weigh these variables.

Position

Where the advertisement is placed in the publication is also subject to negotiation. There are premium positions in every publication, for example, the back cover or the inside front cover. They also command a premium price because they are better read than other positions in the publication.

Positioning for premium positions or adjacent to specific editorial is based on how much you spend in a given publication.

Added Value

Just like broadcast negotiations, a big component of print negotiations is added value. This is the additional items above and beyond the paid advertising in the publication. The following are examples of added-value elements.

- *Bonus distribution.* Free exposure is obtained either through extra copies of the publication being distributed outside of the subscription base or by publishing additional issues.
- *Sponsorships.* A publication may develop a specific event or may simply have an event that can be sponsored. For example, *Southern Living* magazine has a

cooking school that travels to a variety of cities and is sponsored by various food manufacturers.

- *Promotional contests.* A brand develops and sponsors, and may be a part of, a contest for the subscribers of a publication.
- *Advertorial support.* A publication develops an editorial concept that is written with the advertiser in mind. For example, a travel section on Mexico may feature specific hotels within the context of the article.
- *Product mentions.* The brand may be featured in recipes or other normal editorial content.

This is not an all-inclusive list, but it does offer examples of what is negotiated in the consumer magazine area.

Cross Platform

Just like other media, print is rapidly developing other ways for consumers to see their content. This can be in digital form such as websites, audio or video podcasts, and iPad or other e-reader devices. With these additional venues publications can add more reach to their buy. It becomes a negotiation point in the buying process.

Summary

Print negotiation is another highly specialized media activity. Negotiators specialize in a specific medium such as consumer magazines or newspapers. It is a detailed process and results in a contractual obligation. As a result, negotiations are highly scrutinized by senior management of the advertiser. As with all media negotiations, negotiators want to get the most they can for the brand within the budget.

Unit 29 Exercises
Working with Print Negotiations

1. What are the components of print negotiation?

2. Why does print negotiation have such a high profile in a company?

3. Besides Time, Inc., what are other examples of companies that own more than one publication? What is the advantage or disadvantage of negotiating with such a company?

4. In Table 29.1, what is the most cost efficient publication?

5. In which of the two publications in Table 29.1 is the audience composition for the brand higher?

6. In Table 29.1, which of the two publications appears to offer more in the way of extra items for the brand?

7. Based on the information in Table 29.1, put together rationales for why you should select *Epicurean* over *Good Housekeeping* and why you should select *Good Housekeeping* over *Epicurean*. After completing the rationale for each, which one would you select and why?

Part VI
Out-of-Home Media

Unit 30

Working with Out-of-Home Media

While broadcast and print are the traditional mainstays of an advertiser's media plans, there is a growing array of alternative choices for consideration. Out-of-home media is the oldest medium around, yet it has seen an explosion of alternatives. On the other hand, the Internet is a relatively new medium that is still being defined in the marketplace.

Out-of-home media encompasses a wide range of media choices that include outdoor bulletins and posters, transit advertising on buses and cabs, and many other forms of media. Much of this alternative media is called *place-based media*. This means that you are trying to get your message across to your audience at a place where they congregate or at a place that is relevant to them. For example, you can purchase signs called dioramas at most major airports or run ads on airport televisions that carry CNN news and are stationed at the departure gates. So, for a travel advertiser, this type of media exposure would make a lot of sense. Other place-based media run the gamut from ads placed above men's urinals in the bathroom to logos created in the sand at major beaches. Anything is fair game these days as a part of the out-of-home media landscape.

Regardless of the medium, the basics of its delivery remain relatively the same. Out-of-home media are measured using some form of traffic count. In outdoor posters and bulletins, the term *daily effective circulation* (or DEC) is the average number of people 18 and over who are exposed to the advertising on a daily basis. Outdoor companies get this information audited by a third-party research company and then use the information to construct reach and frequency estimates.

Outdoor has moved from selling a showing to selling gross rating points (GRPs) like other media. A *showing* is the percentage of the market reached each day. For example, a 100 showing includes the number of posters or bulletins necessary to reach 100 percent of the daily traffic in the market. Now outdoor companies sell by monthly GRPs. So, a 100 GRP level would be enough outdoor posters or bulletins to generate 100 GRPs on a daily basis. This is very close to the reach level of 100 percent of the market but allows the outdoor company and advertiser to adjust the buy to include a greater degree of frequency in their purchase.

Table 30.1 is a delivery chart for a standard outdoor company using outdoor posters. Across the top are the GRP levels. Under each GRP level are the corresponding reach and average frequency estimates.

Outdoor poster and bulletin companies offer advertisers sophisticated software tools to map their consumers in order to develop targeted outdoor programs. As you move into the

Table 30.1

Outdoor Posters Reach and Frequency

Demographics	25 GRPs		50 GRPs		100 GRPs	
	Reach	Avg. freq.	Reach	Avg. freq.	Reach	Avg. freq.
Ages 18–24						
Adults	80.4	8.7	87.0	15.9	91.6	30.2
Men	81.2	9.5	86.0	17.7	90.6	33.5
Women	79.5	7.9	88.1	14.2	92.5	27.0
Ages 25–34						
Adults	81.7	8.4	88.1	15.6	92.0	29.8
Men	82.4	9.5	88.6	17.7	92.2	34.0
Women	80.9	7.3	87.5	13.5	91.8	25.6
Ages 35–44						
Adults	73.9	7.0	81.1	12.8	86.1	24.1
Men	74.7	8.0	81.2	14.8	84.6	28.3
Women	73.0	6.0	81.0	10.8	87.6	20.0
Ages 45–54						
Adults	73.1	6.7	81.0	12.1	86.8	22.5
Men	72.8	8.3	79.3	15.2	86.2	28.0
Women	73.4	5.2	82.6	9.2	87.3	17.3
Ages 55–64						
Adults	65.5	6.4	75.9	11.0	82.7	20.1
Men	65.7	6.6	74.3	14.3	80.1	26.5
Women	65.2	4.6	77.5	8.0	85.1	14.5
Age 65+						
Adults	64.3	5.3	73.3	9.3	80.6	16.9
Men	59.4	6.6	70.0	11.1	76.2	20.4
Women	67.6	4.6	75.4	8.2	83.5	14.7

Source: Telmar.

Note: Estimates based on 28 days using daily GRP levels.

place-based advertising world, the research tools become less precise and more judgmental. However, that being said, most out-of-home media companies strive to provide some form of circulation measures that can be used by media planners to calculate some form of delivery.

Outdoor posters are sold in groups called showings or as single billboards. Regardless of how they are sold, outdoor costs are based on unit costs.

Out-of-home media can take many forms. Billboards, buses, taxis, and subway stations are all forms of out-of-home media. We are going to focus on the outdoor billboard industry as our cost example. Outdoor is sold in a variety of ways. The largest standard format for all outdoor media is called a bulletin. The most common size bulletin is 14 feet high by 48 feet wide. Posters are also available, and they come in two sizes. The most common is called a 30-sheet poster. A 30-sheet ad panel has a copy area measuring 9.5 feet high by approximately 21.5 feet wide. These posters are typically found on surface roads, while bulletins or 14×48 units are generally on the major freeways and four-lane roads. There are also 8-sheet posters, which are often used in high urban foot traffic areas. These are much smaller units than a 30-sheet poster or a bulletin, with a copy area measuring just 5 feet high by 11 feet wide.

If you were to purchase a bulletin outside your retail establishment, you would pay a monthly leasing fee to put your message on it. If you purchase a 25 GRP poster schedule, you would pay a monthly fee to have your message on a number of posters. If you decide to purchase a variety of bulletins that move to different locations every two or three months to allow you to gain broad market coverage, you are using a *rotary program.* Such programs are sold in GRP increments just like posters. Outdoor costs are usually based on a monthly cost. Many outdoor programs require annual contracts.

Unit 30 Exercises
Working with Out-of-Home Media

Use the reach and frequency chart found in this unit (Table 30.1) to answer the following questions:

1. For an outdoor advertising campaign aimed at women ages 18–24, you are buying 25 GRPs.

   a. Calculate the total number of GRPs gained per showing period. Show your calculations.

   b. Calculate the actual number of GRPs per day achieved by this campaign. Show your calculations.

   c. Compare your answer to question 1b (the previous question) with the anticipated GRP level (25 GRP). Are they the same, and if not, why might there be a discrepancy?

2. Now you are placing outdoor advertising aimed at adults ages 35–44.

    a. What percentage reach would you expect from a showing at the 75 GRP level? Show your calculations.

    b. What would be the average frequency of this outdoor buy? Show your calculations.

    c. What is the actual GRP level per day? Show your calculations.

    d. Referring to question 2c above, what would be the GRP level per day that you would expect?

    e. Are the actual GRP level and the anticipated GRP level the same? If not, by how much are they different? Keep in mind that small discrepancies and "rounding errors" may be acceptable for the purpose of estimating.

Unit 31
Working with Out-of-Home Media Costs

Out-of-home media is the fastest growing medium next to the Internet. Out-of-home media has been changing rapidly in the past years in both type and creative possibilities.

When you typically think of out-of-home media, you think of billboards. Billboards are one of the oldest forms of media. Even this rather staid medium is being changed with new digital ads that turn a static billboard into a giant television screen. The digital revolution is changing what is possible with out-of-home. That coupled with mobile media has put out-of-home media on the radar screen of most media plans.

Out-of-home media comes in many forms. There are billboards, buses, taxis, subway stations, buildings, elevators, pump toppers, and a myriad of other media forms. While each medium has its unique aspects, the fundamental way in which it is priced and sold is fairly much the same. For purposes of this unit we are going to focus on the outdoor billboard industry as our cost example. The following are the components of the cost.

Type and Creative Unit

There are a variety of outdoor types and sizes. The largest standard format for outdoor billboards is a bulletin. The most common size is 14 feet high by 48 feet wide. These are typically seen on freeways and major highways. The next size is posters. Posters come in two sizes. The most common is called a 30-sheet poster. A 30-sheet advertising panel has a copy area measuring 9 feet high by 21 feet wide. These are typically found on surface roads. The second type of poster is an 8-sheet poster. The surface area for the creative unit is 5 feet high by 11 feet wide. Eight-sheet posters are sometimes called pedestrian posters since they are found in urban areas with heavy foot traffic. Each of these types of outdoor billboard has different rate structures.

Coverage

The key component to outdoor cost is the coverage of the outdoor program. Billboards are sold in a number of ways. You can purchase a single billboard that may be used as a directional sign for a retail establishment. This type of purchase is contracted for on an annual basis or

Table 31.1

Working with Out-of-Home Media Costs: Outdoor Costs

| Market | 30 Sheet | | | 14 × 48 Bulletins | |
	GRP schedule	# of units	Est. cost ($)	Avg. unit cost ($)	Avg. DEC (000)
Chicago	100	632	384,907	6,630	36.7
	75	474	289,747		
	50	316	199,494		
	25	158	106,122		
Dallas/Fort Worth	100	190	128,250	3,179	75.3
	75	143	101,530		
	50	95	67,450		
	25	48	34,080		
Detroit	100	167	198,864	5,085	65.4
	75	125	148,850		
	50	83	98,837		
	25	42	50,014		
Houston/Galveston	100	172	113,520	3,139	91.3
	75	129	87,720		
	50	86	18,080		
	25	43	29,670		
Los Angeles	100	532	485,360	6,919	55.8
	75	399	373,117		
	50	266	248,745		
	25	133	124,372		
Philadelphia	100	292	224,566	5,441	68.9
	75	219	173,124		
	50	146	115,416		
	25	73	57,708		
San Francisco	100	261	230,152	8,500	60.3
	75	196	185,306		
	50	131	123,853		
	25	65	61,454		
Washington, DC	100	284	310,980	6,337	31.2
	75	213	238,560		
	50	142	163,300		
	25	71	83,425		

longer. The cost for this type of purchase is typically based on the number of cars that pass by the billboard. This is called the average daily effective circulation, or DEC. The other way you can purchase outdoor billboards is by different levels of coverage. The coverage historically has been called showings. The outdoor industry is now converting showings to GRPs to allow media planners to easily compare outdoor to other media. There is also a relatively new method for calculating GRPs called "eyes-on ratings." Eyes-on ratings is a method that offers a measure of actual people looking at the billboard compared with an estimate of car traffic. So, the GRP levels will be slightly different from the showing level. A showing is the number of billboards needed to reach a certain percentage of the mobile population. Table 31.1 provides an example of poster showings or GRPs for a number of markets. A 25 GRP or poster showing in Chicago requires 158 posters to be purchased. This showing means that 25 percent of the mobile population will potentially see the posters every day. Another way to purchase outdoor advertising is called a "rotary program." This is used for bulletins. The idea of a rotary program is to purchase three or four billboards that will rotate to new locations every three months thereby increasing the reach of the program. Rotary programs are also calculated on a showing and/or GRP basis.

Time Frame

The other variable in the cost for outdoor showings is the time frame. As we mentioned, buying a single unit requires a lease of at least a year and usually three years. Showings, on the other hand, can be purchased in 3-month increments. You can buy 3-, 6-, 9-, and 12-month showings. Some outdoor companies will deviate from this structure but historically that is how the industry has sold their inventory.

Market Size and Traffic

Table 31.1 shows the GRP schedule size, the average number of units that make up that schedule, and the cost. Next to the 30-sheet poster cost is an average unit cost for a 14 × 48 bulletin in these same markets. The average daily effective circulation, or DEC, is also provided.

As you can see, the larger the market, the higher the outdoor costs. Market size correlates with the potential traffic that goes by a billboard. There are a lot more drivers whizzing by billboards in Los Angeles than in the other markets shown in this example. There is a greater chance of reaching 25 percent of the mobile population in Los Angeles than there is in Detroit. And that is reflected in the greater costs.

Market Demand

The final aspect of cost is supply and demand. Just like any other medium, costs will vary widely by market depending on the supply and demand of advertising for that medium. In Table 31.1 there is an interesting example of this. Houston has a DEC level for bulletins that is 50 percent and greater than that for Los Angeles, yet the average cost for bulletins in Houston is less than half that of Los Angeles. This speaks to the greater demand in Los Angeles than in Houston for bulletins.

Outdoor Cost Resources

There are a number of websites that can be accessed to get detailed market cost information for the outdoor industry. The three largest sellers of outdoor billboards are Clear Channel, Lamar, and CBS Outdoor. Each of these companies has a website where you can obtain detailed market information. The outdoor advertising association trade group also provides links to these companies and other resources for cost information.

Unit 31 Exercises
Working with
Out-of-Home Media Costs

1. What is the definition of an outdoor showing?

2. What is the difference between bulletins, 30-sheet posters, and 8-sheet posters?

3. What is the cost of a 25 GRP showing in Philadelphia and Washington, DC?

4. How many 30-sheet posters would you buy to achieve a 75 GRP schedule in San Francisco?

5. How much would it cost to purchase a bulletin for a year in San Francisco?

Unit 32
Working with Out-of-Home Negotiation

Out-of-home negotiation is different from other media negotiation. One difference is that with outdoor advertising your choices are limited. (For example, you may want to purchase a specific media vehicle, such as a directional outdoor board for a retail location.) The second difference is that there are fewer companies to negotiate with. In fact, unlike other media, much of out-of-home media is concentrated in a single company. (As we discussed in Unit 31, three companies—Clear Channel, Lamar, and CBS Outdoor—control the bulk of out-of-home locations.) Out-of-home outcome includes transit, taxis, and most place-based media as well.

As a result, out-of-home negotiation is more about selecting the best package of locations than it is about negotiating with multiple vendors. In the top ten metro markets, there is more than one outdoor company so there is some competition, but in many markets there is only a single company.

Negotiation Process

Just like other media, the negotiation or selection process begins with a request for a proposal from the outdoor company. Based on the media planning parameters, the request is for cost, impressions, and locations that fit the target audience. Many outdoor companies utilize geo-demographic programs that map the brand's audience in conjunction with the outdoor locations. Depending upon the purchase requirements, the outdoor company can provide a detailed view of the possible target audience for each location.

Components of Negotiation

For the purpose of this unit, we are going to focus on 30-sheet outdoor posters. Table 32.1 shows two different packages for the evaluation. There are somewhat different criteria used to negotiate everything from elevator ads to mall displays to billboards, but the fundamentals remain the same. The following are the key components of negotiating outdoor billboards.

Table 32.1

30-Sheet Outdoor Package Comparison[a]

Item	Package A	Package B
Showing size	25	25
No. of panels	150	175
Cost per month	$75,000	$65,000
Cost per unit	$500	$371
Impressions	21,428,570	21,666,670
CPM	3.50	3.00
Location distribution[b]		
% A	20%	10%
% B	40%	30%
% C	30%	40%
% D	10%	20%

[a]Analysis of the visibility of outdoor locations.
[b]Key: A, Excellent; B, Good; C, Average; D, Poor

Costs

The first element is cost. Cost should be viewed as unit cost and package cost. You want to understand the cost per unit as well as the cost for the package. Many times media professionals compare these costs across markets and/or to last year's purchase as points of negotiation.

Audience

The other side of the equation is audience analysis, or how many people you reach. Most media professionals use impressions as a basis for coverage, and reach and frequency are also used. Brand delivery based on geo-demographic mapping as an alternative view of delivery is another method used by media professionals.

CPM

The CPM is based on a demographic target. This is typically used to assess the medium's CPM compared with alternative media choices. It is also a way to view alternative packages as in Table 32.1. Some media professionals will apply a brand CPM to packages.

Location

Location. Location. Location. That is the mantra of the real estate market and it is the same in out-of-home selection. There is a big difference in being able to see a billboard for just a few seconds compared with having it in your line of sight for 30 seconds. Media buyers develop location scales to help them determine whether one location is better than another.

Added Value

There is not as extensive an added-value component in out-of-home media as there is in other media. However, media professionals will request bonus distribution for billboards and assistance in merchandising the outdoor buy to an important stakeholder.

Summary

Out-of-home media is negotiable but only within the context of adding it to the media mix. Much of out-of-home has a single vendor so, when working with the medium, the challenge is to maximize the selection of the inventory.

Unit 32 Exercises
Working with Out-of-Home Negotiation

1. Why is out-of-home not as negotiable as other media?

2. What is the most important component of the selection process?

3. In Table 32.1, which package has the lowest CPM?

4. In Table 32.1, which package has the best locations?

5. Which package would you recommend to the client and why?

Part VII
Digital Media

Unit 33
Working with Online Display Media Estimates

Compared with media like newspapers, magazines, and radio, the Internet is a relatively new advertising medium. Because of the networked nature of online computers, the Internet has proven to be highly measurable. Advertisers can tell how many people look at their ad, which is called *clicking on*. Advertisers can also tell how many people read or engage their ad, which is called a *click through* since clicking on an ad takes a viewer to the brand's website. By monitoring these click rates, some advertisers can track the immediate *return on investment* (ROI) that their advertising is producing, that is, they can tell how much it costs to get one person who sees an online display ad to click through to their website.

There are nearly as many ways to advertise on the Internet as there are websites. Every day there is something new being tried in this medium. The most traditional advertising methods on the Internet are to schedule banners or pop-ups or streaming video that interrupt users as they "surf the net." Other approaches are to sponsor a website or collect e-mail addresses and send out "permission e-mail."

Table 33.1 offers an example of how reach and frequency are built using traditional methods for advertising on the Internet. The first schedule is a *wide dispersion schedule*. A widely dispersed schedule is a schedule in which impressions are focused on the top 100 websites based on total page views.

How do you determine the top websites? One way is to use a ranking website like Web 100 (www.web100.com) or Alexa (www.alexa.com/topsites). Advertising on some type of top 100 sites would generally include the large search engines such as Yahoo! and high traffic sites such as CNN, or a local site such as a local newspaper. All of these schedules would consist of banners on their respective front pages. So, a widely dispersed schedule is a high reach schedule for the Internet.

The second schedule is a *limited dispersion schedule,* which would be focused on specific websites. The limited dispersion schedule would be for a combination of sites beyond that top 100 that have low page views. For example, a limited dispersion schedule could be an academic department's pages on a university's .edu website. Or it could be literally hundreds of smaller sites or niche sites that would make up a low-reach schedule.

Table 33.1 shows weekly GRPs in the far left column. The body of the table shows wide dispersion and limited dispersion schedules, each of which covers one-week reach, four-week reach, and average frequency.

Table 33.1

Wide Dispersion versus Limited Dispersion

Weekly GRPs	Wide dispersion			Limited dispersion		
	1 week reach	4 week reach	Avg. freq.	1 week reach	4 week reach	Avg. freq.
10	5	6	6.7	2	2.25	17.8
25	6	10	10.0	3	3.25	30.8
50	10	12	16.7	3.5	3.75	53.3
75	13	14	21.4	4	4.25	70.6
100	14	15	26.7	4.5	4.75	84.2
150	15.5	15.5	38.7	5	5.25	114.3
200	15	16	50.0	5.5	5.75	139.1
250	15.5	16.5	60.6	5.75	6	166.7
300	16	17	70.6	6	6.25	192.0
350	16.5	17.5	80.0	6.25	6.5	215.4
400	17	18	88.9	6.5	6.75	237.0
450	17.5	18.5	97.3	6.75	7	257.1
500	18	19	105.3	7	7.25	275.9

Source: FKM Agency estimates.

Reviewing delivery on the Internet is key. Because there are so many websites available, it is challenging to build reach levels online versus in traditional media like television and magazines. The value of the Internet is that it is a niche medium and is used to pinpoint selected audiences. If you want to reach people who raise standard poodles, or make their own sausage, or practice day trading, you can easily find them online. And you can reach these niche audiences with virtually no "waste" reach, if that is your goal.

Unit 33 Exercises
Working with Online Display Media Estimates

1. You are advertising at a level of 200 GRPs on an Internet site that achieves wide dispersion.

   a. What will be the percentage reach in one week?

   b. What will be the percentage reach in four weeks?

   c. What will be the average frequency?

   d. How long will it take to achieve that frequency level?

e. If there are 1,600,000 in your target group, how many do you project that you will reach?

2. You are advertising on an Internet site that achieves limited dispersion.

 a. What GRP level would you need to reach 5 percent of the audience in one week?

 b. What GRP level would you need to reach 5 percent of the audience in four weeks?

 c. What GRP level would you need to reach your audience an average of 25 times?

Unit 34
Working with Online Display Media Costs

The Internet is unlike any other medium in terms of how advertising is purchased. In traditional advertising prices are based on delivery. In a television spot a certain number of impressions are delivered and the price is based on those impressions. For radio, newspapers, outdoor, and magazines, ads are priced the same way, that is, based on the number of people (impressions) the seller estimates the advertisement will reach. On the Internet it is possible to generate a virtually unlimited number of impressions. As such, media planners base their Internet plans on how many people they want to reach, as we saw in the previous unit. To do so, the planner can purchase either impressions (the CPM method) or "clicks" (the Pay for Performance method). There is no "best" method; in fact, the decision is often out of the planner's hands as the website itself determines which payment method it will use. Each payment method has its own strengths and weaknesses.

The CPM Method

The standard method for paying for advertising on the Internet is by arranging to pay for a certain number of impressions on the site for a negotiated cost per thousand (CPM). Unlike any other medium, the Internet can deliver a potentially unlimited amount of advertising. As a result, the advertiser must set his or her own limits on how many people he or she wants to reach on that site. Typically, when armed with the standard page views of information about a site, including the site's total audience, a media planner can determine the number of impressions required to deliver. The website will indicate the cost of reaching 1,000 people, and the media planner then estimates how many thousands of impressions needed for that site.

With impressions as the limit for reach and frequency, the creative unit also affects the cost of advertising over the Internet. As a rule, more exotic or technically superior creative units cost more than the more basic ones. Therefore, a rich media ad that contains animation costs more than a basic banner ad that acts like a static billboard. Additionally, the placement of the ad on the website can affect costs. For example, a banner ad at the top of a page is often priced higher than one at the bottom of the page. This is because many people don't like to scroll down and thus the number of people seeing the bottom of the page will most likely be lower.

A benefit of the CPM method is that it is efficient. You can expose your message to a large number of a site's visitors over the course of a few days. The planner has complete control over the budget. Unlike a television spot, underdelivery is not possible when you purchase an ad based on impressions. However, there are some weaknesses to the CPM method. Your ad may be exposed to large numbers of people, but it's possible that no one will click on the ad. And so it's important that you have a mechanism in place on the destination website linked to your ad in order to monitor online engagement.

Table 34.1 shows various Internet sites that include newspapers, magazines, television, and online-only media. Each site sells various ad units with specific dimensions. Placement, that is, the serving of the ad units, can be *run of network* (RON), which allows the site to serve the ads up randomly. Or they can be served in a more fixed manner such as on the home page or on entering the site. The next two columns are cost oriented. The first is the CPM, and the second is monthly costs for executing a 100,000-impression purchase.

As you can see from the table, the creative unit has a dramatic impact on the CPM for most of the websites. For example, on Expedia.com, buttons (a small-sized unit) are 60 percent of the cost of any type of banner (a larger-sized unit). Depending upon the site's activity level, costs may be graduated or fixed. WSJ.com sells their site at a flat $51 CPM regardless of the type of banner.

Placement can also affect costs significantly, since better placement correlates with stronger click-through rates. On the Houston Chronicle.com, a button on the home page is nearly twice the CPM of a banner that is run-of-network. In general, buttons are one of the lowest CPM units available. The same is true for a portal such as Excite.com, where purchasing a unit on a specific channel page such as business or sports costs more than a less-targeted exposure. Just like in magazines, a premium position commands a premium price. This is certainly true in the online world as well as the off-line world.

Pay for Performance

Another way of purchasing on the Internet is called "pay for performance." In the early days of the Internet, computer hardware and software companies would pay the website a percentage of their sales for each time an individual clicked through their ad and purchased their product. This type of payment is analogous to direct response television and was very popular at the onset of the Internet in early 2000. This arrangement has evolved to what is known today as "pay per click." Advertisers pay each time an individual clicks on an ad and clicks through to the advertised website.

Click-through rates for online advertisements are notoriously low. For many sites, a click-through rate (CTR) of .01 percent is considered strong. This means that 1 out of every 10,000 people exposed to an online ad will click through the ad. Take a banner ad on the *Houston Chronicle,* for example. To reach 10,000 people, the cost would be $176.00 (the CPM of $17.60 multiplied by 10, the number of thousands of people you wish to reach). Therefore, the cost to get one person to click through the ad on the *Houston Chronicle* would cost $176.00 (assuming a CTR of .01 percent). The benefits and weaknesses should be clear to you: while you are only paying for those people who take action relative to your ad (a strength), oftentimes that cost could be very high (a weakness). The media planner, of course, should ask the sales rep at the Houston Chronicle what the average CTR of ads on the site was to make a decision as to whether this would be a good placement for the brand. Comparing the data to other website data is also valuable.

Table 34.1

Online Advertising

Online site	Ad size	Placement	Est. CPM ($)	Monthly costs ($)
Houston Chronicle.com				
Banner	468x60	RON	17.64	1,764
Super tower	120x600	Business page	25.88	2,588
Button	120x90	Home page	35.29	3,529
HBJ.com				
Button	120x60	RON	15.00	1,500
Square button	125x125	RON	18.00	1,800
Banner	468x60	RON	23.00	2,300
Tower	120x600	RON	33.00	3,300
Super tower	160x600	RON	28.00	2,800
Island	300x250	RON	33.00	3,300
Island	336x280	RON	33.00	3,300
WSJ.com				
Tower	120x600	RON	51.00	5,100
Super tower	160x600	RON	51.00	5,100
Island	300x250	RON	51.00	5,100
Banner	468x60	RON	51.00	5,100
CBS Marketwatch.com				
Introductory message	480x640 50k 10 sec.	Before entering site	100.00	10,000
Skyscraper	120x600	Home page	25.00	2,500
Skyscraper	120x600	RON	25.00	2,500
Rich Media Windows	336x280 30k, 3 loop, rich media	RON	25.00	2,500
Yahoo! Finance				
Super banner	728x90	RON	13.50	1,350
Super banner	728x90	RON	14.50	1,450
Skyscraper	120x600	RON	8.00	800
Skyscraper	120x600	RON	10.00	1,000
Excite Network				
Full banner	468x60	RON	15.00	1,500
Horizon	550x150	RON	10.00	1,000
Full banner	468x60	Channel banner	50.00	5,000
Full banner	468x60	Home page	21.00	2,100
Rectangle	180x150	Home page	21.00	2,100
Expedia.com				
Button	120x90	RON	15.00	1,500
Banner	468x60	RON	25.00	2,500
Half banner	234x60	RON	25.00	2,500
Vertical banner	120x240	RON	25.00	2,500
Cnet.com				
Leaderboard	728x90	RON	72.00	7,200
Skyscraper	160x600	RON	85.00	8,500
Messaging Plus Unit (MPU)	300x250	RON	95.00	9,500
Rectangle	180x500	RON	54.00	5,400
NYTimes.com	160x800	RON	40.00	4,000
	336x280	RON	40.00	4,000
	240x400	RON	40.00	4,000
	768x90	RON	40.00	4,000
	468x60	RON	30.00	3,000
	234x60	RON	50.00	5,000
Adage.com	125x125	Home page	60.00	6,000
	120x240	Targeted sites	85.00	8,500
	120x600	RON	70.00	7,000
	468x60	Home page	85.00	8,500
	160x600	Targeted sites	110.00	11,000

Source: FKM Agency estimates.

Note: 100,000 monthly impressions for all sites.

Unit 34 Exercises
Working with Online Display Media Costs

1. Your interactive group has developed a 120×600 pixel unit for your Internet plan. What is the most efficient way to gain 1 million impressions per month using at least three different websites?

2. Your client has asked what the highest cost would be to reach 500,000 impressions per month using a mix of WSJ.com and CBS Marketwatch to reach stockbrokers. What is the cost ceiling for such a plan?

3. You are developing a media plan with skyscrapers and banners.

   a. If you put two plans together, one using each unit, how would the cost compare if the goal was to reach 2 million impressions per month?

b. What would the cost be to reach 2 million impressions per month where 1 million impressions were generated from banners and 1 million from skyscrapers?

c. Of these three options, which would you recommend to the client and why?

Unit 35
Working with Search Engine Marketing

In the previous unit, we introduced you to the concept of Pay for Performance pricing. This type of pricing is used most often in search engine marketing (SEM). SEM is a type of Internet marketing that promotes websites by increasing their visibility on a search engine result page (SERP). Advertisers and marketers pay to include their websites on the search results page, appearing at the top of the search listings or on a sidebar on the page: often this fee is based on the number of clicks an ad gets, not the number of impressions. On many search engines, these paid listings are labeled as sponsored listings. SEM differs from search engine optimization (SEO), which is improving the placement of a website or a web page on a SERP in the "natural" or unpaid search results.

To start a search engine marketing program, the advertiser or marketer thinks about the brand to be promoted and considers what search terms people generally use to find websites in that brand category. These search terms, also known as keywords, will be used to determine when the sponsored ad would be displayed on the SERP. If you're advertising a restaurant, for example, you might want to use keywords such as "Italian restaurant," "pasta restaurant," "pizza restaurant," and the like. Often advertisers have several words and phrases in their list of keywords.

Once keywords are determined, two ways of paying for results are available: the flat-rate and the bid-based. In both cases the advertiser must consider the potential value of a click from a given source, and that is why having appropriate keywords that will reach potential customers is important. The day and time that the click is made may also be valuable to know: a click made closer to the dinner hour may result in more customers than a click made at 10:00 A.M.

Flat Rate Pay per Click (PPC)

In the flat-rate model, the advertiser and Web publisher (e.g., the search engine) agree upon a fixed amount that will be paid for each click; this data may be available on a rate card similar to a magazine rate card. Flat rates may differ for a single site based on the placement on the SERP. Advertisers generally set up a maximum spend for each day, usually starting at about $50 per day for the larger search engines like Google.

Bid-Based PPC

In the bid-based model, advertisers sign a contract that allows them to compete against other advertisers in a private auction hosted by the publisher. Each advertiser informs the host of the maximum amount that he or she is willing to pay for a given ad spot (often based on a keyword). The auction plays out in an automated fashion every time a visitor triggers the ad spot. In situations where there are bids from different advertisers (a common occurrence on SERPs), the ad's positions on the page are influenced by the amount each has bid. The ad with the highest bid generally shows up first.

For instance, if you wanted to appear in the top listings for searches using the keywords "Italian restaurants in San Francisco," you might agree to pay $1.25 per click. If no one agrees to pay more than this, then you would be in the number-one search result. If someone else later decides to pay $1.26, then you slip into the number-two position. You could then bid $1.27 and move back to the top if you wanted to. Like the flat-fee system, you would indicate a maximum spend per day. Therefore, even if your bid for a keyword isn't the highest bid, you will probably still get exposures every day—either in a position secondary to the top bidder or a premium spot once the top bidder's maximum spend level has been reached.

How much should be bid per click? It all depends. The key is to determine how often someone will click on a link appearing on that search engine results page. The major search engines have tools that will allow you to see how popular keywords are, how many clicks per day one could expect, and how much an average click costs. Visit a site like Google AdWords to learn more. Agencies themselves also have pay per click management systems that allow for bids to be controlled through an automated system. These systems are generally tied into the brand's website and fed the results of each click, providing there is a feedback loop for future bids.

Unit 35 Exercises
Working with Search Engine Marketing

A small Italian restaurant in the Greenwich Village neighborhood of New York City is trying to select an advertising vehicle for an upcoming campaign for their "Italian Wine Month" promotion. The campaign will last one month and the restaurant has a budget of $500. The owners have identified several opportunities by searching online. These include:

- A banner ad in the restaurant section of the *Village Voice* website. The *Village Voice* is the leading entertainment and lifestyle newspaper in New York; its website receives over 350,000 page views per month. The average click-through rate is .006 percent. Banner ads are flat rate priced at $10 CPM.

- A banner ad on Eater.com, a blogging site about restaurants in New York. The blog receives 50,000 impressions per month, and is priced at a flat rate of $475 per month. Click-through rate is .01 percent.

- A banner ad in the weekly *Village Voice* newsletter. This is an opt-in newsletter that is e-mailed to 110,000 subscribers, and covers theater, music, and dining in New York once per week. The cost is $500 per week. The click-through rate is .008 percent.

- A banner ad in the *Village Voice* weekly dining e-newsletter. This is an opt-in newsletter that is e-mailed to 6,000 subscribers. These individuals eat out at least twice per week. The cost for a banner ad at the top of the newsletter is $150; a banner at the bottom is $100. Click-through rate is .02 percent.

- A text ad on a Google SERP using the keywords "Italian restaurant New York" and "Italian restaurant Greenwich Village" and "Italian Wine." The recommended bid is .56 per click. The click-through rate for a Google-sponsored ad is 7.5 percent.

1. Why is the click-through rate on a Google ad so much higher than on the other ad vehicles?

2. Given the budget of $500 per month, how many impressions could be expected from each vehicle? (Remember, a click-through rate of .006 percent means that you multiply the total impressions by .00006 to determine the actual number of clicks.)

3. How many click-throughs could be expected from each vehicle?

4. Which vehicle would you recommend?

5. Given the efficiency of Google ads, is there a value to considering other types of digital marketing? Why or why not?

Unit 36
Working with Social Media

Social media sites like Facebook and Twitter are very popular with online users, and as such have attracted the attention of advertisers and marketers who wish to get their brands engaged with regular customers and potential customers alike. One key to success in social media is for the brand to be involved and engaged: not just to set up a social media presence, but to have staff committed to participating in the conversations that occur. Therefore, a brand's social media presence really isn't without cost: personnel costs are essential. In addition, to attract people to their social media presence, many brands choose to place paid advertisements. For some brands this can be imperative in order to break through the social media clutter and start to create a vital community in the social media space.

The leading social media services constantly experiment with optimal advertising solutions. Given the huge amount of content available at these services, advertising opportunities usually allow targeting via both demographics and keywords. Facebook and YouTube both currently use this model. Twitter allows for sponsors' tweets, and as of this book's publication the specifics are still being tested and are not available to most advertisers. You can learn more at the Twitter website.

Facebook and Advertising

The most popular social media site at this writing, Facebook, allows brands to set up a "page" for their brand or company (see, for example, the Facebook page for the burger chain In-N-Out Burger: http://www.facebook.com/innoutEssentially); "liking" a company becomes an online word-of-mouth recommendation from the person who clicked on the "like" button. Online participants who "like" a brand page may be able to post on the brand's wall, upload videos and photos, and respond to comments or questions posted by the brand.

Facebook's Social Ads are text-based ads (with a small image) that appear on an individual's news feed and profile. Social Ads are somewhat analogous to search engine marketing (SEM), but instead of identifying and bidding on keywords, advertisers identify and bid on demographics and areas of interest to target. Advertisers also have the choice of paying for impressions (the CPM model) or for clicks (the pay for performance model). Advertisers can also identify a maximum spend per day for the campaign.

Here's an example: Let's say that In-N-Out was expanding into the states of Washington and Oregon, and wanted to let Facebook users know. The first target audience selected for analysis is all adults 18 and older who live in Oregon and Washington. The group consists of 4,706,200 people. The recommended bid per click with a $10 daily limit is $1.13 per click and the bid per thousand on a CPM basis is .48.

The second target is all adults 18 and older who live in Oregon and Washington and who have "liked" a competitor (McDonald's, Burger King, Burgerville). The group consists of 85,160 people. The recommended bid per click with a $10 daily limit is $1.26. The recommend bid for 1,000 impressions is .54 CPM.

The third target is men 18–34 who live in Oregon and Washington and who have liked a competitor. The group consists of 25,700 people with a recommended bid of .98 per click or .42 on a CPM basis.

The most cost efficient target is the third one. It is also the smallest target, and the most specific. It is likely that this group is often on Facebook and even though it is highly specific, it would not be difficult to reach them. As the age in the target audience increases, the costs increase as well, reflecting the fact that it is more difficult to reach those individuals.

What will the audience delivery be? The daily deliver estimate can be calculated using the following:

$$\frac{Daily\ maximum\ spend}{CPM\ bid} = Daily\ impressions$$

$$\frac{Daily\ maximum\ spend}{CPC\ bid} = Daily\ clicks$$

With the third group and a $10 maximum spend per day, the calculations would be:

Impressions: $\frac{10}{.42} = 23.8$, or 23,800 impressions per day (almost the entire target audience!).

Click: $\frac{10}{.98} = 10.2$, or approximately 10 clicks per day.

For a company expanding its business to a new geographic area where they likely have few people who are part of the community, it may be enough to have an impressions-based campaign that simply announces the opening of new locations. The value to purchasing clicks is that the brand's online network will start to be built.

Agencies can manage these campaigns via the "ads and pages" application on Facebook. YouTube uses a similar targeting and bid system, but allows video ads to be placed around content.

Unit 36 Exercises
Working with Social Media

Remember the three targeting choices for In-N-Out Burger's Facebook campaign? The first target audience selected for analysis is all adults 18 and older who live in Oregon and Washington. The group consists of 4,706,200 people. The recommended bid per click with a $10 daily limit is $1.13 per click and the bid per thousand on a CPM basis is .48. The second target is all adults 18 and older who live in Oregon and Washington and who have "liked" a competitor (McDonald's, Burger King, Burgerville). The group consists of 85,160 people. The recommended bid per click with a $10 daily limit is $1.26. The recommended bid for 1,000 impressions is .54 CPM. The third target is men 18–34 who live in Oregon and Washington and who have liked a competitor. The group consists of 25,700 people with a recommended bid of .98 per click or .42 on a CPM basis.

1. Calculate the daily impressions for each targeting option with a $10 daily spending limit.

2. Calculate the daily click-throughs for each targeting option with a $10 daily spending limit.

3. Which targeting option would you recommend to the client?

4. What other targeting options might you investigate for the type of campaign detailed in Unit 36?

Unit 37
Working with Mobile Media

Mobile media advertising is considered the next big thing, and the advertisers are closely watching the mobile phone user segment. Already highly popular in Europe and Asia, mobile media advertising is slowly becoming more utilized in the United States as increasing numbers of individuals rely on their smart phones: blackberries, iPhones, and other devices that offer more advanced computing ability and connectivity than a traditional cell phone. Most Americans feel that their mobile phone is their communications tool of choice.

Mobile media advertising is becoming popular due to the ubiquitous nature of cell phone usage. While consumers have a choice to view or avoid traditional advertising, one's mobile phone almost never goes unnoticed. Individuals take and make calls, check texts, keep updated on news, and find out weather reports via their mobile phones. Since advertisements on cell phones are still relatively new, there is a novelty factor that creates a higher than average interest in the messages. For a while at least, click-through rates on mobile phones are likely to be a lot higher than other forms of digital advertising.

Mobile media offer a lot of variety in ad types. While text messages are the most popular in early 2011, ads also feature videos, graphics, pictures, and banners to attract users. Additionally, many advertising services work on an opt-in basis, that is, the phone user indicates the types of messages he or she wishes to receive. For example, some ad services will alert phone users about news and information on their favorite bands and sports teams.

With GPS (Geographical Positioning System), another possibility is location-based advertising. A coffee shop, for example, can send messages to users who "opt-in" to their system whenever they are near an outlet. Newer location/social services like FourSquare and Gowalla allow users to "check in" at various locations and use that check-in to share their status with friends and earn rewards for visiting establishments.

Search engine marketing is also used on mobile sites for the popular search engines such as Google. Google recently purchased a company called AdMob, which gave them the ability to use the adwords technology with mobile phones. Advertisers can extend their existing AdWords campaigns to target desktop or laptop computer users or to create a unique, mobile-specific campaign. Begin testing and learn how this growing advertising opportunity can fit into your marketing plans.

The effectiveness of a mobile ad campaign is measured in a variety of ways, and the main measures are the same as other types of digital media we've discussed: impressions (views) and click-through rates. Click-throughs can be designated as clicking through to a website, or clicking to automatically call back the advertised business. Both flat-rate and bid systems are used.

Unit 37 Exercises
Working with Mobile Media

Remember the small Italian restaurant in the Greenwich Village neighborhood of New York City from Unit 35? They are now trying to select a mobile media advertising vehicle for an upcoming campaign for their "Italian Wine Month" promotion. The owners have identified several opportunities by searching online.

- A banner ad on the *Village Voice* mobile website. The mobile site gets 100,000 views per month. The price for a banner ad at the top of the site is $1,400 per month and at the bottom of the site is $1,000. The click-through rate is 3.0 percent for the top banner and 1.3 percent for the bottom banner. The banner ad can include flash animation.
- A text message alert sent to 1,000 *Village Voice* subscribers who have opted in to receiving text messages about restaurants. The message consists of 125 characters and costs $150. There is a 4 percent click-through.
- A mobile display ad on the Google mobile search site sent to adults who live in New York City. The cost per click bid would be 55 cents. There are about 300,000 possible impressions per month. Click-through rate is 3.0 percent.
- A text ad on the Google mobile SERP page using the keywords "Italian restaurant" and limited to adults in New York City. The term is searched for about 22,000 times per month. The cost would be .30 per click with a click-through rate of about 5 percent.

1. Estimate the number of impressions for each vehicle at three budget levels: $500, $1,000, and $1,500.

2. Estimate the number of click-throughs for each vehicle at each budget level.

3. Why are the banner ads on the *Village Voice* mobile website priced so much higher than other options? What benefits to the creative unit are available?

Part VIII
Media Tools, Analysis, and Resources

Unit 38
Combining Sources and Data

Now that you understand the basic processes in making advertising media calculations and you know how to make some of those calculations yourself, it is time to realize that the actual work plans may be somewhat more complicated.

For example, the information you need may not be contained in a single source. So, you may have to go to two or more places to get the right information, and then manipulate those numbers and values until they fit the problem you want to solve.

For example, you want to estimate the unduplicated reach in Washington, DC, of placing four advertisements in the *Washington Post*. So you go to a newspaper audience estimating table and you find this information.

Adult Reader Reach: Daily Newspapers

Daily DMA HH Coverage	Reach of Adult Readers		
	1 insertion	2 insertions	4 insertions
10	17	20	23
20	22	28	33
30	28	36	44
40	36	45	55
50	44	53	65

However, you don't know offhand what the market penetration is in Washington for the *Washington Post*. So you find another media source that gives you these figures.

Daily Newspaper Costs: Top Ten U.S. Markets

Market	Adult coverage in DMA (%)	Number of newspapers required
New York	38	2
Los Angeles	30	1
Chicago	31	1
Philadelphia	33	2
San Francisco	32	2
Boston	35	1
Washington, DC	49	1
Dallas	36	1
Detroit	36	1
Houston	38	1

So now you know that the largest-circulation newspaper in Washington (the *Post*) reaches about 49 percent of the population in that city. Using that figure, you go back to the first table and estimate that, in Washington, with a market coverage of close to 50 percent, four insertions in the *Post* will likely provide about 65 percent unduplicated (combined) reach in Washington, DC.

In another situation, you might want to estimate the cost of reaching an audience of a certain size through a certain advertising medium, but the cost guide may require you to have an estimate of the audience size first. So you will need to consult an audience-estimating guide to help you calculate a realistic estimate of the size of audience, and then go back to the cost-estimating guide to help you calculate the likely costs involved.

As with using other sources of information, you will save time if you avail yourself of data that are already available. Combining sources takes some creativity and thinking but will result in a better plan while perhaps requiring less original research on your part.

Unit 38 Exercises
Combining Sources and Data

1. Look up the population of your city in three different sources (e.g., U.S. Census, local chamber of commerce, state development department). Write down the population and the source. Also write down the population base: city, county, metropolitan area, etc., as well as the population type: individuals, households, adults, etc. If the figures do not all agree, explain why. Also, how would you report these figures if your supervisor had requested this information?

2. You are the media planner for Budweiser. The brand manager has come to you to begin work on a new project for the company. Anheuser-Busch has decided to tap into the bottled water market with a new brand of bottled water called Clydesdale Springs. Since the brand doesn't have any information on the bottled water target, the client has asked you to look at Miller beer drinkers as a target. The ad people at Budweiser were able to obtain seasonality data on water consumption from a salesperson and want some help with understanding the information. Your task is to develop the target audience profile and advise the brand on when the best time is to launch this new water product.

3. The brand manager for Sears is confused. He is not sure if he should do a local campaign or a national campaign. He has a goal of 90 reach and a 5 average frequency for his month-long campaign. He has $5 million to invest in the promotion which targets women. His sales are in line with the population of each U.S. market except New York. He has only 2 percent of sales in this top market. The president of Sears wants the promotion to cover at least 40 percent of Sears's business. Is it better for him to run locally or to schedule a national television campaign using a 30-second creative?

4. You are traveling to your next client presentation when you happen to meet a former classmate of yours who is now president of a hot new video gaming company. He is in a bind. He could really use a media plan to help him raise $20 million of venture capital money to promote his new video game. He begs you for help, but all you have with you is your *Media Workbook*. However, being resourceful, you know that his target market is teens and young adults. They are twice as likely as older adults to be radio listeners and Internet users and less likely to be heavy viewers of television. The cost to reach this group is roughly one-third of the adult marketplace. He is launching his game in November to lead into the Christmas holiday shopping season. What would be your one-page media recommendation for him?

Unit 39
Manipulating Data

Not all the information you find for your media plan will be in the exact format you require, or it may not cover the exact periods or locales or companies that you want to research. So you will need to manipulate the research data that you find.

The three most common ways of manipulating data are interpolation, extrapolation, and disaggregation. There are a few other useful ways to manipulate research data to fit the problem at hand as well.

Interpolating

You may need to extrapolate data (estimate based on already known information) or interpolate data (insert between known values). If you know that Dyerville's grocery sales in the year 2000 were $220 million, and in 2002 they were $260 million, then you may be able to interpolate that the sales in 2001 were about $240 million.

Year	Grocery sales
2000	$220,000,000
2001	_____
2002	$260,000,000

If the sales grew by $40,000,000 over two years, they may likely have increased by $20,000,000 per year, or up to $240,000,000 for 2001.

Extrapolating

Similarly, if you know those year 2000 and 2002 figures, you may be able to extrapolate that the 2003 sales went up to about $280,000,000.

Year	Grocery sales
2000	$220,000,000
2001	$240,000,000
2002	$260,000,000
2003	_____

If the sales grew by $20 million a year in the first two years, they are likely to have increased by about another $20 million during the next year, or up to $280 million.

But be careful. If you know that the average movie ticket sales in Larksburg were $25,000 in October and $45,000 in December, it is not safe to assume that the movie sales were $35,000 in November. Movie sales depend on what films are showing, not on annual trends.

Disaggregating

Sometimes you can easily put together new estimates of your own. Imagine that you are planning advertising for a local fast-food chain, Burger Boy, which competes directly with another local fast-food chain, Pop's Hamburgers. You would like to know the annual sales for Pop's Hamburgers, but you also realize that Pop's is unlikely to share that kind of information with a direct competitor.

So you count how many locations Pop's has in your area. Then you go into a few Pop's locations and buy some food and also watch what other people buy and how much it costs them. From this, you can calculate the cost of an average order at Pop's. Then you hire an intern to sit in a car across from each of Pop's locations for a day and count how many people go into the place. From this, you can calculate the average store traffic for a Pop's location. So with the number of customers per store, multiplied by the number of stores, you know the approximate total number of customers for all Pop's locations on an average day. Multiplying that figure by the average sales estimate gives you the estimated total sales per day for Pop's. Multiplying that figure by the number of days per year gives you a good estimate of the total annual sales for Pop's hamburgers. Your figures might look something like this.

600	Number of customers per store per day
× 10	Number of stores
6,000	Total number of customers per day

6,000	Total number of customers per day
× $4	Average sales per customer
$24,000	Estimated total sales per day
$24,000	Estimated total sales per day
× 365	Days per year
$8,760,000	Estimated annual sales

Your figures will not be exact, but you will likely be close—and your estimate will be much better than a wild guess.

Manipulating Data

You may also need to manipulate data. Let's say you have these figures.

Age	Monthly average of gasoline purchases (000)
18–24	$1,500
25–34	$1,750
18–49	$3,250

If you need to know the average monthly gasoline purchase amount for persons ages 25–49, you can manipulate the data this way: subtract the purchase amount for those ages 18–24 from the purchase amount for those ages 18–49 and you will have your answer.

18–49	$3,250,000
– (18–24)	–1,500,000
25–49	$1,750,000

Of course, working with lots of varied sources can be complicated and time consuming. Remember, though, that these sources are actually *saving* you time, making it easier for you to get along with your work because they have already gathered the information, charted the media and audience levels, and calculated the average costs, audience levels, and media weights.

It may help if you remember to label every statistic and figure that you use, so when you need to refer to an item later, you know what it means. Suppose that your boss asks you to find the level of sales for your major competitor in San Diego last year, and you write down the figure 2,200,000. That figure could refer to cases of the product, dollars of sales, units consumed, or some other measure; it could even be a rounded number (such as expressed as 000, so that the real value is 2.2 billion rather than 2.2 million). Only by labeling each figure can you keep track of the work you have already done.

Unit 39 Exercises
Manipulating Data

1. Your staff has begun planning a spot radio buy on several stations in the Seattle area, but the plan has not been completed. You decide to complete the calculations for the various audience levels on each station. Fill in spaces in the table where data are missing.

Station	Reach	Frequency	Impressions	Gross Rating	Reach GRPs	Cost/Ad	Total Cost	Cost/ Rating Pt.
KAAA	400,000	5	2,000,000	20	100	$1,000	$5,000	$50
KBBB	600,000	5	3,000,000	30	___	$1,650	$8,250	___
KCCC	700,000	5	___	___	175	___	$10,500	___
KDDD	300,000	7	___	___	___	$675	___	___
KEEE	___	7	___	10	___	___	___	$45
KFFF	___	___	___	40	200	___	___	$55

2. When you look up the annual sales of automobiles in Stanleytown, you find the following figure.

Auto sales   ($000,000)
Stanleytown   12.465

How would you express this figure in a research report?

3. When you add up the total advertising spent last year on your brand and on your major competitors, these are the figures you find.

Brand A	$6,520,000.00
Brand B	$8,400,000.00
Brand C	$9,124,500.00
Your Brand	$7,453,221.88

   How might you report these figures on a research report? Why might you decide to round off some of the figures?

4. Here are sales figures that you found for two years of sales.

2005	132,000,000 units
2007	174,570,000 units

Using these figures, can you estimate the sales figures for 2006? Why or why not?

Unit 40

Working with Basic Media Math

Working with media involves working with some basic mathematical concepts. Most media problems involve little more than being able to add, subtract, multiply, and divide. In today's media environment, the majority of sophisticated mathematics is done via media research software programs developed specifically to meet the needs of media planning and buying. Advertising media problems often engage thinking and logic, so any difficulties people might have with these media problems rarely involve arithmetic. Instead, there may be problems with discovering exactly what is being asked and what information or other resources are available to aid with the solution.

Occasionally there may be an equation to solve, but the equations are usually simple and involve finding a single missing element or number. For example, in the equation $10 + X = 12$, you can easily figure out that the missing number is 2, so $X = 2$. Similarly, in the equation $4 \times Y = 12$, you can easily figure out that the missing number is 3, so $Y = 3$.

Fractions and Decimals

Much of media audience information is reported in decimals and fractions. As a result, there are times when you may need to convert a fraction to a decimal, a decimal to a fraction or a percentage, or a fraction to another fraction of equal value.

The term *percent* means per hundred. So

$$40\% = 40/100$$

Another way to express that value is

$$0.40$$

which reads as *forty hundredths*. Remember the importance of the decimal place:

$$0.40 = 0.40000 = 0.4$$

So, most of the time, the figure

$$0.40$$

would be shortened and expressed as

$$0.4$$

You also need to know how various fractions compare with one another. Thus,

$$\frac{4}{10} \; = \; \frac{2}{5} \; = \; \frac{40}{100} \; = \; \frac{8}{20}$$

Therefore, the following figures are all equal in value:

$$\frac{4}{10} \; = \; \frac{40}{100} \; = \; \underline{0.4} \; = \; \underline{40\%}$$

Notice that as a fraction's numerator (the top number, above the line) gets larger, the overall value of the fraction gets larger as well.

$$\frac{1}{5} \quad \text{is smaller than} \quad \frac{2}{5} \quad \text{which is smaller than} \quad \frac{3}{5}$$

But as the fraction's denominator (the bottom number, below the line) gets larger, the overall value of the fraction gets smaller.

$$\frac{1}{2} \quad \text{is larger than} \quad \frac{1}{3} \quad \text{which is larger than} \quad \frac{1}{4}$$

Incidentally, a *change in percent* is not the same as a *percentage change*. If last year your advertising was communicating with 16 percent of the target audience, and now you communicate with 20 percent, the increase was four percentage points, but the percentage increase was 25 percent.

$$\frac{\text{Amount of increase}}{\text{Original percentage}} \; = \; \frac{4\%}{16\%} \; = \; \frac{1}{4} \; = \; 25 \text{ percent}$$

Mean, Median, and Mode

It is useful to know an *average* for a set of numbers because that average gives you some sense of the collective value of all the numbers in a single figure. This is particularly important as you analyze a media schedule or face the challenge of putting together a media plan or buy.

But you may recall that there are three kinds of averages: the *mean,* the *median,* and the *mode*. The mean is the traditional average, which typifies the entire set of numbers. To find the mean, you simply add up the scores or numbers and divide that total by how many items there are (which is symbolized by *n*). As a simple formula,

$$\text{Mean} = \frac{\text{Sum of scores}}{\text{Number of scores}} \quad \text{or} \quad \text{Mean} = \frac{\sum X}{n}$$

when $\sum$ means the sum (or the total of addition), and *X* means each value or score, and *n* is how many scores or numbers there were that you added; add up all the *X*s and divide the total by *n*.

The median is the middle score when the values are arranged in either ascending or descending order, and the mode is the score or value that comes up most often. In the scores

12
11
10
10
10
9
9
8
7
4
3

the mean is 8.45, that is, the sum of the scores ($\sum = 93$) divided by how many scores (*n* = 11), or

$$\frac{93}{11} = 8.45.$$

The median, which is the middle value, is 9. The mode, which is the value that comes up most often, is 10 (because it appears three times in the set of scores).

Indexes

Many times, media information is provided in the form of an *index* (the plural can be indexes or indices). An index sets some standard value against which other values can be compared.

For example, if the value of the U.S. dollar in the year 2000 is set at an index value of 100, media cost inflation can be measured against that year 2000 standard. If media costs went up by five percentage points in 2001, the indexed figure would be 105 (100 + 5% = 100 + 5 = 105).

Another type of index sets the value of 100 as the average for a set of data or scores. If the ability to reach adult females by advertising in magazines is set at an average index score of 100, a magazine that does better than average will have an index score higher than 100, while a magazine that does poorer than average will have an index score of less than 100. Thus, a magazine with an index score of 108 is 8 percentage points better than the average (index = 100) of all magazines in that particular ability (108 − 100 = 8), while a magazine with an index score of 86 is doing 14 percentage points poorer in that particular capacity when compared with the average (again, index = 100) for all magazines (100 − 86 = 14).

Be aware that a difference of a few points from one index to another may not be very meaningful. If one television network has an index of 102 and another has an index of 98, there is only a four-point difference, which may not be statistically significant—and may, in fact, be within the range of sampling error, which is often within a margin of three or four points. Some advertising experts use 120 as the necessary point for an index to be adequately above average, and below 80 as the point to be adequately below average.

Specialized Indexing

In marketing and advertising work, there are some specialized indexes used in the industry. Indexes are also a very common way to show differences between various media alternatives or media vehicles.

A *brand development index,* or BDI, indicates how strong a company's sales are in a particular market in relation to the population of that market. The average market would have a BDI of 100. A market that does twice the average amount of business per capita (i.e., per person in the population) would have a BDI of 200, while a market that had sales just half the average would have a BDI of 50. If Tupelo, Mississippi, has 4 percent of your target population but accounts for 6 percent of your sales, it would have a BDI of 150.

$$\frac{6}{4} \times 100 = 150$$

The quotient is multiplied by 100 to provide an index number that is easy to use. Applying the BDI to a market's share of the advertising budget requires you to use the BDI of 100 as equal to 1, so a BDI of 125 would be applied as 1.25 and a BDI of 150 would be applied as 1.50.

Original budget allocation to Tupelo	$50,000
Multiplied by the BDI of 150	× 1.50
	$75,000

As you have just seen, the BDI is most often applied as an adjustment to the marketing or advertising budget allocation for each market, changing the per capita or pro rata (i.e., per person) budget allocation upward or downward, depending on the relative sales patterns.

If you are working with a brand or service that is relatively new or that has been drastically repositioned in the marketplace, you may not have a history of your brand's sales that you can use to calculate a BDI. In this case, you might use sales figures from the entire product category or service category, which would allow you to calculate a *category development index* (CDI). A CDI can be applied to sales or budget figures in the same way as a BDI can.

Keep in mind that it is preferable to use brand data (i.e., a BDI) if you have that information because it applies solely to your brand; product or service category figures (a CDI) would not likely be as close to your own brand's sales data.

Agency Commission

Advertising agencies are paid for their work in many ways, including a mark-up on costs (known as "cost-plus"), a fee that has been negotiated, a payment that reflects the value of the work done, a fee that represents the sales trends resulting from the advertising campaign, or some combination of these compensation approaches. Traditionally, advertising agencies have been compensated through a commission from the media in which the agencies place advertisements.

Over the years, the standard advertising agency commission has settled at 15 percent. The commission might look like this:

Cost of advertising	$1,000
Amount sent to media	$1,000
Commission returned to agency by media (15%)	$ 150

In practice, however, the agency may simply retain the 15 percent commission and transmit the balance to the media.

Cost of advertising	$1,000
Commission retained by agency (15%)	$ 150
Amount sent to media	$ 850

As we said, the 15 percent advertising agency commission is a standard figure.

$$\frac{\text{Agency commission}}{\text{Cost of advertising}} \quad \frac{\$150}{\$1,000} \quad = \quad 15\%$$

However, some advertising media may claim that they grant a commission of 17.65 percent. Actually, they are still granting the standard 15 percent commission, but since the media never received the entire advertising amount, they calculate the commission as a percentage of the money they actually received.

$$\frac{\text{Agency commission}}{\text{Amount received by media}} \quad \frac{\$150}{\$850} \quad = \quad 17.65\%$$

The agency commission is the same amount of money either way. The only difference is whether that commission is calculated as a percentage of the gross amount (i.e., the total cost of the advertising, or $1,000 in this case) or calculated as a percentage of the net amount (the gross amount less the commission, or $850 in this example).

Mental Calculations

Although most people use calculators for complicated mathematics, there are times when you may not have a calculator available, such as in a meeting, when talking on your cell phone, or sitting in your boss's office. In times like these, you'll be more successful if you can do simple calculations in your head.

For example, you want to multiply

$$6 \times 14$$

and you don't know your multiplication tables up to 14. But you do know that if you double one value and cut the other one in half, you'll get the same answer. Thus,

$$2 \times 6 = 4 \times 3$$

where you double the 2 (to 4) and halve the 6 (to 3).

So in the problem above,

$$6 \times 14,$$

you can double the 6 and halve the 14, making the problem

$$12 \times 7.$$

And because you know your multiplication tables up through 12, you know that

$$12 \times 7 = 84, \text{ so } 6 \times 14 = 84 \text{ as well.}$$

Similarly, you can calculate 16×7 very easily.

If $8 \times 7 = 56$,
then 16×7 must be twice as much, or 112.

In fact, you may find it useful to remember such things, because it means that

$$\frac{1}{7} = \text{ about } 14\%$$

and that

$$\frac{1}{14} = \text{ about } 7\%.$$

Similarly, if $11 \times 9 = 99$, then you can calculate in your head that

$$\frac{1}{11} \; = \; \text{about } 9\%$$

and that

$$\frac{1}{9} \; = \; \text{about } 11\%.$$

Being able to do simple calculations in your head, without the aid of a calculator and without paper and pencil, can make your job easier, faster, and more efficient.

Unit 40 Exercises
Working with Basic Media Math

1. Enter the proper values for the following figures:

$$\frac{80}{100} = \frac{}{10} = \frac{}{50} = \frac{}{20}$$

$$0.62 = \frac{}{100} = \underline{\qquad}\%$$

2. What is 4% of 100? _____
   What is 10% of 110? _____
   What is 9% of 117? _____
   300 is what percent of 1,200? _____
   16 is what percent of 88? _____
   42 is what percent of 20,600? _____

3. Below is an advertising budget for several markets. What percentage of the total does each market receive?

Market	Allocation	Percentage
1	$62,000	_____
2	$77,500	_____
3	$55,350	_____
4	$81,075	_____

4. Here are local television audience figures for a city at 8 P.M. on a Monday night. What percentage did each station receive of the total audience?

Station	No. of TV households	Percentage
KLLL	234,000	_____
KMMM	189,000	_____
KNNN	366,000	_____
KOOO	297,000	_____
KPPP	147,000	_____

5. There are 250,000 television households in a certain market area. Use the percentages of households reached to project the number of households tuned to each station. (The percentages do not add to 100 percent because not all households have their television sets on at any one time.)

Station	Percentage of households reached	Projected no. of households
KQQQ	17.1	_____
KRRR	22.7	_____
KSSS	7.9	_____
KTTT	11.2	_____

6. Give the mean, median, and mode for the following set of values.

6
4
6
2
8
1
6
8
2
1
9
6
7

Mean   = _____
Median = _____
Mode   = _____

7. Calculate the following index figures.

   a. If the total amount of advertising expenditures in the United States in the year 2010 has an index figure of 100, what would be the index for the year 2011 if advertising expenditures increased by 9 percentage points?

   b. Using the answer from question 7a, what would be the index for the year 2011 if advertising expenditures increased by another 9 percentage points?

8. If the average television station in West Alto has an index of 100 in reaching teenagers, would each station below be above or below the town average for reaching teens, and by how much?

Station	Index	Above or below average?	By how much?
WFFF	86	_____	_____
WGGG	101	_____	_____
WHHH	100	_____	_____
WJJJ	93	_____	_____

9. Your client has supplied you with the following market data for her product. Calculate the BDI for each market. Place your answers in the blank spaces provided under BDI.

Market	Percentage of U.S. population	Percentage of brand sales	BDI
A	12	10	_____
B	18	18	_____
C	18	20	_____
D	30	25	_____
E	22	27	_____
	100%	100%	

10. Using the CDI figures provided below, adjust the advertising budget allocations to reflect the sales ratios in each market.

Market allocation	Advertising budget allocation	CDI	Revised budget allocation
W	$275,000	96	_____
X	$340,000	111	_____
Y	$555,000	89	_____
Z	$670,000	102	_____

11. An average newspaper in one U.S. region reaches 60,000 adult women readers. Using the index figures below, calculate the number of adult women readers for each newspaper.

Newspaper	Index for reaching adult women	No. of adult women
News	102	_____
Tribune	89	_____
Gazette	94	_____
Post	112	_____

12. If an advertising agency places $4,734,000 of advertising time with a certain radio network, what would be the amount of the agency's standard commission? Show your calculations.

13. Try the following calculations in your head, without using a calculator or writing down the problems. Then, if you wish, check your work by using a calculator.

$7 \times 14 = ?$

$\dfrac{100}{9} = ?$

$10 \times 40 = ?$

$6 \times 18 = ?$

$9 \times 2.2 = ?$

14. Fill in the missing numbers.

$$3/4 = \underline{\hspace{2cm}} / 20$$

$$3/4 = \underline{\hspace{2cm}} \%$$

$$6/8 = \underline{\hspace{2cm}} / 4$$

$$3/4 = \underline{\hspace{2cm}} / 16$$

$$3/4 = 0. \underline{\hspace{2cm}}$$

$$3/4 = \underline{\hspace{2cm}} / 100$$

$$3/4 = \underline{\hspace{2cm}} / 24$$

15. Here is an index for magazines that reach male teens.

Magazine	Index
AA	101
BB	97
CC	116
DD	102
EE	77
FF	99

a. Is magazine CC above or below average in its ability to reach male teens, and by how much?

b. Is magazine EE above or below average in its ability to reach male teens, and by how much?

16. Here is a table of how many residents there are in each age category for Centreville.

Age	No. of males	%	% of males
2–11	16,000	_____	_____
12–17	17,500	_____	_____
18–24	22,000	_____	_____
25–34	19,250	_____	_____
35–49	20,500	_____	_____
50–64	21,000	_____	_____
65 and older	24,000	_____	_____

Age	No. of females	%	% of females
2–11	17,000	_____	_____
12–17	19,750	_____	_____
18–24	25,500	_____	_____
25–34	22,250	_____	_____
35–49	19,750	_____	_____
50–64	27,000	_____	_____
65 and older	30,000	_____	_____

a.   Calculate what percentage each group is of the total population (males and females) in Centreville and enter those figures in the percentage columns.

b.   For the remaining column, calculate what percentage each male age group is of the total male population of Centreville and what percentage each female age group is of the town's total female population.

Unit 41
Working with Media Websites

The Internet is a wonderful invention, one that provides access to almost the entire store of information of the entire world while saving time and effort. As with most inventions, there are advantages and disadvantages in using the Internet. Knowing where to look, gaining experience with Internet searches and websites, and having confidence in the information that has been found are all important—as is using some particular websites that relate to your specific field and job.

General Information

Although it may be a tedious task to find quality content on the World Wide Web, don't get frustrated. Instead, learn to conduct productive searches. If you cannot find what you seek, maybe you need to try another search engine.

There are a number of good general search engines. Even though they are general and cover all topics and categories, they can still find advertising and media data that you may need, as well as population and marketing information.

Google (www.google.com) is the largest and most widely used search engine currently available, covering more than 8 billion web pages. It is especially useful for finding local-market information that may not be available in the large specialized advertising and marketing sources. Learn to use the advanced search tools to narrow your task.

Ask.com started as a question-and-answer site, but now you can also use it for more conventional searches. Using www.ask.com/webadvanced can help you restrict searches to a particular geographical area or time period.

MSN (www.msn.com) is a service of Microsoft that serves both as an Internet portal and as a search engine. The portal facet lets you browse certain categories rather than search through the entire Internet.

Yahoo! (www.yahoo.com) also combines an Internet portal with a search engine. You can click on "advanced search" to look for a particular domain (e.g., .org or .gov), for pages updated within a recent time frame, or to find more advanced features.

Bookfinder.com searches for sellers of used and new books you may need.

Meta-search engines such as SurfWax (www.surfwax.com) and lxquick (www.lxquick.com) may save time by combing through several other search engines. Use a meta-search to get a quick overview of the range of information available on a subject.

Media-Specific Information

You will benefit from Internet sites that contain information relating specifically to marketing, advertising, media, or media planning.

Here are several good Internet sources, organized by function.

Marketing and Market Information

Mediamark Research Inc.	www.mediamark.com
Scarborough	www.scarborough.com
Simmons Market Research Bureau	www.smrb.com
Information Resources, Inc. (IRI)	us.infores.com

Basic Media Information

Magazine Dimensions	www.mediadynamicsinc.com
Radio Dynamics	www.mediadynamicsinc.com
TV Dimensions	www.mediadynamicsinc.com

Media Audience Information

Audit Bureau of Circulations	www.accessabc.com
Bacon's Directories	www.baconsinfo.com
Business Publications Audit of Circulation	www.bpai.com
Certified Audit of Circulations, Inc.	www.certifiedaudit.com
Verified Audit Circulation Corporation	www.verifiedaudit.com

Broadcast Audience Estimates

Arbitron	www.arbitron.com
Nielsen Media Research	www.nielsenmedia.com

Message Research Sources

Gallup & Robinson	www.gallup-robinson.com
Nielsen Media Research	www.nielsenmedia.com
Readex	www.readexresearch.com
VNU	www.vnu.com

Advertising Rates

Marketers Guide to Media	www.adweek.com/stores/directoriesl.asp#MGM
Media Market Resources, Snapshots	www.mediamarket.com/snap.htm
Standard Rate & Data Service	www.srds.com

Media Research Software

Interactive Market Systems	www.imsms.com
TapScan	www.tapscan.com
Telmar	www.telmar.com

Cautions

Huge amounts of information are available on the Internet; unfortunately, however, not all of it is reliable. In fact, there are some experts who claim that not even a majority of the "facts" on the Internet are actually true.

So how can you be sure whether the information you find is reliable? You can't be, at least, not absolutely, but you can use care and caution to make your search findings more trustworthy and reliable. Keep in mind that before a book or journal is published, it is usually vetted or scrutinized by editors and subject experts who have checked on the claims and facts; that is not the case with much Internet information. There is no regulatory group that monitors the reliability or accuracy of information found on the Internet.

Be careful of sources that can be edited by anyone who goes to that website. For example, although information from "wiki" sites, such as Wikipedia, may generally be reliable, you should know that such sites allow visitors to add, remove, and otherwise edit or change some of the content, sometimes without the need to register. Consequently, the same ease of interaction and operation that makes a wiki an effective tool for collaborative authoring also means that anyone may have posted a belief or opinion that may or may not be true.

So you may need to conduct your own research. Who is the author of the information, and what credentials does that person hold?

What type of site is it? Is an .edu or .gov site more likely to contain reliable information than, say, a .com or .biz site?

What is the purpose of the site? Are there reasons to suspect bias on the part of those who write for or control the site? And did an original reliable site switch you to another site that may not have the same level of credibility?

How recently was the site updated? Can you find other sites that corroborate the information that you have found? And even if a particular site or page may not seem credible, you still may be able to use it to help you generate some ideas of your own or to lead you to other, more reliable sources.

Finally, watch for page protections, such as copyright protection. If there is a copyright symbol, it may mean that the author or site owner wants to protect the accuracy of the information found there. It may also mean, however, that you cannot legally use the information without permission, such as a signed release.

Remember, to be safe, you can always check your findings against references in a good research library.

Unit 41 Exercises
Working with Media Websites

1. What are the annual sales for Ruby Tuesday's restaurants for the most recent year you can find? For what year are the figures valid? What was your source? Do you consider the data valid?

2. Use at least two different sources to learn the current population of Bloomington, Indiana. What are the two sources? What are the population figures? Do they agree—and if not, why not?

3. What percentage of the adult residents of St. Paul, Minnesota, smoke cigarettes? What is your source? Do you consider the data valid?

4. How many students are enrolled in U.S. colleges and universities? What percentage of the total U.S. population are enrolled? What is the most popular college major? What are your sources for each of these figures?

5. What are the ten biggest advertising program enrollments among U.S. universities, and at what schools?

6. What is the cost of advertising during prime time on Monday night on WCBS-TV in New York City?

7. How many households or persons can be reached with outdoor advertising in Los Angeles?

8. If you want to advertise to people who travel regularly to Asia from the United States, what is the best website to use for placing your advertising?

Unit 42
Working with Competitive Media Information

In the course of developing a media plan, it is important to analyze the brand's competition to determine what their media strategy is and how you might align your strategy to its greatest advantage.

There are two national competitive media tracking tools available today to help a media planner assess the competition. Kanter Media has a suite of tools that track competitive advertising spending and creative. The second service is called AdViews. It is owned and operated by Nielsen Media Research.

Each service offers consumer media spending reports for a wide variety of media, including network television, cable television, local or spot television and radio, network radio, outdoor, newspapers, magazines, and Sunday supplements. CMR also provides a business-to-business competitive media service that tracks many trade magazine categories. Each service has its pros and cons for analyzing consumer media spending.

There are some caveats to any competitive spending analysis. The first is to use the spending numbers as directional guides and not as absolute spending. Because media are highly negotiable, the actual spending may be higher or lower than the reported numbers. Second, both CMR and AdViews do an excellent job of capturing television spending, particularly on a national basis, but capturing local radio spending is problematic at best. Neither service captures direct mail expenditures and other out-of-home media beyond traditional outdoor posters and rotary bulletins. With that being said, it is still important to understand the relative spending levels and media approaches that your competitors are employing. After all, they are trying to take business from your brand. You need to understand the enemy.

There are many analyses that you can perform with competitive spending information. The traditional exercise is called *share of spending* or SOS. Share of spending is the percent of spending that your brand has relative to all the brands in its category. For example, if your brand were Bob's Baked Beans with media spending of $5 million dollars, it would have a 20 percent share of spending if the category spending was $25 million.

You can also analyze how your brand's media mix compares to another brand. With appropriate software, you can study the monthly schedule of each brand's spending, as well. There are also ways of drilling down to analyze the individual media vehicles that your competitors are scheduled in. Some software programs allow the media professional to convert the reported dollar spending to rating points. That way, you can determine the weight levels at which your competitors are scheduling their activity. This analysis is called a *share of voice* or SOV. Share of voice is a comparison of the percent of impressions that your brand is delivering compared to other brands in the category. Many media professionals use SOS and SOV interchangeably, but they are very different concepts. For purposes of this workbook, we will deal strictly with SOS.

Like most media information, competitive spending is available online and can be manipulated by media planners to reflect the way they choose to see the information. Typically, the reported spending numbers are shown in thousands or (000). There are appropriate percentages reported for the percent of spending in total for each brand and the percent of spending by medium for each brand.

As an example of competitive media information, Table 42.1 summarizes advertising expenditures for different brands of beer from January to December 2002.

For a more complete discussion of competitive analysis, see Larry D. Kelley and Donald W. Jugenheimer, *Advertising Media Planning: A Brand Management Approach*, 3d ed., (Armonk, NY: M.E. Sharpe, 2012), chap. 8.

Table 42.1

Media-Wide Brand Summary for Beer, January–December 2002 (in U.S. dollars)

Subsidiary	Brand	Total	Television expenditures				
			Cable TV	Hispanic network TV	Network TV	Spot TV	Syndicated TV
Anheuser-Busch Inc.	Bud Light Beer	130,666,421	10,716,644	6,797,445	81,279,700	19,628,317	3,687,822
Anheuser-Busch Inc.	Budweiser Beer	151,961,271	10,536,353	10,518,711	94,799,668	18,175,221	5,268,943
Anheuser-Busch Inc.	Busch Beer	9,732,399	3,479,948	0	2,746,800	672,856	0
Coors Brewing Co.	Coors Light Beer	141,102,606	9,178,956	9,973,288	95,456,333	18,147,255	1,411,141
Diago North America Inc.	Guinness Beer	8,434,199	1,858,839	0	3,074,900	1,191,025	1,256,248
Heineken USA	Amstel Light Beer	22,830,097	1,246	0	673,600	12,375,904	6,774
Heineken USA	Heineken Beer	54,582,354	12,528,186	1,927,300	25,475,600	7,792,523	2,525,364
Miller Brewing Co.	Miller Genuine Draft Beer	37,929,874	6,456,597	11,306,295	4,557,100	13,699,233	0
Miller Brewing Co.	Miller Lite Beer	143,589,181	18,055,582	22,348,001	72,406,300	13,431,618	3,398,375

(continued)

Table 42.1 (continued)

Subsidiary	Brand	Radio expenditures		Magazine expenditures		Newspaper expenditures		Outdoor
		Network radio	Spot radio	Local magazine	National magazine	Local newspaper	National newspaper	
Anheuser-Busch Inc.	Bud Light Beer	0	4,380,102	30,690	1,865,383	20,618	294,749	1,964,951
Anheuser-Busch Inc.	Budweiser Beer	95,000	5,517,449	2,735	4,018,764	76,757	142,000	2,809,670
Anheuser-Busch Inc.	Busch Beer	0	158,596	0	104,565	0	0	2,569,634
Coors Brewing Co.	Coors Light Beer	0	2,733,424	30,902	690,220	34,462	0	3,446,625
Diago North America Inc.	Guinness Beer	0	405,348	5,108	0	0	0	642,731
Heineken USA	Amstel Light Beer	5,947,685	2,974,269	0	850,619	0	0	0
Heineken USA	Heineken Beer	0	60,690	10,817	3,389,954	37,790	0	834,130
Miller Brewing Co.	Miller Genuine Draft Beer	0	1,465,547	54,075	378,400	12,627	0	0
Miller Brewing Co.	Miller Lite Beer	0	3,487,567	27,219	9,717,339	70,202	71,000	575,978

Source: Nielsen AdViews; report dated January 26, 2004. Copyright © 2004 Nielsen Media Research.

Notes: Reported National Spot TV data is based on Nielsen Adviews spot television markets survey and does not reflect all Nielsen DMA's. 0 spent on local Sunday supplement, national Sunday supplement, and FSI coupons.

Unit 42 Exercises
Working with Competitive Media Information

Use Table 42.1, Media-Wide Brand Summary, to answer the following questions:

1. Rank the brands in terms of share of spending from high to low.

2. What is the share of spending for Coors compared to Anheuser-Busch?

3. Compare the media mix of Bud Light to Miller Lite. What are their strengths and weaknesses?

4. What brand has the highest percentage of its media allocation dedicated to Hispanic television? Why do you think the brand allocated its dollars that way?

5. What is the ratio of all television (national, local, cable, and syndication) to all radio (national and local) dollars spent in the category?

6. How does the total share of spending for each brand compare to the share of spending they do on cable television? Why do you feel that certain brands spend more or less than their total share of spending on this particular medium?

7. If Guinness Beer had an extra $50 million to invest in media, where would you allocate it to compete against Heineken?

Appendix A
A Primer to Media Math

Now that you understand the basic processes in making advertising media calculations, you no doubt realize that advertising is a complex business. Among other tasks, advertisers and marketers must concern themselves with devising a focused, effective message that builds and reinforces such intangible concepts as brand identity, and then they must plan a method for communicating that message to consumers. Planning a method to communicate the message is a particularly complex task. First, one must choose from among all the media outlets available, from television and radio to a myriad of potential print publications. Next, one must decode each medium's unique method of measuring its reach and influence among consumers.

Media measurements generally fall into two categories: broadcast and print. Each category is divided into subcategories to measure audience information, ranging from simple concepts relating to the number of people likely to see an advertisement down to details as specific as the demographic makeup of the audience. Additionally, each category has several different ways to assess advertising costs. Media planners and media buyers use all this information to purchase and monitor advertising campaigns. The goal of this tutorial is to promote an understanding of the mathematical relationships behind media concepts and measures.

Role of the Media Planner and Buyer

Most marketers hire professional help before launching an advertising campaign. A large part of that help comes from media planners and media buyers. Some media planners and buyers work in specialized firms. Often, however, they are a part of a larger advertising agency. Such full-service agencies can work with marketers from start to finish, devising marketing messages, creating advertising to communicate that message, and selecting outlets to air the message.

Media experts specialize in monitoring the performance of advertising on various media outlets. Their first job is helping marketers select outlets that enable access to specific groups of people, which can be divided by age, income, race, occupation, gender, and a myriad of other criteria. This is primarily the role of the media planner. In addition to picking outlets, the media planner is responsible for devising a schedule that balances a marketer's need to get a message to consumers against a marketer's need to stay within his budget.

Once the media planner and marketer agree to a plan, the media buyer takes over. The media buyer's job is to negotiate rates for the advertising. Additionally, the media buyer tracks the effectiveness of those advertising runs. Traditionally, media planners were paid a 15 percent commission on the value of the advertising they placed. In fact, the advertising industry got its start as a media buying service, not as a creative vendor; the first advertising agencies acted as brokers between marketers and media outlets, which were predominantly print and radio outlets at the time.

Some media planners still work on a commission plan, but, increasingly, advertising agencies are using different formulas to earn their money. Media planners and buyers are changing with them. Many advertising and media professionals work on a flat-fee system. The fee structure varies among firms. Generally, however, rates are devised by looking at an agency's fiscal-year billings and level of staffing. That way, firms with experience running larger, more complex campaigns can justify a higher rate. Typically, the costs for paying the media advisors and advertising staff would already be incorporated into the media plan.

Broadcast Media

Television has three basic units of measurement:

- Households using television (HUT)
- Share
- Rating

Households Using Television (HUT)

HUT is the percentage of households in a given market that have their television sets on at a particular time. The measure is expressed as a percentage of the total number of televisions. HUT can be used to measure the percentage of the entire country with the television on, or it can be drilled down to specific markets.

Generally, HUT is a predictable number. More television sets will be turned on during prime time (8 P.M.–11 P.M. EST) and during specific seasons of the year. HUT is another way of saying "total available audience."

Obviously, households with the television off will not see a commercial, so it makes no sense to include them in calculations of rating and share.

Share

Share is the percentage of the audience with TV sets on (HUT) who are tuned to a particular station. For example, say six out of ten televisions are turned on (HUT = 60%). Of those six, two are watching CBS, two are watching NBC, one is watching ABC, and one is watching Fox. In this example, CBS has a 33 percent share (2 out of 6). One-third of the televisions in use in the market are tuned to CBS.

Share is basically a percentage of a percentage. It measures a particular program or network's piece of the available viewer pie.

Rating

Rating is a percentage of the total television audience (whether or not their television is turned on at the time) in a given market that is tuned to a particular program.

To borrow from the share example above, in a hypothetical market with ten televisions where two sets are tuned to CBS, CBS has a rating of 20 percent (2 out of 10). ABC, since it has only one viewer, has a rating of 10 percent. If you know the formulas to calculate HUT, share and rating, you only need two of the numbers to calculate the third.

Other Measures to Gauge TV Programming and Advertising Success

Not content with HUT, share, and rating, television has several more measures used to gauge the success of television programming and advertising.

- Performance factors
- Gross rating points (GRPs)
- Reach
- Frequency

Gross rating points, reach, and frequency are also used to measure advertising in other vehicles such as radio, mail pieces, and print.

Performance Factors

Performance factors are an index of market performance compared with the national average for a particular program or station within a certain time period. It is a tool to measure differences in viewership in different markets around the country.

For example, let's look at the program *20/20*. The performance factor for *20/20* in Miami was 104 and in Boise it was 91. This means that the program had more viewers in Miami than the national average, but fewer in Boise.

Gross Rating Points (GRPs)

GRP is a measure of the total gross weight delivered by a media vehicle. If a commercial runs more than once during a program, the audience has an opportunity to be exposed to it more than once. Gross rating points are a tool to reflect that exposure in a way that a simple look at the audience size would not measure. One rating point means one percentage point of the coverage base.

Because gross rating points are duplicated ratings that measure exposure to an advertisement, the number can exceed 100.

Reach

Reach measures the percent of households exposed to a specific media vehicle at least once. It is also referred to as the unduplicated audience.

Frequency

Frequency is the average number of times an audience is exposed to a media vehicle. The average frequency is not the number of occasions or insertions (spots). For example, although a media plan will run only 43 advertisements, the average frequency is only 4.7. Why? The frequency is lower because not everyone was watching each spot.

Frequency is an average number, not an absolute one. To determine how many times the majority of a plan's target audience was exposed to a message, media planners need a frequency distribution. With a frequency distribution, planners can determine whether or not a message has an *effective reach*. Effective reach is the percentage of an audience that has been exposed to an advertisement (frequency) enough times to cause a change in behavior, such as purchasing a product.

Effective reach is often defined as those viewers exposed to the advertising three times or more (this level will vary depending on the product and advertising goals).

Effectiveness Analysis

Following are some analysis techniques used to evaluate whether a marketing message is effectively reaching the target audience:

- Quintile Analysis
- Universe Base
- Rating Point
- Audience
- GRPs
- Gross Impressions

Quintile Analysis

Quintile analysis is a measurement to assess the target audience at various levels of exposure to advertising. The heavy-to-light scale is divided into five parts; hence, the term *quintile* is used to describe each section. This analysis is used primarily to determine commercial "wear out," meaning that it is overexposed and the target audience tunes it out. There is no industry standard for when a commercial is worn out. However, consumer packaged-goods (CPG) companies often consider the quintile with the second-highest exposure viewing the advertisement 26 or more times to be worn out.

Universe Base

This is the population of the group being measured. The number is expressed in thousands (000). For example, a household base of 100,800 is looking at a universe of 100,800,000 actual households. Women ages 18 to 34 would represent a universe of 34,335,000 people, based an audience estimate expressed as a percentage of a target population exposed to an advertising message. So five rating points would mean 5 percent of the target audience universe was exposed to the advertising message.

Audience

The audience counts the total number of people or households exposed to an advertisement.

GRPs

Gross rating points are the total of all rating points achieved for a specific schedule without regard to duplication. For example, if an advertising campaign running in *Good Housekeeping* earns 25 rating points and the same campaign runs during *Scrubs* on television and delivers 13 rating points, the GRP for the total advertising schedule is 38 (25 + 13).

Gross Impressions

Gross impressions are the raw number of potential times an advertisement has been exposed to a particular audience. This is the sum of the gross audiences of all vehicles in the media plan without regard to duplication. Impressions are used to compare delivery in different markets. They are also used to compare delivery between different target markets or demographics. Impressions are usually expressed in thousands (000).

Cost Measurements

Media planners use several basic cost measures to calculate the overall cost of a media schedule:

- Cost per thousand (CPM)
- Cost per point (CPP)
- Cost per lead (CPL)
- Cost per unit (CPU)

Cost per Thousand (CPM)

The cost of delivering a marketing message to 1,000 households is referred to as a CPM (M is the Roman numeral for thousand). CPMs are used to compare and evaluate the cost efficiency of different media vehicles. It does not consider qualitative factors such as the value of the environment or synergy between multiple exposures.

Cost per Point (CPP)

CPP is the cost of reaching one rating point, or one GRP. In other words, CPP measures the cost of reaching 1 percent of a target population. Both CPP and CPM can be used to estimate the anticipated cost of a media schedule.

Cost per Lead (CPL)

CPL is used in direct-response advertising campaigns to evaluate the cost for each lead generated by an advertisement.

Cost per Unit (CPU)

This is the cost for purchasing a single unit or advertising spot. The cost for a particular spot is determined by the rating of the program or time period on the broadcast. For example, a 30-second spot on *American Idol* received an 18.0 rating in New York. The CPP for 30 seconds of prime time in New York is $800. In this case, the cost for airing a 30-second commercial in New York during *American Idol* is $14,400 (18 × $800).

Print Media

Print publications have their own terminology and audience measures independent of those used for television and broadcast media:

- Circulation
- Audience
- Rate Base
- Composition
- Coverage
- Comp/Coverage
- Duplication

Circulation

The number of copies of a particular issue of print media that are sold or distributed is called the circulation. There are two kinds of circulation: paid and nonpaid. Paid publications are distributed to subscribers or sold at newsstands. Nonpaid publications are distributed free of charge. Trade publications are more likely to be nonpaid, while consumer-oriented publications are more likely to be paid.

Audience

The total number of readers of an issue is referred to as the audience. Audience is calculated by multiplying the circulation by the readers per copy. This tells media planners not only how many issues of a magazine are distributed, but also how many people read it. Usually the audience number will be higher than the circulation number. This is simply because a single issue of a magazine can be read by more than one person. The audience figure gives a better idea of how many people would be exposed to an advertisement in the magazine.

Rate Base

Rate base is the circulation number that a magazine guarantees to deliver. Publication advertising rates are based on this number. For example, if *Family Circle* has a CPM for a full page of $15.30 and a rate base of 5,150,000, then the unit cost is $78,795. Bonus circulation is the number of issues that are delivered over the guaranteed rate base.

Composition

This is the percentage of the total audience of a publication that a specific demographic group represents. It is useful in targeting advertising to specific demographic groups. For example, 48.7 percent of *Cosmopolitan*'s readership is in the 18- to 34-year-old women demographic.

Coverage

A closely related concept is coverage, the percentage of a specific demographic group that is reached by a publication. This again is a useful tool to target advertising to a specific group. For example, *Cosmopolitan* reaches 22.4 percent of the population of 18- to 34-year-old women.

Comp/Coverage

The composition and coverage numbers are usually presented together; they are essentially the equivalent of a rating figure for print publications. For example, there are 34,335,000 women ages 18–34 in the United States. *Cosmopolitan*'s total audience is 15,816,000. Of those, 7,703,000 (48.7 percent) are in that demographic group. As a result, *Cosmopolitan* is read by 22.4 percent of 18- to 34-year-old women. If a media planner were looking to advertise to this demographic group, an advertising insertion in *Cosmopolitan* magazine would reach a significant portion of them.

Duplication

This is the percentage of the total audience in a print media schedule reached by more than one magazine. If a media planner can only afford to place an advertisement in two publications, he wants the least duplication possible so the advertising will reach a greater total audience.

For example, suppose a media planner is running an advertisement in *Good Housekeeping* magazine to reach an audience of women 18+ years old. He can afford one other publication; should it be *Family Circle* or *Woman's Day?*

Family Circle has 20 percent duplication. *Woman's Day* has 16 percent duplication. In this case, *Woman's Day* would be the better choice because it has a lower level of duplication.

Conclusion

Media planning is obviously a complicated subject. Learning all the terminology and mathematical formulas behind the various measurements takes some time but will prove to be very helpful. Marketers looking to use media advertising as a tool for reaching potential customers would be well advised to hire professional help for the media planning and campaign tracking. This tutorial should help make sense of it all, but it is in no way a replacement for having an experienced hand at the wheel.

Appendix B
Some Commonly Used Advertising Media Formulas

Cost per Thousand (CPM)—Print Media

$$\text{CPM} = \frac{\text{Advertising rate}}{\text{Circulation}} \times 1{,}000$$

Answer is expressed in dollars and cents.

Cost per Thousand (CPM)—Broadcast Media

$$\text{CPM} = \frac{\text{Advertising rate}}{\text{Audience size}} \times 1{,}000$$

Answer is expressed in dollars and cents.

Readers per Copy (RPC)—Print Media

$$\text{Readers per copy} = \frac{\text{Number of readers of an average issue}}{\text{Circulation of an average issue}}$$

Answer is usually taken to one decimal place.

Program Rating—Broadcast

$$\text{Rating} = \frac{\text{Households tuned to program, station, or network}}{\text{Total number of television households (TVHH)}}$$

Answer is expressed as a percentage.
Audience numbers can be used instead of households.

Share of Audience—Broadcast

$$\text{Share} = \frac{\text{Households tuned to program, station, or network}}{\text{Households with television sets operating}}$$

Answer is expressed as a percentage.
Audience numbers can be used instead of households.

Gross Rating Points (GRPs)

$$
\begin{array}{rl}
 & \text{Rating} \\
+ & \text{Rating} \\
+ & \text{Rating} \\
+ & \text{Rating} \\
\pm & \underline{\text{Etc.}} \quad \text{(for every commercial placement)} \\
 & \text{GRP}
\end{array}
$$

Also, Reach % $\times$ Frequency = GRP.
Answer is expressed as a whole number.

Total Audience Impressions (TAI)

Also known as gross impressions.

Audience member A $\times$ number of exposures = impressions
Audience member B $\times$ number of exposures = impressions
Audience member C $\times$ number of exposures = impressions
Etc., for every audience member and each one's impressions

Then, add together all the impressions figures.
Also, Reach # $\times$ Frequency = TAI.
Answer is expressed as a whole number.

Average Frequency

Also known as effective frequency.
Also known as exposure frequency.

$$\text{Frequency} = \frac{\text{Total audience impressions}}{\text{Unduplicated audience}}$$

Answer is often taken to one decimal place.

Appendix C
Advertising Media Glossary

Accumulative audience: *See* Cumulative audience.

Ad click-through: When a viewer clicks on an advertiser's advertisement to access a website.

Ad click-through rate: The ratio of ad click-throughs to advertisement impressions.

Ad impression: Ad that is served to a user's browser. Measurement of responses from an ad delivery system to an ad request.

Ad impression rate or click rate: Click-throughs divided by ad impressions.

Adjacency: A broadcast program or a commercial that is adjacent to another on the same station, either preceding or following the other.

Ad serving: The delivery of ads by a server to an end user's computer on which the ads are displayed by a browser.

Agency commission: Amount, usually 15 percent, paid to advertising agencies by advertising media on the agencies' purchase of media space or time.

Agency of record: An advertising agency that coordinates an advertiser's promotion of several products or services that are handled by more than a single agency.

Agency recognition: An acknowledgment by media that advertising agencies are good credit risks and fulfill certain requirements, thus qualifying for a commission.

Announcement: An advertising commercial that is broadcast between programs (*see also* Station break, Participation, ID, Billboard); an advertisement within a syndicated program or feature film; any broadcast commercial.

Arbitron: A national radio ratings service.

Area of Dominant Influence (ADI): Arbitron measurement area that comprises those counties in which stations of a single originating market account for a greater share of the viewing households than those from any other market; similar to Nielsen's designated market area.

Audience: Persons who receive an advertisement; individuals who receive and pay attention to a mass media vehicle.

Audience composition: Audience analysis, usually expressed in demographic terms.

Audience duplication: Those persons who see or hear an advertisement more than once in a single media vehicle or in a combination of vehicles.

Audience profile: The minute-by-minute viewing trend for a program; a description of the characteristics of the people who are exposed to a media vehicle.

Audimeter: Nielsen Media Research automatic device attached to radio or television receiving sets that records usage and station information. (*See also* People meter.)

Availability: A broadcast time period that is open for purchase by an advertiser (slang "avail").

Average audience: The number of homes or people that are tuned in for an average minute of a broadcast.

Average exposure: The mean (average) number of times that each audience member has been exposed to an advertisement.

Banner: A graphic image shown on an HTML page in the form of an ad. Banners come in many sizes and shapes, but the most common of the original standard ad units is the "full banner," which is defined spatially as 468 x 60 pixels. Banners are usually linked to the advertiser's website.

Barter: Arrangement where advertising time and space are offered in return for merchandise or other nonmonetary returns; also, a broadcast advertising offer where a station is offered a syndicated program in exchange for commercial positions within the program.

Billboard: An outdoor poster; production information that follows a broadcast program; a six-second radio commercial; a short commercial at the start and close of a program, announcing the name of the sponsor.

Billing: The value of advertising that is handled by an advertising agency on behalf of its clients (often called billings); invoices for media space and time.

Bleed: Magazine printing to the edge of the page, with no margin or border.

Brand development index (BDI): A comparative measure of a brand's sales in a market relative to the size of the market. (*See also* Category development index.)

Break: Broadcast time available for purchase between two broadcast programs or between segments of a single program.

Bulk discount: A discount offered by media for buying in quantity. (*See* Quantity discount.)

Bulk rate: *See* Bulk discount.

Business paper: A magazine intended for business or professional interests.

Button: Online image that, when clicked, precipitates some form of action such as displaying an ad, connecting to a website, linking to a different page within the site, and so on.

Buy: Negotiating, ordering, and confirming the selection of a media vehicle and unit; the advertising that is purchased from a media vehicle.

Buyer: *See* media buyer and media planner.

Buying service: A company primarily engaged in the advertising media planning and buying; also called media buying specialist or time/space buying specialist/service.

Call letters: The letters that identify a broadcast station; for example, WBZ-TV.

Campaign: A coordinated advertising effort for a particular product or service that extends for a specified period of time.

Car card: Transit advertisement in a bus, subway, or commuter train car.

Carryover effect: The residual level of awareness or recall that remains after a flight or campaign period; accounts for lag effect and is used to plan the timing of schedules.

Cash discount: A discount, usually 2 percent, by media to advertisers for prompt payment.

Category development index (CDI): A comparative of a market's total sales of all brands of an entire product category compared with the market size; used to evaluate the sales potential of a market for a product category or a brand. (*See also* Brand development index.)

CC: The conclusion of a broadcast program; for example, the conclusion (CC) of *Law and Order* is 11:30 P.M.

Center spread: An advertisement on two facing pages printed on a single sheet in the center of a publication.

Chain: A broadcast network, a newspaper, or a magazine group of single ownership or control.

Chain break (CB): The time during which a broadcast network allows stations to identify themselves; usually a 20-second spot (abbrev. "twenty" or ":20").

Checking: The process of confirming that an advertisement actually appeared as ordered.

Checking copy: A copy of a publication that is supplied by a print vehicle to show that an advertisement appeared as specified.

Circulation: The number of print copies distributed; the number of broadcast households within a signal area that have receiving sets; in outdoor, the number of people with a reasonable opportunity to see a billboard.

City zone: A central city and the contiguous areas that cannot be distinguished from it.

Class magazines: Special-interest publications with desirable upscale audiences.

Classified advertising: Advertising arranged according to categories or interests.

Classified display advertising: Classified advertising with some of the characteristics of display advertising. (*See also* Display advertising.)

Clear time: The process of reserving available broadcast advertising time.

Click: Metric that measures the user to an Internet ad.

Click-through: The action of following a hyperlink within an advertisement to another website or another page within the website.

Clipping bureau: An organization that checks print advertising by clipping the advertisements from print media.

Closing date: The deadline for print advertising to appear in a certain issue; in broadcast, sometimes called closing hour.

Column-inch: Advertising space that is one column wide by one inch high.

Combination rate: A discounted advertising rate for buying space in two or more publications owned by the same interests.

Commercial impressions: The total audience impressions for all commercial announcements in an advertiser's schedule. (*See also* Gross impressions.)

Confirmation: A statement from a broadcast vehicle that a specific time is still open for purchase by an advertiser.

Consumer profile: A demographic description of the households or people who are prospects for a product or service. (*See also* Target group.)

Contiguity rate: A reduced broadcast advertising rate for sponsoring two or more commercials in succession.

Controlled circulation: Circulation limited to persons who qualify to receive a publication; sometimes distributed free to qualified persons.

Cooperative advertising: Retail advertising that is paid partly or fully by a manufacturer; two or more manufacturers or two or more retailers cooperating in a single advertisement (abbrev. "co-op").

Cooperative announcement: Broadcast commercial time made available in network programs to stations for sale to local or national advertisers.

Cooperative program: A network broadcast sold on both a national and local basis; for example, *Saturday Night Live*. (*See also* Cooperative announcement.)

Cost per thousand (CPM): A comparison that shows the relative cost of various media vehicles; indicates the dollar cost of advertising exposure to a thousand households or individuals.

Cover position: An advertisement on the cover of a magazine, often at a premium cost; 1st cover is the outside front cover; 2nd cover is the inside front cover; 3rd cover is the inside back cover; 4th cover is the outside back cover.

Coverage: The number or percentage of households or persons who are exposed to a medium or to an advertising campaign.

CPA: Cost per action, sales transaction, customer acquisition.

CPC: Cost per click.

CPL: Cost per lead.

CPP: Cost per (rating) point; indicates the dollar cost of advertising exposure to one percentage point of the target group, audience, or population.

Crossplugs: In alternating broadcast sponsorships, permitting each advertiser to insert an announcement into the program during the weeks when the other advertiser is the sponsor, maintaining weekly exposure for both advertisers.

Cumulative audience (slang "cume"): Total number of persons exposed to any insertion of an advertisement in multiple editions of a single vehicle; unduplicated audience is those persons who were exposed to any insertion of an advertisement in a combination of vehicles or media, counting each person only once.

Cumulative reach: The number of different households exposed to a medium or campaign during a specific time.

Cut-in: The insertion of a local broadcast commercial into a network or recorded program.

Dayparts: Segments of the broadcast day; for example, daytime, early fringe, prime access, prime time, late fringe, late night.

Deadline: Final date or time for accepting advertising material to meet a publication or broadcast schedule. (*See also* Closing date.)

Dealer imprint: A local dealer's identification inserted into a nationally prepared advertisement.

Dealer tie-in: A manufacturer's advertisement that lists local dealers; not the same as co-op.

Delivery: The ability to reach or communicate with a certain kind or size of audience by using a particular advertising schedule.

Demographic characteristics: The population characteristics of a group.

Designated market area (DMA): A term used by Nielsen Media Research; those counties in which stations of the originating market account for a greater share of the viewing households than those from any other area (*see also* Area of dominant influence); for example, Lake County, Illinois, belongs to the Chicago DMA because a majority of household viewing in Lake County is of Chicago stations rather than stations from Milwaukee or any other market.

Digest unit: *See* Junior unit.

Direct advertising: Advertising under complete control of the advertiser, rather than through some established medium; for example, direct mail, free sampling, and so on.

Direct mail advertising: Advertising by mail; advertising in other media that solicit orders directly through the mail.

Direct marketing: Sales made directly to the customer rather than through intervening channels; includes direct mail, direct advertising, telemarketing, and so on.

Directory advertising: Advertising that appears in a buying guide; for example, Yellow Pages advertising.

Display advertising: Print advertising intended to attract attention and communicate easily through the use of space, illustrations, layout, headline, and so on, as opposed to classified advertising.

Double spotting: *See* Piggyback.

Double spread: *See* Two-page spread.

Downloading: The process of transferring a copy of a file or files from a host computer to the user's own computer.

Drive time: Radio broadcast time during morning and evening rush hours.

Earned rate: The advertising rate actually paid by the advertiser, after discounts and other calculations.

Effective frequency: Level of audience exposure that provides what an advertiser considers to be the minimal effective level or within the goal objectives; also called effective reach.

Effective reach: *See* Effective frequency.

E-mail: Electronic mail or message files sent from user to user on the Internet.

Facing: Outdoor advertising location with the panels facing the same direction and visible to the same lines of traffic.

Fixed rate: A broadcast advertising rate that cannot be taken away or preempted by another advertiser; usually the highest advertising rate; commonly used in broadcast advertising.

Flat rate: An advertising rate not subject to a discount.

Flight (flight saturation): Concentrated advertising within a short time period; an advertising campaign that runs for a specified length of time, followed by a period of inactivity (*see* Hiatus), after which the campaign may resume with another flight.

Forced combination: A policy to require newspaper advertisers to buy advertising in both morning and evening newspapers owned by the same publisher within a market.

Forcing distribution: The use of advertising to increase consumer demand, thereby inducing dealers to stock a product.

Fractional page: Print advertising space of less than one full page.

Free circulation: A publication sent without charge; often controlled circulation.

Free-standing insert (FSI): Advertisement in a publication that is not on a regular page; bound into a magazine as a separate item.

Frequency: The number of times that an individual or household is exposed to an advertisement or campaign (frequency of exposure); number of times that an average audience member sees or hears an advertisement; the number of times that an advertisement is run (frequency of insertion).

Frequency discount: Reduced advertising rate offered by media to advertisers who use a certain number of advertisements within a given time frame.

Frequency distribution: A chart showing the percentage or number of audience reached at certain levels of exposure frequency.

Fringe time: Broadcast time periods before or after prime time; television time following daytime is called early fringe, and the television time immediately following prime time is called late fringe.

Full run: One transit advertising car card in every transit vehicle.

General magazine: A consumer magazine that is not aimed at a special-interest audience.

Grid card: Broadcast advertising rates set in matrix format to allow a station to set rates based on current audience ratings and advertiser buying demand; for example:

	60-sec.	20/30-sec.	10-sec.
A	$350	$275	$125
B	345	272	223
C	340	270	221
D	330	265	220

Gross audience: The total number of individuals or households "delivered" or reached by an advertising schedule, regardless of any possible duplication that might occur; also called total audience.

Gross impressions: *See* Total audience impressions; Gross audience.

Gross rating points (GRPs): The sum total of broadcast rating points delivered by an advertiser's television schedule, usually in a one-week period; an indicator of the combined audience percentage reach and exposure frequency achieved by an advertising schedule; in outdoor, the standard audience level upon which a market's advertising rates are based.

Gutter: The inside page joint where a publication is bound.

Half run: Transit advertising in half the vehicles of a system.

Head of household: The person within a household or family who is responsible for the major purchasing decisions; sometimes the male head and female head of household are considered separately.

Hiatus: A period during a campaign when an advertiser's schedule is reduced or suspended for a time, after which it resumes.

Hit: When users access a website their computer sends a request to the site's server to begin downloading a page.

Hitchhiker: A broadcast commercial at the end of a program that promotes another product from the same advertiser.

Holdover audience: Those persons tuned to a program who stay tuned to that network or station for the following program.

Home page: The "front screen" for a website (or collection of websites) that is unique to a particular individual or business.

Horizontal cume: The total number of different people who are tuned to a broadcast network or station at the same time on different days of the week.

Horizontal publication: A business or trade publication that is of interest to one level or to one job function in various businesses or fields.

House agency: An advertising agency that is controlled by an advertiser.

House organ: A company's own publication or media outlet.

Households using radio (HUR): *See* Households using television.

Households using television (HUT): The percentage of households that have broadcast receiving sets operating at one time within a market. (*See also* Persons using television.)

ID (Identification): A television commercial 8 to 10 seconds in length, during a station break; a 10-second broadcast commercial, sometimes referred to as a "ten."

Impact: The degree that an advertisement or campaign affects its audience; the amount of space (full-page, half-page, etc.) or of time (60-second, 30-second, etc.) that is purchased, as opposed to reach and frequency measures; also, the use of color, bleed, large type, powerful messages, or other devices that may induce audience reaction. (*See also* Unit.)

Independent station: A broadcast station not affiliated with a network.

Index: A numerical value assigned to quantitative data for ease of comparison.

Insert: An advertisement enclosed with bills or letters; a print advertisement that is distributed with the publication and that may or may not be bound into it.

Insertion order: A statement accompanying the advertisement copy indicating specifications for the advertisement.

Integrated commercial: A broadcast advertisement delivered as part of the entertainment portion of a program.

Interactive media: Communication channels that provide for two-way interaction, such as CD, DVD, or Internet.

Internet: Literally a global network of computers, the Internet encompasses all computers that tap into cyberspace and communicate with each other from the largest servers to a single person's home computer. This term is not synonymous with World Wide Web.

Internet service provider (ISP): A company that offers access to the Internet through its computers for a fee.

In-unit clicks: Response that generally causes an intra-site redirect or content change.

Island position: A print advertisement surrounded by editorial material; a print advertisement not adjacent to any other advertising; a broadcast commercial scheduled away from any other commercial, with program content before and after; often at premium advertising rates.

Isolated 30: A 30-second broadcast commercial that runs by itself, not in combination with any other announcement; usually found on network television.

Junior unit: Permitting a print advertisement that has been prepared for a smaller page size to be run in a publication with a larger page size, with editorial matter around it in the extra space; similarly, using a *Reader's Digest*-sized advertising page in a larger magazine is usually called a digest unit.

Key: A code in an advertisement to allow tracing which advertisement produced an inquiry or order.

Life: The length of time an advertisement is used; the length of time an advertisement remains effective; the length of time when a publication is retained by its audience.

Lifestyle profiles: Classifying advertising audiences by career, recreation, and leisure patterns or motives.

List broker: A company that prepares and rents the use of mailing lists.

Local rate: An advertising rate offered by media vehicles to local advertisers that is lower than the rate offered to national advertisers.

Log: A broadcast station's record of on-air programming.

LOH (Ladies of the House): A term used by Nielsen Media Research in some of its reports, referring to female heads of households.

M: One thousand.

MM: One million (MM is $1,000 \times 1,000 = 1,000,000$).

Mail-order advertising: Advertisements that ask for direct orders of merchandise through the mail; the advertisements themselves may be distributed through the mail or may appear in other advertising media.

Make-good: Repeating an advertisement to compensate for an error, omission, or technical difficulty with the publication, broadcast, or transmission of the original.

Market: *See* Target group; Target market.

Market potential: The reasonable maximum sales level or market share that a product or service can be expected to achieve.

Market profile: A geographic description of where prospects are located. (*See also* Target market; Target profile.)

Market share: A company's or brand's portion of the generic sales of a product or service category.

Mat service: A service to print media that supplies pictures and drawings for use in advertisements; entire prepared advertisements may be offered; mat is slang for "matrix."

Media buyer: A person responsible for purchasing advertising space or time; often someone skilled in negotiation with the media.

Media planner: A person responsible for determining the proper use of advertising media to fulfill the marketing and promotion objectives for a specific brand or advertiser.

Merchandising: Promotion of an advertiser's products, services, and the like to the sales force, wholesalers, and dealers; promotion other than advertising to consumers through the use of in-store displays, services, point-of-purchase materials, etc.; display and promotion of retail goods; display of an advertisement close to the point of sale.

Message distribution: Measurement of media audience by the successive frequency of exposure; for example, saw once, saw twice, and so on.

Metropolitan area: A geographic area consisting of a central city of at least 50,000 population plus the economically and socially integrated surrounding area, as established by the federal government; usually limited by county boundaries; slang: "metro area."

Metro rating: A rating figure from within a metropolitan area.

Mouse-over: User places mouse over an ad to view without clicking.

NCR (or NCIR): Abbreviation for "no change in rate," used when some other format or specification has changed.

Net: The money paid to a media vehicle by an advertising agency after deducting the agency's commission; also slang for "network."

Net unduplicated audience: The total number of different people who are reached by a single issue of two or more publications, counting each person only once. (*See* Cumulative audience; Unduplicated audience.)

Network: In broadcast, a cooperative group of stations; a company that supplies programming to a group or chain of stations.

Network option time: Broadcast time on a station when the network has the option of selling advertising.

Newspaper syndicate: A firm that sells special material such as features, photographs, comic strips, cartoons, and the like for publication in newspapers.

Next to reading matter: An advertising position in print media adjacent to news or editorial material; may be at premium rates.

Nielsen: The A.C. Nielsen Company; Nielsen Media Research; a firm engaged in television ratings and other marketing research.

NSI: Nielsen Station Index; a television rating service for individual television stations.

NTI: Nielsen Television Index; a national television rating service for network programming.

O&O station: A broadcast station "owned and operated" by a network.

One-time rate: *See* Open rate.

Open-end transcription: A transcribed broadcast with time for the insertion of local commercials.

Open rate: The highest advertising rate before discounts begin; also called basic rate and one-time rate.

OTO: "One time only"; a commercial announcement that runs once only.

Overrun: Additional copies of an advertisement beyond the number ordered or needed; extra copies to replace outdoor posters or transit car cards that have been damaged.

Package: A series of radio or television programs that an advertiser may sponsor.

Package plan discount: A spot television discount for buying a certain number of spots, usually within a one-week period.

Packager: A company that produces packaged program series; also called syndicator.

Page views: The number of times users are exposed to a page that contains editorial content or an advertiser's ad.

Paid circulation: The number of print copies that are purchased by the audience.

Panel: An outdoor billboard.

Participation: A commercial announcement within the body of a broadcast program, as compared with one scheduled between programs; also called participating announcements.

Participation program: A broadcast program in which each segment is sponsored by a different advertiser.

Pass-along readers: Readers of a publication who get copies other than by purchase or subscription. (*See also* Secondary audience.)

Penetration: The percentage of households having a broadcast receiving set; a measure of advertising effectiveness; the percentage of households exposed to an advertising campaign.

People meter: Slang for a broadcast ratings device that records individual audience members who are present during a program.

Per issue rate: A special publication advertising rate determined by the number of issues used during the contract period; similar to a frequency discount, except based on the number of issues in which an advertising campaign appears rather than on the number of advertisements.

Persons using television (PUT): The percentage of total population who watch television at a given time.

Piggyback: Slang for two of a sponsor's commercial announcements presented back-to-back within a single commercial time segment; for example, two 30-second commercials in a 60-second time slot; also called double spotting.

Pilot: Sample production of a proposed broadcast program series.

Plans board: An advertising agency committee that reviews message, media, or campaign plans for clients.

Plug: Free mention of a product or service.

Point-of-purchase advertising (POP): Promotions in stores, usually displays.

Portal: A "virtual" door or pathway that a user goes through whenever she/he accesses the Internet; as the starting point, it usually provides options for shopping, news, and other popular options, and often includes a search engine.

Position: Location of an advertisement on a page; the time when a program or commercial announcement will air in a broadcast; special positions often cost premium prices.

Potential audience: The maximum audience possible.

Preemptible rate: Advertising rate subject to cancellation by another advertiser's paying a higher rate, usually in broadcast; the protection period varies by station and ranges from no notice to two-weeks' notice or more. (*See also* Fixed rate.)

Preemption: Cancellation of a broadcast program for breaking news or special material; a station's or network's privilege to cancel a regular program to run a special program; a commercial announcement that may be replaced if another advertiser pays a higher (fixed) rate.

Premium: An item offered to help promote a product or service; a higher-cost advertising rate. (*See also* Premium price.)

Premium price: A higher advertising rate for special positions or other considerations.

Preprint: Advertising material printed in advance of the regular press run, perhaps on another printing press with greater capability for color, and so on.

Primary audience: Print audience members who purchase or subscribe to the publication. (*See also* Secondary audience.)

Primary household: A household where a publication has been subscribed to or purchased.

Primary listening area: The geographic area where a broadcast transmission is static-free and easily received.

Primary readers: People who purchase or subscribe to a publication; readers in primary households.

Prime access: Broadcast time immediately before prime time; for example, 7–8 P.M. Eastern time.

Prime time: Hours when television viewing is at its peak; usually the evening hours.

Product allocation: Various products that are assigned to specific times or locations in an advertiser's schedule when more than one brand is advertised; the amount of the advertising budget allocated to individual products.

Product protection: Time separation between the airing of broadcast commercial announcements for competitive goods or services.

Profile: Used interchangeably with audience composition to describe the demographic characteristics of audiences.

Program compatibility: Broadcast programming or editorial content suitable for the product or service that is being promoted; suitability of the advertising campaign theme with program content.

Progressive proofs: Test press run of each color in the printing process.

Projected audience: The estimated number of audience members calculated from a sample survey of audience size; the estimated number of broadcast viewers, either in total or per receiving set, based on the sample for the rating percentages.

Publisher's statement: Certified circulation of a publication, attested by the publisher and subject to audit.

Pulp magazine: A publication, often printed on low-quality paper, with sensational editorial material; for example, a mystery, detective, or TV movie magazine.

Qualified circulation: The distribution of a publication restricted to individuals who meet certain requirements; for example, member physicians are qualified to receive the *Journal of the American Medical Association.*

Qualified reader: A person who can prove that he or she read a publication.

Quantity discount: A lower advertising rate for buying a certain amount of advertising space or time.

Quarter-run: One-fourth of the car cards required for a full run in transit; a card in one-fourth of the transit system vehicles.

Quintile: One-fifth of some group; in advertising, often refers to audience members who have been divided into five equal groups (quintiles), ranging from the heaviest to the lightest product or media usage levels.

Rate: The price or charge for advertising media space or time.

Rate book: A printed book or online tool designed to provide advertising rates for several media vehicles; for example, Standard Rate and Data Service (SRDS).

Rate card: A printed list of advertising rates for a single media vehicle.

Rate differential: The difference in costs between the local and the national advertising rates in a vehicle.

Rate guarantee: Commitment on the part of a media vehicle that an advertising rate will not be increased during a certain calendar period.

Rate holder: A small printed advertisement run by an advertiser to meet contract requirements for earning a discounted advertising rate.

Rate protection: The length of time an advertiser is guaranteed a certain advertising rate without an increase.

Rating: The percentage of the potential broadcast audience tuned to a particular program, station, or network; audience of a vehicle expressed as a percentage of the total population of an area.

Rating point: Rating of one percentage point; 1 percent of the potential audience; the sum of the ratings from multiple advertising insertions (e.g., two advertisements with a rating of 15 percentage points each will total 30 rating points).

Reach: Total audience a medium actually reaches; size of the audience with which a vehicle communicates; total number of people in a media audience; total percentage of the target group actually covered by an advertising campaign.

Readership: The number or percentage of people who read a publication or advertisement.

Reading notice: Print advertisement intended to resemble editorial matter.

Rebate: Payment that is returned by the media vehicle to an advertiser who has overpaid, usually because of earning a lower discount rate than was originally contracted.

Reminder advertising: An advertisement, usually brief, intended to keep the name of a product or service before the public; often a supplement to other advertising.

Rep: Slang term for a media sales representative.

Replacement: A substitute for a broadcast commercial announcement that was not broadcast as specified on the advertiser's order.

Retail trading zone (RTZ): Geographic area where most of a market's population makes the majority of their retail purchases.

Roadblock or roadblocking: Slang term for placing broadcast commercials at the same time on two or more networks or at the same time on several stations in a single market; used to reach audience members who switch channels during a commercial break.

ROP color: Run-of-press color; color printing done during the regular press run.

Run of paper (ROP): Advertising positioned anywhere in a publication, with no choice of a specific place for the advertisement to appear.

Run of schedule (ROS): Broadcast commercial announcements scheduled at the station's discretion anytime.

Run of site/network: Internet ad placement terms referring to where an ad will appear; "run of site" means that ads may appear in various areas on a specific site. "Run of network" usually refers to a content-based series of sites (e.g., entertainment, sports) where an ad can appear. Choosing run of site/network depends on the options that are available when buying ad space through a particular service, the desired specificity of targeting, and how such offers are priced by the seller.

Satellite station: A supplemental broadcast station located in a fringe reception area to boost the effective range of the main station's signal.

Saturation: Advertising media schedule with wide reach and high frequency, concentrated over a time period to achieve maximum coverage and impact. (*See also* Flight.)

Scatter plan: Broadcast commercials scheduled during a variety of times; usually, the advertiser is permitted to specify general time periods during which the commercials will be run; also called scatter package.

Schedule: List of media or advertisements to be used in a campaign; calendar of the advertisements that have been planned.

Schedule and estimate: Form submitted by an advertising agency to the advertiser prior to a firm media purchase, containing price and audience goals and the proposed schedule.

Secondary audience: Members of a print media audience who do not subscribe to or purchase the publication. (*See also* Pass-along readers.)

Secondary listening area: Outlying area where broadcast transmissions are subject to fading or static; in television, the Grade 2 or Grade 3 signal contour.

Self-liquidating point-of-purchase: A display for which the retailer pays the costs.

Self-liquidating premium: An item paid for by the customer; the price that the consumer pays covers the manufacturing and distribution costs of the premium.

Self-mailer: Direct-mail item mailed without an envelope.

Share of audience ("share"): The percentage of households with a broadcast receiving set in use that are tuned to a particular station, network, or program.

Shopping newspaper ("shopper"): Publication devoted to advertising, often distributed free to shoppers or to households.

Short rate: Money owed to a media vehicle by an advertiser to offset the difference between the earned rate and the lower contracted rate.

Showing: Number of outdoor posters necessary to reach a certain percentage of the mobile population in a market within a specified time; most outdoor markets are now purchased by gross rating points. (*See also* GRPs.)

Sixty: Slang for a one-minute broadcast commercial.

Soap opera: Slang for a continuing broadcast dramatic serial program, usually a daytime program.

Space buyer: Person responsible for purchasing advertising in newspapers and magazines and sometimes outdoor and transit. (*See also* Media buyer.)

Space position value: Measurement of the effectiveness of an outdoor poster location.

Spectacular: Large lighted outdoor sign.

Split run: Testing two or more print advertisements by running each to a different portion of the audience, usually in a single issue.

Sponsor: Advertiser who buys all the commercial time available in a given broadcast program or segment.

Spot: Purchase of broadcast slots by geographic areas; purchase of slots at certain times, usually during station breaks; the term *spot* can refer to the time used for the commercial announcement or it can refer to the commercial itself.

Standard Metropolitan Statistical Area (SMSA): *See* Metropolitan area.

Station break: Time between broadcast programs for station identification and spot announcements; slang for a 20-second broadcast announcement.

Station clearance: *See* Clear time.

Station identification: Broadcast announcement of station call letters, usually with frequency or channel and station location.

Station option time: Broadcast time when the station has the option of selling advertising.

Station posters: Advertising posters in transit stations.

Strip programming: Broadcast commercial scheduled at the same time of day on successive days of the week, usually Monday through Friday or Monday through Sunday.

Sunday supplement: Sunday newspaper section in magazine format; also called magazine supplement, magazine section, or, simply, supplement.

Sustaining period: Advertising campaign period when advertisements are used to remind the audience of the product or service or of the campaign; often, a time of reduced advertising expenditures following an introductory flight.

Sweep: Time period during the year when a ratings service measures the broadcast audience in the majority of the markets throughout the country, usually three or four weeks in length; for example, surveys that are scheduled for November 2 through 24 would be referred to as the "November sweep."

Syndicated program: Broadcast program sold to individual stations rather than appearing on a network.

Syndicator: Television program distributor who offers reruns or new programs on a market-to-market basis. (*See also* Packager.)

Tabloid: Newspaper with the approximate page size of a standard newspaper folded in half; slang "tab."

Tag: Dealer identification added to the end of a broadcast commercial announcement indicating where the advertised product or service can be purchased in the local market.

Target group: People to whom a campaign is directed; persons with similar characteristics who are prospects for a product or service; also called consumer profile.

Target market: Geographic area where a campaign is aimed; areas where a product or service is being sold or introduced; sometimes called market profile.

Target profile: Description of the target groups, often including the demographic or geographic target markets.

TBA: Abbreviation for "to be announced"; notification in broadcast program schedules.

Tearsheet: Publication page where an advertiser's message appears; sent to the advertiser for approval or for checking.

Teaser: An advertisement preceding the major portion of an advertising campaign, intended to build curiosity.

Telemarketing: Selling by telephone, either initiating the calls or receiving orders.

Ten: Slang for a 10-second broadcast commercial.

Thirty: Slang for a 30-second broadcast commercial.

Throwaways: Free shopper newspapers.

Tie-in: *See* Cooperative advertising; Dealer tie-in.

Time buyer: Person responsible for purchasing advertising on radio and television. (*See also* Media buyer.)

Time sheet: Form used to keep track of a media buy; also called a buy sheet; also, the form used to track how advertising agency personnel use their time, for billing purposes.

Total audience: The number of all the different households or individuals tuned at any one time to a broadcast program.

Total audience impressions (TAI): The total number of times an advertisement or campaign is seen and/or heard; total audience or numerical reach multiplied by average frequency.

TPR: Abbreviation for "time period rating"; the rating for a particular broadcast time period without attention to the program that was broadcast.

Trade paper: A specialized publication for a specific trade, industry, or profession; term for some business publications.

Traffic count: Number of persons passing an outdoor panel location.

Trim size: The final magazine page size after it is cut to the final size.

Turnover: Frequency of audience change for a broadcast program over a period of time.

Twenty: Slang for a 20-second broadcast commercial; also called a chain break or station break.

Two-page spread: A single print advertisement on two facing pages; also called double spread or double truck. (*See also* Center spread.)

Unduplicated audience: Total number of different people exposed to an advertisement or campaign through multiple insertions in more than one media vehicle; compare with Cumulative audience.

Unique user: Unique individual or browser who has accessed a site. They are identified by either user registration or cookies.

Unique visitors: The number of different visitors to a given website, network, or ad schedule in a particular time frame. This is the equivalent of "reach" for conventional media.